READERS AND
WRITERS IN CUBA

LATIN AMERICAN STUDIES
VOLUME 10
GARLAND REFERENCE LIBRARY OF THE HUMANITIES
VOLUME 1935

LATIN AMERICAN STUDIES

DAVID WILLIAM FOSTER, *Series Editor*

READERS AND WRITERS IN CUBA
A SOCIAL HISTORY OF PRINT CULTURE, 1830s–1990s

PAMELA MARIA SMORKALOFF

GARLAND PUBLISHING, INC.
NEW YORK AND LONDON
1997

Library of Congress Cataloging-in-Publication Data

Smorkaloff, Pamela Maria, 1956–
  [Literatura y edición de libros. English]
  Readers and writers in Cuba : a social history of print culture, 1830s–
1990s / Pamela Maria Smorkaloff.
      p.   cm. — (Garland reference library of the humanities ; v. 1935.
Latin American studies ; v. 10)
  Rev. and updated English language version of: Literatura y edición de
libros. 1987.
  Includes bibliographical references and index.
  ISBN 0-8153-2099-X (alk. paper)
  1. Publishers and publishing—Cuba—History. 2. Cuban literature—20th
century—History and criticism. 3. Cuban literature—19th century—History
and criticism.   I. Title.   II. Series: Garland reference library of the
humanities ; vol. 1935.   III. Series: Garland reference library of the humanities. Latin American studies ; vol. 10.
  Z515.3.C9S6613   1997
  070.5'097291—dc21   96-39152
                                                                  CIP

Printed on acid-free, 250-year-life paper
Manufactured in the United States of America

CONTENTS

ACKNOWLEDGMENTS

Far too many individuals and institutions have contributed over the years to the making of this book, both the original study in Spanish and the revised, updated English-language version, to ever adequately thank and acknowledge them all.

In addition to the individuals and institutions in Cuba cited in the text, I remain grateful to all those who helped make its research and writing possible: those in the Ministry of Culture, the Alejo Carpentier Center, the José Martí National Library, and particularly Tomás Fernández Robaina, writer/bibliographer, who remains a loyal friend and colleague. My thanks to all those who lent the crucial support I needed to get started nearly ten years ago.

To Cuban scholar, Alberto Batista Reyes, for his camaraderie and unflagging interest in the project, and for providing me with the current statistics on print culture in Cuba in the late 1980s and 1990s that allowed me to complete Chapter 8 and update, spirit and letter, my original research.

To Haydée Vitali, my brilliant yet down-to-earth muse and teacher, for inspiring the birth of and subsequent developments in this study, and for providing essential direction for its revision, reading chapters of the manuscript with her ever keen and critical eye. And for having given me more than I could have ever imagined for the last twenty years.

To Christopher Mitchell, Director of the Center of Latin American and Caribbean Studies at NYU, for his friendship and constant efforts on behalf of interdisciplinary regional studies; Carmen Díaz, Assistant Director, for her friendship, guidance and sense of humor; and the changing, supportive staff at the Center where I have been teaching, broadening and deepening my scholarship on problems of culture and society. With special thanks to my sharp and profoundly intelligent graduate students, now graduated, Lisette Rodríguez and Faith Hancock, who tackled the manuscript and unfamiliar software to produce a fine conceptual index to the study. And my appreciation for all the graduate students at the Center who have helped shape my thoughts as a Latin Americanist and Caribbeanist, over the years.

To Bill Hinchey, companion through thick and thin in my writing life; to my mother, María Eugenia Smorkaloff, always; and in memory of my grandmother, América Ana Garrigó y Salido, whose spirit still hovers over much of what I research and write.

To Wilfrido Corral, a kindred spirit in scholarship and in life whose nobili-
ty and constructive engagement with the world, academic and beyond, never
ceases to astonish and inspire. Special thanks for directing me to unexplored
theoretical readings which greatly improved the framework for this study, and
for dozens of invaluable suggestions made while the manuscript was in preparation.

Finally, and most importantly, my deepest thanks to David William Foster
of Arizona State University, scholar extraordinaire, for embracing this study as
part of the Garland Latin American Studies Series, and so many other things for
which I am eternally in his debt. Most especially, for having had the unerring
vision and profound wisdom to acknowledge, as opposing points on the spectrum, the emergence of Casa de las Américas, as an alternate cultural center for
the Americas, and the horrors of the military dictatorship in Argentina as the two
single events to produce the most profound impact on cultural production in the
Americas in our time. My most heartfelt thanks to David for making this book
possible.

PREFACE

> Behind every edition or title lies the question of identity, technical limitations, the supremacy of certain languages, monopoly control over the production of paper, domination of the means of distribution, and particularly, its use as an instrument of cultural penetration. Selecting a book is a cultural act which constitutes, at the same time, a political decision. Few readers in the world are conscious of this.[1]

Those who study the problems surrounding books from Michel de Montaigne to Ariel Dorfman—both in their material and spiritual dimensions—their creation, production and distribution, all agree that they are complex and varied. Hence, their study invokes fear and fascination. The complexity, diversity and ignorance that shroud the problems of book production and print culture are at once the raison d'être and the frustrated lament of the researcher. Where to begin? What types of data will shed light on the problems of print culture in its totality? How should they be organized? There are so many aspects to research, from the dialectics of production to theories of readers' reception of literary works in a given context, that one runs the risk of getting lost, of not finding solid ground on which to proceed. Ambrosio Fornet, the Cuban writer and critic, in his introduction to *En blanco y negro*, a sociohistorical study of twentieth-century Cuban fiction, compares the task of writing "a sociological essay on literary matters or a literary essay with sociological pretensions" with that of "a cosmonaut flailing about in space," fearing that he may end up "like the man who tried to find the heart of an onion: teary-eyed and empty-handed."[2]

---

[1] Enrique González Manet, *Cultura y comunicación* (Havana: Editorial Letras Cubanas, 1984). This, and all subsequent quotations from Spanish-language sources, have been translated by the author, unless otherwise indicated.

[2] Ambrosio Fornet, *En blanco y negro* (Havana: Instituto del Libro, 1967): 7, 9-10.

The sociology or social history of literature is much like literary translation in that it borrows from many disciplines without constituting an autonomous discipline in and of itself. The very same text, in the hands of ten translators, will generate ten distinct versions. Were this not so, the effort would lack the creative impulse, would lose its richness and potential. The same is true of studies in the sociology of literature; identical data can generate quite dissimilar studies, according to the researcher's selection, organization, analysis and orientation. The example cited by Rodolfo Stavenhagen, the Mexican sociologist, clearly illustrates the importance of method and analysis in defining the role of the social scientist:

> The fact that we accept theories that attempt to explain "peasant conservatism" or prefer those that underline "peasant rebellion" will depend on the orientation of our values, and our selection will, in turn, determine the importance we attribute to different types of empirical data.[3]

Both Rodolfo Stavenhagen and C. Wright Mills have criticized severely, and not without reason, the growing tendency toward trivialization in the social sciences. Literary sociologist Jacques Leenhardt notes a similar trend in the call for a "gratuitous literature" on the part of some writers and critics:

> In believing that really modern literature must lay aside any concern with meaning, some critics and writers have in fact produced the theory of total reification of consciousness. While they thought they were "democratizing" writing by liberating it of the necessity to communicate an exceptionally felt experience, these writers and critics have led, in spite of themselves, to the theoretical expression of the radical disappearance of any human consciousness. If literature were only a long verification of someone's inexistence, it would prove that Marcuse's worst fears in *One-Dimensional Man* have been realized.[4]

---

[3] Rodolfo Stavenhagen, *Sociología y subdesarrollo* (Mexico: Nuestro Tiempo, 1981):11.

[4] Jacques Leenhardt, "Toward a Sociology of Reading," in *The Readers in the Text*. Susan R. Suleiman and Inge Crosman, eds. (Princeton: Princeton University Press, 1980): 9.

Seeking the security of established models and "molds," the researcher tends to select problems more and more limited in scope, specialized and arcane, and as a result the fruits of his or her research grow more and more useless and unintelligible to those outside the "guild" of specialists within a particular area. Mills and Stavenhagen propose,[5] in order for the social sciences to redeem themselves, that researchers set out, accepting the challenge implied, to study the most crucial problems of their time, with an approach that is synthetic rather than reductionist. This implies a willingness to follow paths uncharted, to cultivate the "sociological imagination," and open new fields of research without theoretical or methodological models from the archives to fall back on.

---

[5]See Rodolfo Stavenhagen, "¿Cómo descolonizer las ciencias?," in *Sociología y subdesarrollo* and C. Wright Mills, "On Intellectual Craftsmanship," in *The Sociological Imagination* (Oxford, 1959).

CHAPTER 1. TOWARD THE TWENTIETH CENTURY: LITERARY CULTURE FROM COLONIALISM TO INDEPENDENCE

> A million thanks for the copy you were kind enough to send me of your wonderful novel *Cecilia Valdés*. I read the work with an equal mix of pleasure and surprise, because, to be truthful, (I say this in all sincerity, hoping that you will not misunderstand) I never thought a Cuban could write anything so good.[1]

This is the letter Spanish novelist Pérez Galdós wrote to the Cuban Villaverde in 1883. Villaverde himself had sent Pérez Galdós a copy of the novel begun in Cuba in the 1830s and completed in New York in 1882. He was a romantic when he began *Cecilia Valdés* and a realist when he finished, forty-two years later, still a self-described "unknown novelist" in spite of having authored the first Cuban novel ever to be published in book form in 1838.[2] Despite the existence of more than half a million slaves condemned to illiteracy, the Cuban colony in the first half of the nineteenth century saw the rise and fall of what was to be considered its Golden Age of literature. The renaissance of the 1830s and 1840s would give birth to Latin America's first Indianist narrative as well as its first abolitionist novel.[3] The events of the nineteenth century were crucial in determining the direction the economy would take and in bringing out the characteristics that would come to define national culture in the struggle against

---

[1]Ana Cairo, ed., "Villaverde y Pérez Galdós sobre 'Cecilia Valdés'." *Letras. Cultura en Cuba*, Vol. IV (Havana: Pueblo y Educación, 1987): 95. Correspondence originally published in *La ilustración cubana*, Barcelona, June 20, 1887.

[2]Ambrosio Fornet, "Literatura y mercado en la Cuba colonial (1830-60)." *Casa de las Américas* 84 (May-June 1974): 43. The first bound Cuban novel referred to was Villaverde's *El espetón de oro*.

[3]These were, respectively, Ramón de Palma's "El ermitaño de Niágara" and Anselmo Suárez's *Francisco*, discussed in the opening pages of Ambrosio Fornet, *En blanco y negro* (Havana: Instituto del Libro, 1967): 15-17.

Spain. Most of Cuba's novelists of the period were abolitionists and separatists, if not advocates of outright independence. Villaverde's own political convictions which evolved from advocacy of annexation to the U.S. to national sovereignty, led to his arrest, near imprisonment and exile in New York. Like most of the "progressive" intelligentsia, while in Havana he sought refuge in the *tertulias*, literary circles held in private homes, protected from public scrutiny and the persecution of the colonial authorities. Villaverde offers eloquent testimony in his *Autobiografías* to the importance of Domingo del Monte's *tertulia*, then the most influential of the Havana groups, in the formation of many young writers, as well as the plight of the Cuban novel:

> Anselmo Suárez finally wrote and read his novel *Francisco* in Del Monte's *tertulia*, which was unpublishable in Cuba at that time. That was why Mr. Madden, the abolitionist, while on a visit to Havana around 1840, had taken the manuscript with him to England. I had of course come to understand that it was useless to attempt to publish anything in the novelistic genre in Cuba; it would be like writing a novel only to preserve it in manuscript form for a long, long time. I had no lack of material for novels. It was right around that time that I had copied the *Official Diary of a Runaway Slave Catcher*, which contained an inexhaustible store of bloody and tragic incidents in which slaves figure as the heroes or as Scottish clansmen. But in order to write that as a historic novel, I would have had to turn the runaway black slaves into Indians and transfer the scene of events to someplace that had Indians, all of which was repugnant to my ideas on the novel whose local character I believe to be indispensable.[4]

Villaverde belonged to the last wave of nineteenth-century intellectuals who had forged a creole culture in the period of transition toward a Cuban culture. It was not, in fact, until the eighteenth century that the groundwork was laid for cultural development of any sort in the colony. The printing press arrived in 1720 and close on its heels followed the establishment of the first two institutions of learning on the island; the seminary of San Carlos, in 1722, and the University of San Gerónimo, in 1728. But it was not until 1774 that higher education would extend beyond theology at the Seminary of San Carlos. Founded

---

[4]Cirilo Villaverde, *Autobiografías*, in *Letras. Cultura en Cuba*, Ana Cairo, ed. (Havana: Pueblo y Educación, 1987): IV.5-6.

by a Cuban bishop at the school suddenly left vacant when the Jesuits were expelled in 1767, it was the first educational institution not strictly limited to filling the ranks of the priesthood. Although the grounds for admission were extremely rigid, in terms of race and class, excluding "all those not descended from ancient Christians ... all those who descended from blacks, mulattoes or mestizos" along with "the sons of mechanics,"[5] students received a liberal, enlightened education at San Carlos. It was there that Father Varela, an early advocate of independence for all the Latin American colonies, having been appointed to the Chair of Philosophy, revolutionized education on the island by lecturing exclusively in Spanish instead of the traditional Latin, from 1813 on. A Spaniard by birth, Varela became one of the most influential figures in the cultural life of the colony due to his accessibility to a wide audience and popularity as an educator, philosopher and advocate of the colonies' right to independence. He was also, and not coincidentally, author of Cuba's first local best-sellers, along with the poet Heredia. Their islandwide renown as authors, together with their modestly successful print-runs, gave the impression of a "literary market" in the first part of the century. But in Varela's case it was the Seminary that allowed for his publishing success. In 1821 he had roughly 150 students and by 1822, nearly 300, which would indicate a total of 500 copies in circulation, at best.

Ambrosio Fornet, Cuba's foremost scholar of nineteenth-century literary life, has studied Heredia's correspondence in order to calculate the number of copies of his works in existence at that time. He printed two editions of his poems: the first in New York in 1825 and the second in Mexico in 1832. Of the first edition, costing approximately 1.50 pesos, around 200 copies circulated in Cuba; of the second edition, around 150 copies were sold at 2.50 pesos each. All in all, Fornet concludes, 400 copies of his poems were sold over a ten-year period. This was a typical average: during Cuban literature's boom in the first half of the nineteenth century, the greatest sales of any Cuban book costing more than one peso fluctuated between 200 and 250 copies. And this, at a time when Havana was, along with Mexico City, New York, Philadelphia, Rio de Janeiro

---

[5]Antonio Bachiller y Morales, *Apuntes para la historia de las letras y de la instrucción pública de la Isla de Cuba* (Havana: P. Massana, 1859: I.1534, cited in Hortensia Pichardo Viñals, *La actitud estudiantil en Cuba durante el siglo XIX* (Havana: Editorial de las Ciencias Sociales): 4.

and Bahia, one of the six cities in the Americas with more than 100,000 inhabitants.[6]

There is a historical relationship in both the "old" and "new" worlds between the growth of educational institutions and literature's circulation in society at large, between textbook production and the rise of publishing and distribution, as is somewhat reflected in the interdependence between Varela the author and Varela the philosophy professor. However, in Cuba the ups and downs in the movement to establish a literary tradition came in rapid succession; the pendulum swung more violently in the last of the colonies. And Cuba's unstable yet always active literary life in the nineteenth century is all the more astounding when viewed against its demographics: by the end of the 1800s only a third of the population was literate. Conditions were markedly different from those in Europe where universalization of education, and the demand for textbooks, laid the basis for the development of a publishing industry:

> Compulsory education was established in most of the industrialized countries by the middle of the nineteenth century. In France, general education was made compulsory in 1833 and in Britain in 1870, but by this time literacy was fairly general because of the many schools already in existence. A number of publishing houses built up a stock of school textbooks....[7]

Sugar, coffee, slavery, the abolitionist movement and upheaval within the Spanish monarchy made the nineteenth century alternately productive, inspired, chaotic and ultimately frustrated, with regard to its literary production. In the Cuban colony, the trend was the opposite of that occurring in the European nations. Over the course of the nineteenth century, illiteracy on the island grew as the population increased. Ever suspicious of their educated subjects, all the Spanish administration had to do in order to swell the ranks of the illiterate was to allow the population to grow without providing more schools, as Fornet has

---

[6]Research into Varela and Heredia's publishing and distribution histories, as well as population statistics, was done by Ambrosio Fornet and published in his article on nineteenth-century literary journals, "Lo que viven las rosas." *Revolución y cultura* (May 1981): 27-31.

[7]Per Gedin, trans., George Bisset, *Literature in the Marketplace* (New York: Overlook Press, 1977): 28.

pointed out. His research indicates that in 1827 the illiteracy rate was 85% in a population of 700 thousand; in 1861, it was 80% in a population of one million; in 1887, it was approximately 72% in a population of one million six hundred thousand. "That is to say, that while the illiteracy rate dropped, the number of illiterates was on the rise. The 85% in 1827 equalled 595 thousand; the 72% in 1887 equalled 1,152,000. This phenomenon sealed the fate of books and literary journals in Cuba....."[8]

Over the course of the nineteenth century the battle for Cuban culture was waged among the literate minority, a minority distributed between the literati, the university and the sugar elite. The changing policy and tactics of the monarchy toward its overseas possessions had immediate repercussions in educated society, often pitting one group against another and aggravating divisions within each. The colonial administration's vigilance of the activities of the literati indirectly affected literary production since it caused the "sugarocracy" to remain aloof, thus depriving Cuban writers of patronage, their natural base of economic and social support. Censorship was a much more direct obstacle to literary development. It was not, however, among the literati or the plantation owners but on the grounds of the university and seminaries that a protracted struggle to win the "hearts and minds" of the educated minority—their political and cultural loyalty—was occurring. Initial tranquility in the cloistered university gave way to increasing unrest as a result of tensions between the religious orders and the military. The military command considered the universities the perfect source for conscripts for the Voluntary White Militia and the military presence on campus only contributed further to anti-Spanish sentiments. While the religious attempted to improve and expand curriculum, the administration placed more and more restrictions on what the university could offer, first prohibiting the study of law for all creoles and ultimately eliminating advanced study on the island in all disciplines other than theology. To pursue those studies, you had to go to Spain. The colonial administration was convinced that all literate, educated Cubans either were or had the potential to become Spain's enemies, and to that end, when the Ten Years War broke out General Antonio Peláez wrote in a pamphlet published in Madrid in 1869: "I received verbal orders that, since they were the

---

[8]Fornet, "Lo que viven las rosas," 31.

principal factors in the rebellion, any doctor, lawyer, notary or teacher that was apprehended with the rebels should be immediately shot."[9]

A general's report from the same year includes a list of prestigious individuals apprehended in the insurrection in Camagüey; among the 200 arrested, 18 were lawyers, 10 doctors, two dentists, a pharmacist, a professor, five university students, a university graduate, and a notary. The rest included 98 *hacendados*, 48 peasants, two writers and a handful of artisans and employees.[10] This prompted then Governor Lersundi to conclude that: "Public education, from the University down to the town schoolhouse had become a conspiracy against national unity."[11]

Lersundi's successor to the governorship, Count Valmaseda, embarked on an even fiercer campaign of *españolización* of the Cuban elite. It was he who passed the decree eliminating the granting of doctorates on Cuban soil in all disciplines other than theology, hoping in this way to channel the children of the elite toward the motherland and thus cultivate greater loyalty—a new generation of hispanophiles. But forced university study in Spain had the opposite effect; their years on the Peninsula convinced many students, among them José Martí, of the need for separation at any price.

The organic links between education, letters and insurrection date back almost to the founding of the first seminaries and universities on the island and were strengthened, in the early part of the nineteenth century, by the teachings and influence of Varela, many of whose students went on to become professors themselves and influence a new generation. Medardo Vitier, who wrote on Varela's works, declared: "I don't know if Varela ever fully realized that his teachings undermined the foundations of the colony.[12]

Under the general censorship governing all literature pertaining to the Americas since the sixteenth century, an 1837 decree further prohibited the entry into Cuba "of all printed matter that attempted to provoke discontent and foment

---

[9]Fernando Portuondo, *Estudios de historia de Cuba*, 98, cited in Pichardo Viñals, *La actitud estudiantil en Cuba durante el siglo XIX* (Havana: Editorial de Ciencias Sociales, 1893): 73.

[10]Pichardo Viñals, *La actitud estudiantil*, 73.

[11]Fernando Portuondo, cited in *La actitud estudiantil*, 73.

[12]Medardo Vitier, cited in Pichardo Viñals, *La actitud estudiantil*, 34.

disunity,"[13] aimed at preventing the circulation of works by such Cuban authors as José Antonio Saco and Gertrudis Gómez de Avellanada. Her novels, published in Spain, were banned from the island in 1844. Governor Lersundi backed up the decree by banning all gatherings, in workshops or other locales, for the purposes of reading and commenting on literary works and periodicals, to little or no avail. The university students quickly stepped in to fill the gap; those at home corresponded with those forced to study abroad, requesting the latest works of philosophy, history and literature unavailable on the island. Figures such as Del Monte opened their homes to the intelligentsia and the *tertulia* arose as the primary means of dissemination of European literary works and those of its members. These gatherings also served as a forum for artistic and social concerns, the primary social concern of the day being the slave question. *Sab*, *Francisco*, *El negro Francisco* and *Romualdo*, among the novels published in the first half of the century, all take their titles from the names of their slave protagonists. Whereas the majority of the upper classes were proslavery plantation owners, the literary intelligentsia was overwhelmingly abolitionist. Del Monte's group actively promoted the emancipation of slaves and its leader encouraged the elaboration of literary works which addressed that question. The abolition of slavery in 1840 dealt a harsh economic blow to the creole bourgeoisie and in working toward that goal, Del Monte's group had acted as both cultural and political vanguard. The membership of the Del Monte group spanned all sectors of Cuban society, from the emancipated slave, Francisco Manzano, to artisans such as the poet Plácido, to the middle strata, represented by Heredia, as well as the bourgeoisie to which Del Monte belonged, evidencing a high degree of cohesion among the proponents of a national literary movement within the larger struggle for nationhood.

None of the young men who had "come out" publicly as writers in Havana under the tutelage of Del Monte in the 1830s had a profession. They would later become teachers, journalists or lawyers, the traditional vocations of aspiring "men of letters," but they had all initially nurtured hopes of making some money as authors and editors.[14]

In the 1830s a number of Cuban poets began to put out books of verse, and it appeared that these works, previously confined to newspapers and magazines, had found a market. As we noted earlier, Villaverde's novel, *El espetón de oro*,

---

[13]Pichardo Viñals, *La actitud estudiantil*, 47.

[14]Fornet, "Lo que viven las rosas," 42-43.

was published in book form in the late 1930s after its successful episodic printing in the magazine *El album*. Two books of poetry by Plácido, the pen name of Gabriel de la Concepción Valdés, the most widely disseminated Cuban poet of the nineteenth century, also appeared around the same time but only after he had gained popularity by writing a poem a day, at roughly 82 cents per poem, under contract to the editor of the newspaper *La aurora de Matanzas*.

That decade saw as many titles of poetry published as in the preceding two decades and three times as many books as in the first thirty years of the century, as the following table indicates:[15]

Decade	Books	Booklets	Titles
1800-09	-	15	15
1810-19	2	7	9
1820-29	6	33	39
1830-39	25	25	50
TOTAL	33	80	113

Between 1838 and 1839, either in book form, literary journals or manuscripts that circulated among the literati, the novels, plays and poetry that would, as a corpus, offer the first coherent image of what today is considered national literature appeared, among them *Francisco*, by Suárez Romero, *Antonelli*, by Echeverría, the early version of *Cecilia Valdés* and *Poesías de Plácido*.[16]

The proliferation of titles and editions of the 1830s, the cohesion of the literary movement and the growth of the printing industry would all seem to point to the existence of a strong market, at least in Havana. There were, at that point, ten printing presses in Havana and the cost of raw materials—paper which used to be imported from Spain could now be imported from the U.S.—had gone down. Soon, an edition of 300 copies of a one-hundred-page book, modestly printed and bound, would cost as little as 112 pesos , or less than forty cents a copy. "Publishing a book would still be a risk but no longer a luxury,"[17] or so

---

[15]Ambrosio Fornet, "Literatura y mercado en la Cuba colonial," 41.

[16]Fornet, "Literatura y mercado," 41.

[17]Fornet, "Literatura y mercado," 44.

it appeared. European correspondents who received copies of many of the titles published over the decade attributed the literary renaissance to the interest and economic support of the prosperous sugar- and coffee-producing class. But, in truth,

> The splendid literary movement which, when viewed from a distance, gave the country a renaissance image, existed in spite of the ruling classes, the censorship, the absence of a broad-based reading public, and the hostile atmosphere. It was an ontological scandal. In less than five years, it had gone through a cycle of development that should have taken fifteen: at its high point in 1838, by 1841 the literary movement was in decline.[18]

Havana's short-lived literary renaissance, the rise and fall of book publishing in the capital, was certainly affected by political upheaval in Spain and its repercussions in the colonies, royal decrees on the circulation of printed matter and the cost of production and distribution, but the root cause was much more elemental: lack of readers for literary works. The literary movement, having gained momentum, required a national public to sustain its growth. Without universal education and the birth of a mass market for books, literature would not break out of the marginal, elite circle within which it was confined. The reading public was still a minority and within that minority the most dedicated and dynamic vanguard confronted an elite indifferent to the movement to promote national cultural expression in literature and the arts. These conditions inevitably brought on a cycle of failure and retreat in both book publishing and periodicals alike, as vehicles for the dissemination of literature. Desperation led authors to try the "subscription" method of book publishing, the same method employed with varying degrees of success by the literary journals of the period, although the history of instability among Cuban periodical publications dates from the founding of the first, *El papel periódico*, in 1790, to the influential although no less doomed *Orígenes* of the 1950s.

The crisis of book publishing that led authors and editors to turn to literary journals as an alternate outlet for their works in the 1840s was in reality the crisis of readership and the colonial indifference to education. Even at the peak of the small literary renaissance, the average print-run of 300 copies of a 100-page book was determined by the maximum level of consumption one could

---

[18]Fornet, "Literatura y mercado," 42.

hope to attain from the Havana-Matanzas market. Rarely were more than 200 copies of a literary work ever sold, and neither authors nor printers were willing to go beyond that limit.[19]

Without wealthy patrons willing to take them under wing, or a stable readership that would allow books to pay for themselves, Cuban authors devised a means of printing "on credit" which they would continue to resort to through the 1950s. Book publishing by subscription was the equivalent of a collective patronage network and depended on the author being viewed as a solvent citizen by the printer in order for it to work. Under the subscription method, the author approached the printer with a list of subscribers, each of whom had pledged to purchase a predetermined number of copies once the book was published. Although still extremely limited in terms of readers and distribution, subscription publishing had a number of advantages: it placed the author in direct contact with the reading public and delivered the printer a guaranteed market. The subscription method did not promote the development of a stable reading public for literature; it merely took advantage of a small, captive audience of friends and relations. Thus, the life of Cuban letters cannot be traced by studying the movement of limited editions through society but rather by examining the relationship that developed between readers, writers and their patrons in the pages of periodicals. These prove a more accurate indicator of the state of Cuban literature and its reception because the price and distribution mechanisms for periodicals allowed them to aspire to a much broader reading public.

El plantel, a literary journal established in 1838 by the Del Monte group, began its life with over a thousand subscribers, a full two-thirds of the literate, educated reading public of Havana, composed of lawyers, notaries, surveyors, pharmacists, university professors and members of the prestigious Sociedad Económica de Amigos del País. The well-known *Revista bimestre*, as a point of comparison, never had more than 280 subscribers.[20] Although in crisis three months later due to a dispute between the editors and printers, *El plantel* continued to publish for another nine months and was one of the most promising edito-

---

[19]There was traditionally a planned surplus of 100 copies for the author to give away to friends and family, bringing the price up from the deceptively low 40 cents to 60 cents a copy. Transportation for the 200 copies destined for the market brought the cost up to nearly a *peso* which, in the end, kept the book out of reach of a greater number of potential buyers.

[20]Fornet, "Literatura y mercado," 45.

rial projects of its day. In order for a literary journal to build readership and aid in sustaining the burgeoning literary movement, it was not enough to find willing subscribers but to retain them in sufficient numbers to keep the enterprise afloat economically. The indifference of the educated Havana public is the primary reason why none of the literary journals of the period survived much beyond two years. *El album*, *La mariposa* and *El plantel* lasted 12 months; *La siempreviva*, 24; *La cartera cubana*, 30, a record which would only be surpassed by the *Revista de la Habana* (1853-57). Havana's literary journals experienced the same meteoric rise and fall that signalled the crisis of book publishing in the capital, over the same period. At the start of 1839 all five literary journals were in circulation, by the end of that year two had folded and in early 1841, none was left.

The sudden demise of the journals had less to do with the nature and quality of the literature being produced and disseminated in their pages than with the composition of Cuban society, its profound divisions. Literary journals have never found a solid base among the very poor or the very rich, and nineteenth-century Cuba offered little middle ground. Some editors sought to fill the void by wooing female readers, but still had to overcome the reluctance of the wealthy creoles to support literary pursuits which, by manifesting a cultural life separate from that of Spain, were likely to arouse the suspicion if not the wrath of the colonial authorities. The most stable of the periodicals, *La cartera cubana* (1838-40), *La revista de la Habana* (1853-57) and the later *Revista de Cuba* (1877-84) and its successor *La revista cubana* (1885-94) were financed by their founders and editors without having to depend on subscribers. In losing the battle to keep the literary journals—founded with such enthusiasm and high expectations—alive, Havana's authors and editors had lost their one remaining hope of achieving professional status, of guaranteeing literature's social life through the development of a stable print culture, and once again retreated to the *tertulias*, the narrowing circle of support offered by the "guild," sheltered from the alternating indifference and hostility of the *hacendados*.

As Fornet reveals in his study "Literature and Market in Colonial Cuba (1830-60)," the greatest irony of Cuba's brief "golden age" of literature was that, objectively, conditions favorable to the consolidation of a national literary movement actually did exist, making the succession of editorial projects gone awry all the more frustrating. There was a dynamic group of writers with a clear sense of vocation, growing economic prosperity and development in Havana and Matanzas, and a significant increase in the number of modern printing presses. There was also the potential for opening up a national market for literature. In 1840, the nonslave, and therefore potentially literate, population was 42% of the total population, twice what it had been at the turn of the century.[21] It was, however, neither the literary journals nor aspiring authors who benefitted from these conditions, but the newspapers. *El faro* and *La prensa* were founded in 1841, entering into competition with the more established newspapers, the *Diario de La Habana* and *Noticioso y lucero*. There were roughly 5,000 newspaper subscribers in total, for whose loyalty they competed, primarily on the basis of their literary sections offered as a *divertissement* between the columns of finan-cial and other "hard" news. *La prensa* was soon to shake up the newspaper world by following up on the results of a crude "market survey" with a change in format. Having determined that there were two distinct markets for the paper, with differing interests and purchasing power—one interested in financial news and advertising space; the other, only in fashion and literature—the editors estab-lished a two-tier subscription structure. To please the *hacendados*, they charged the high rate of $1.20 but placed ads and notices at no additional charge; for the middle-and upper-class women, they charged only sixty cents and committed themselves to publishing a chapter of a novel a day. These chapters were format-ted so that they could be easily cut out, bound and transformed into *books* of ap-proximately 240 pages. *La prensa* also gave away attractive, colorful bookcovers to its female subscribers.[22]

The success of *La prensa*'s literary section prompted rival newspapers to devote equal space to literature. *La prensa* responded by publishing installments of two novels a day, and the tradition continued through the end of the nine-teenth century. *La prensa* had uncovered a market for literature not in evidence due to both the inaccessibility of books and the indifference of the elite to local culture. The newspapers found it more expedient and economical to import European novels, thus Cuban literature found itself deprived of editors and "sub-scribers" at the very moment when more novels were being consumed than ever before. The literature circulating massively on the island was not produced there; imports supplanted the native product and the link uniting writers and readers was severed. When newspaper installments eclipsed the problematic literary journals and the limited Cuban editions as the principal means of dissemination,

---

[21]Fornet, "Literatura y mercado," 47.

[22]For a detailed history of *La prensa*, see Ambrosio Fornet, "Literatura y mercado," 48-50.

literature was "denationalized."[23] The one positive legacy of the newspapers' strangulation of Cuban letters were the new mechanical and steam presses installed in most of the print shops in Havana. This, paradoxically, made it possible to cut the price of book production as well. In the 1840s, the cost of having a book printed was reduced by half, and literary production, for some genres, doubled. Poetry rose from 50 titles in the late 1830s to 97 in the 1840s.[24] Literary production rose by 94% in a decade; book production by 156%. This increase, though due primarily to technological advances and a change in the method of production, had a social impact which altered the Cuban book's image and the writer's status in society. The act of publishing a book,

> by becoming relatively accessible, lost its aura of magic: from then on it would be a transaction, not a rite. The new rhythm of production demystified books. As a consequence, the social image of the writer also changed, as well as the writer's relations with other writers, critics and the public. The rise in literary production was viewed, through the camera obscura of the age, as an inverted image; people began to speak of the decline of Cuban letters, the deterioration of the literary product. Naturally, the quality of the works fell in direct proportion to the quantity. It was not that the writing was worse but that even the worst works were being published. Since the nature of this phenomenon has been overlooked by literary historians, the period of transition between one form of book production and appropriation and another came to be known simply as the age of "bad taste."[25]

While readers and writers in Havana appeared locked into a vicious cycle of false starts, of editorial projects incapable of broadening literature's narrow channels, significant changes were occurring in the provinces. A *national* reading public was making its presence felt outside the capital. In 1855, *Cantos del Siboney*, by the poet Fornaris, became a national best-seller. Copies of Fornaris' work were being sold all over the country, and there were five editions in all of

---

[23]Fornet, "Literatura y mercado," 49.

[24]Fornet, "Literatura y mercado," 50.

[25]Ambrosio Fornet, "Criollismo, cubanía y producción editorial (1855-1885)," *Santiago*17 (March 1976): 51.

the *Cantos* between 1855 and 1863. It was more than a literary "hit" or a purely artistic phenomenon, and Fornaris himself, in a prologue to the last edition in 1888, attributed the success of his poems to their political significance. For his readership, "the Siboney Indians represented the oppressed Cuban people, and the Caribe Indians, their unjust oppressors."[26] Readers embraced as their own the symbols of an emerging nationality:

> This was a different reading public, both quantitatively and qualitative-ly, from that which had up until then determined literary/editorial suc-cess or failure. To distinguish it from the traditional reading public, the privileged classes of Havana and Matanzas, Fornaris called it simply "el pueblo."[27]

His readers were to be found in the provinces, from all social sectors and even the rural areas, especially the Eastern region which around 1860 could be consid-ered the most creole section of the country: 85% of the population were non-slaves and only 5% were Spaniards.[28]

At the same time, journalism was becoming more prevalent outside Havana due to a developing communications network, with 16 of the 30 periodicals in existence in 1856 based in the countryside. Although journalism was growing, publishing activity was the most significant indicator of a rise in print culture outside of Havana in the late 1850s. Twenty-five of the fifty titles of poetry pub-lished in Cuba between 1856 and 1858 were published outside of Havana (11 in Matanzas, 8 in Villaclara and 6 in Oriente).[29]

Bayamo was at the center of the cultural "awakening" in the countryside. It was there that Fornaris had composed his *Cantos del Siboney*, and Carlos

---

[26]Fornaris, cited in Ambrosio Fornet, "Criollismo, cubanía y producción editorial (1855-1885)," 109.

[27]Fornet, "Criollismo, cubanía y producción editorial," 110.

[28]Fornet, "Criollismo, cubanía y producción editorial," 110.

[29]Fornet, "Criollismo, cubanía y producción editorial," 111.

Manuel de Céspedes[30] founded the Philharmonic Society in 1851, around which its cultural life revolved. With a nonslave population of 30,000, Bayamo could sustain the literary renaissance that produced a stream of works by local authors in the 1850s and 1860s, put out by small presses there and in Santiago. Santiago, with a free population of 60,000, was developing its own literary movement under the direction of the printer Miguel A. Martínez, editor of the newspaper *El orden*, and Francisco Javier Vidal who founded the magazine *Semanario cubano* in 1855. Santiago was another important cultural center, with its own Philharmonic Society, three printing presses and a considerable market for children's books, judging by the success of Juan Bautista Sagarra's collection of children's books, "Librería de los niños cubanos," which by 1855 included eight titles. Martínez' press put out an edition of *Poesías* by Luisa Pérez and two titles by Sagarra. And it was in Santiago in 1862 that *Cantos guajiros de varios jóvenes*, edited by Eliseo A. Martínez, appeared, possibly the first anthology of traditional rural poetry to be published.[31]

It appeared that any author could now afford to do without the Havana reading public:

> The success of *Cantos del Siboney* was not an isolated phenomenon. Books had discovered a new reading public and with it the editorial possibilities of creole and popular literature. For that reason, Fornaris and El Cucalambé faced the problem of national literature on a concrete level, as producers who must satisfy the needs of the consumer. They didn't have a *mission* but rather a *function* to fulfill. For the "classic" authors, this had always been a theoretical problem: no one—except Del Monte—demanded of them an autochthonous literature which they, nevertheless, had to create if they wanted to assert their own artistic personality.[32]

---

[30]Carlos Manuel de Céspedes (Bayamo, 1819-74). Cuban patriot, author, director of the Philharmonic Society. He was declared President of the Republic in Arms during the Ten Years War.

[31]Fornet, "Criollismo, cubanía y producción editorial," 112.

[32]Fornet, "Criollismo, cubanía, y producción editorial," 111.

The success or failure of the literary endeavors of the poets Fornaris and El Cucalambé was not determined by their reception in *tertulias*, through the inter-mediary elite, but directly in terms of the literary market. In this sense, Fornaris may have been the first Cuban author to seriously address the problem of con-sumption, of literature in the marketplace, of the publishing needs of the national literary movement. [33]

From this brief history of literature and the market outside of Havana,[34] it becomes clear that the reading public for poetry—as Fornaris' island-wide suc-cess brings to light—was far more prevalent in the rural areas where the trouba-dor tradition lived on. The readership in Havana, from the middle and laboring classes, was primarily for prose narrative and theater.

Costumbrista literature experienced a boom in the 1860s, along with its equivalent in theater, *el teatro bufo*. Two plays, within the *teatro bufo* tradition, were written in 1868 at the outset of the Ten Years War: *Los negros catedráticos* by Francisco Fernández and *Perro huevero, aunque le quemen el hocico* by Juan Francisco Valerio. During a wartime production of Valerio's play in the Villa-nueva Theater in Havana in 1860, members of the Voluntary Militia in atten-dance considered many of the passages to be in support of the revolution and responded to the audience's enthusiasm with a volley of shots.

Over the course of the Ten Years War, a national identity had been forged, that of the *Cuban* people, with the resulting transition from creole to the more assertive *Cuban* cultural expression. Toward the end of the war, Francisco de Paula Galabert's *Cuadros de costumbres cubanas* (1875), made explicit reference, for the first time in the tradition of *costumbrista* literature, to national identity in the title, and in 1876 a volume entitled *Los tres primeros historiadores de la Isla de Cuba* appeared. The growing yet unsatisfied demand for national litera-ture over this period resulted in a sudden proliferation of bookseller-editors in postwar Cuba. In 1879, booksellers Miguel de Villa and José Gutiérrez embarked on a short-lived but important publishing experiment, making them the first

---

[33]Fornet, "Criollismo, cubanía y producción editorial," 112.

[34]For a complete history of literature and society in nineteenth-century Cuba, on which this brief overview is based, see Ambrosio Fornet, "Literatura y merca-do en la Cuba colonial (1830-60), *Casa de las Américas* 84 (1974): 40-52; "Crio-llismo, cubanía y producción editorial (1855-1885)," *Santiago* 17 (1975): 109-21; and "Lo que viven las rosas," *Revolución y cultura* (May 1981): 28-31. All are excerpts from his, then, forthcoming study *El libro en Cuba*.

professional editors to emerge in the second half of the century. As booksellers, they had first-hand knowledge of the possibilities and limitations of the market, and one can therefore consider their editions a barometer of preferences and concerns of Cuban readers following the Zanjón pact, which brought the insurrection to a halt, and its influence on postwar intellectual production.

The printers and editors who had made a name for themselves in the decades before the insurrection responded to the postwar demand with poetry anthologies of *cantos* and *décimas* for distribution in the provinces. Ambrosio Fornet attributes the popularity of the décima and its predominance in postwar literary production to the role played by the peasant masses during the war and the newly won social and political importance of the rural zones.[35] They were also extremely significant in terms of literary production and market: between 1876 and 1880, in the years immediately before and after the signing of the Zanjón pact, more titles were published in the *décima* genre than in any other period.

Although many of the rural small presses remained active after the war, primarily in Güines, Sagua la Grande and Cienfuegos, these areas were for the most part devastated by the war and the Havana-Matanzas printers easily regained the upper hand. The unequal distribution of nineteenth-century book publishing by geographic region reflected the economic disparity between the eastern and western provinces. The war merely exacerbated the imbalance by further concentrating resources for agricultural and industrial development in Havana and Matanzas after Zanjón. The graphics industry underwent a similar process after the war although it did not immediately lead to a systematic reduction in the number of printing presses and small shops. In fact, the printshops which first appeared in the countryside in the 1850s had increased in number by the 1880s. In 1885 there were at least 20 relatively important small presses outside of Havana, without counting those operating in other provincial capitals.[36]

But the communications and transportation network, the infrastructure laid in the 1850s, which had once facilitated the emergence and development of provincial printshops, would squeeze them out of the market toward the end of the century. The relative prosperity of postwar Havana would allow its printers to modernize their shops, equipping them for the mass production that was to

---

[35]Fornet, "Criollismo, cubanía y producción editorial," 119-20.

[36]Fornet, "Criollismo, cubanía y producción editorial," 121.

monopolize the national market. Havana presses flooded the island with newspapers and textbooks whose price and quality rivaled those of the provincial shops:

> From 1880 on, cases like that of Sagarra in Santiago would no longer be possible: intellectual and editorial production supported almost exclusively by the local market, with a few exceptions such as the newspaper *Aurora del Yumurí* which as late as 1886 put out 3,000 copies for the internal consumption of Matanzas alone. Havana-based production swept away all possible competition from the provinces and turned the other urban centers into mere parasites, consuming Havana's goods. In that sense, you could say that Zanjón was Havana's definitive triumph over the provinces. [37]

In terms of book production, in the last two decades of the century only a handful of presses outside of Havana, in Matanzas, Cienfuegos and Santiago, remained active.

Parallel with the ongoing campaign to create and sustain vehicles for autonomous literary expression which we have attempted to outline—the economic battle to keep the literary journals alive without broad readership and the political battles with the colonial administration over "national unity" versus Cuban culture—nineteenth-century literature evolved from a vaguely differentiated creole expression to a critical inward examination, the kind of long, hard look at Cuban colonial society we find in the novel *Cecilia Valdés*, not surprisingly published in exile. Over the course of the nineteenth century Cuban literature began by focusing on the land, in the period of political liberalism (1762-1819), then seeking refuge within the *individual*, with the restoration of absolutism in Spain and a period of severe restrictions for the colonies (1820-49), followed by an examination of colonial society itself in the works of the late nineteenth century[38] such as *Cecilia Valdés*, 1882, and *Mi tío el empleado*, 1887, by Ramón Meza, which was published in Barcelona.

The literary movement of the nineteenth century made astounding advances in laying the foundations for a national literary tradition, despite the agonizing history of the literary journals and the tremendous effort involved in publication.

---

[37]Fornet, "Criollismo, cubanía y producción editorial," 121.

[38]For an overview of literary tendencies and themes corresponding to historical periods within the nineteenth century, see Francisco López Segrera, *Cuba: cultura y sociedad* (Havana: Letras Cubanas, 1989): 42-60.

It is important to bear in mind that until the end of the century, Cuban literary culture could not be openly manifested on the island and in fact had few direct legal channels to society. Many of the major journals and works of the intelligentsia were published in exile and circulated clandestinely through the *tertulias*. It is well known that little of José Martí's work, nearly 30 volumes, was published in Cuba during his lifetime. Nevertheless, the last decades of the nineteenth century were marked by intense cultural and intellectual activity, on the part of those who remained and those in exile, which carried over to the early years of the twentieth century. The Spanish-American War of 1898 did not seem to have an effect, in terms of *volume*, on literary production, but the inauguration of the Republic would produce a change in the collective consciousness that in time brought literary production on the island to a near standstill:[39]

> Upon attaining independence, so mediated...Cubans' superficial, incredulous, and mocking character came to the surface. There was no longer a defined historical ideal to draw them like a magnet; there was no longer a Martí to stand over and inflame them.... They no longer confronted the tremendous Spanish *resistance*, in the face of which the human and poetic phenomenon of the *mambí* was created. Homeland, flag and hymn quickly degenerated into a decorated void.[40]

The momentum of the 1890s sustained literary production for the first few years of the Republic, but from 1908 on, following the second U.S. intervention in 1906, there was a marked decrease in literary activity attributed to the anticlimax of formal independence without substantive change which came to be known as the "mortal leap" into the twentieth century. Although one of Cuba's major novelists, Miguel de Carrión, published *Las honradas* in 1918, and *Las impuras*, in 1919, the hiatus in literary production would last, with few such exceptions, until the 1920s.

---

[39]López Segrera, *Cuba: cultura y sociedad*, 109-10.

[40]Cintio Vitier, cited in Jorge Ibarra, *Un análisis psicosocial del cubano: 1898-1925* (Havana: Editorial de Ciencias Sociales): 20-21.

CHAPTER 2. WRITING AT THE TURN OF THE CENTURY: PRINTING PRESSES AND LITERARY CIRCLES

Conditions prevalent in the republican period differed remarkably little from those of the nineteenth century with regard to literary life. Cuba had become a Republic without eradicating the many ills inherited from the colony and writers and thinkers responded with pessimism or silence. Censorship practices of the Spanish colonialists, the lack of material and cultural resources, together with a 75% illiteracy index toward the end of the nineteenth century, constituted insurmountable obstacles for the development of a national publishing industry. A comparison of resources available for literary production in the Spanish colony and then in the latter half of the twentieth century reveals how little material, social and economic conditions had improved. As we have seen:

> From the very beginning, the production and diffusion of books had to be limited to about 200 copies per title because of the small number of educated people. These copies were distributed at very high cost on subscription in advance. In the beginning distribution was restricted to Havana and Matanzas; during the second half of the 19th century it was extended to other provincial capitals.[1]

And, in the first half of the twentieth century:

> Cuba continued to be a nation without a significant production of books. Book production was restricted to textbooks, sold at a high price, basically for the private schools. From the Ministry of Education's budget, corresponding to the years 1949-50, out of $54,994,059.75, only .01

---

[1]Sigried Taubert, ed., *The Book Trade of the World* (Hamburg: Verlag für Buchmarkt-Forschung; New York: R.R. Bowker, 1976): II.148.

percent was allocated for purchasing books for libraries and public schools. The Cuban State does not have a policy regarding books, does not concern itself with this problem.[2]

Those writers who published their works, from the 1920s on, when literary production revived, with their own money or taking subscriptions to finance the edition, *still* had only the most limited access to the reading public—a minority—and its impressions and reactions. Readership was generally restricted to a small circle of friends to whom autographed copies of their published works were distributed as gifts. The writer's condition was not unlike that of the Cuban physician who, on the one hand, could barely earn a living in the public clinics for those who could not pay full fees and, on the other, didn't dare charge well-to-do patients in whose social circles he moved.

Poet Nicolás Guillén was able to publish his first volume of poems when he had the good fortune to win the lottery, but that was the exception not the rule. The fate of most Cuban writers in the 1930s and 1940s without personal resources to invest in publication is summed up by short story writer Onelio Jorge Cardoso. Publishing one's work in the Cuban Republic was once again both a luxury and a risk:

> I never had publishers and could not publish my books. There were writers who made great efforts to obtain money in order to be able to publish their books. Of course, all copies had to be given away to friends as presents because there was no one who was interested in the Cuban author.[3]

The conditions for the formation of an independent nation—traditionally, universal education and industrialization—have tended to stimulate literary production. If European publishing had had to rely, as Cuba did in the 19th and early 20th century, on literary works alone to foster its development it would not have prospered. It was not until 1960, a full century after the birth of the publishing industry in Europe, that Cuban book production received the impetus of free, universal education which European publishing and, by extension, literary

---

[2]*El libro en Cuba* (Havana: Cámara Cubana del Libro, 1949).

[3]Cardoso cited in Sigfred Taubert, ed., *The Book Trade of the World*, II.148.

production—particularly the novel—had benefitted from in the mid-nineteenth century.

El libro en Cuba, a string of laments and observations concerning the vicissitudes of book publishing and distribution in the Republic, published in 1949, adopts a businessman's perspective in order to analyze the problems faced by book importers, as if Cuban books were either nonexistent or so few and far between that they did not warrant consideration. While it is true that relatively few works were published in Cuba annually before 1959, the greater tragedy for the literary historian is that even fewer records were kept on literary production, as such. Trelles y Govín and Peraza y Sarausa's bibliographical works (compiled and subsidized by the bibliographers themselves) indicate title, author, date and press, without specifying the number of printed copies of each work. The commonly cited figure of less than a million books produced annually in Cuba before 1959 was arrived at by combining existing data with the recollections of booksellers and printers' foremen from the last decades of the Republic:

> Completing and perfecting my Bibliography in the manner I had intended constitutes a new and increased expense (without recompense) which I am not prepared to face. I have already sacrificed too much in the printing of numerous and extensive volumes to continue my *via crucis* amidst the glacial indifference of *all the Cuban administrations* who have not had, in spite of a Treasury that had amassed hundreds of millions, a single cent to contribute, even on a small scale, to the publication of this patriotic work...and yet found $9,285 to pay Messrs. Miranda, López and Co. for the publication of an insignificant, 44 page pamphlet titled "The Cuban Republic in 1909"; $25.00 to subsidize another 76 page pamphlet put out by the *Avisador Comercial* titled "The Cuban Republic" (1910), printed on very good paper, which is its principal virtue; $10,000 as a gift to the "San Francisco Chronicle" of California (1914) for having published an issue in homage to Cuba.[4]

The Republic was founded in 1902 with few printing presses, even fewer schools, almost all private, and an illiteracy rate of sixty-four percent. Two decades later, Cuban radio broadcasting was inaugurated from the presidential palace with a speech addressed to the U.S. public, in English. Shirley Temple

---

[4]Carlos M. Trelles y Govín, *Bibliografía cubana del siglo XIX* (1900-1916) (Matanzas: Imprenta de la Viuda de Quiros, 1917): II.ii-iii.

had arrived, according to a children's ditty: "on an American ship / to teach the Cubans / how to play *one, two, three*."[5]

This ditty provides insight into popular attitudes in the 1920s toward the "mortal leap" from colony to Republic and is an early indication of the pervasive influence the U.S.-based mass-media would have on cultural channels, particularly from the 1940s on. Of all the literature of national origin printed and circulated on the island, the majority were textbooks and "in the first schoolbooks, Martí's name did not appear; the poets, essayists and prose writers of the nineteenth century remained unpublished or were never granted a second edition, languishing in archives and libraries."[6] Achieving nationhood and forming a national culture are, to a large degree, parallel processes. In Cuba, a semicolonial Republic had been founded whose officials appeared to have declared a war against national culture, its historical origins and continuity:

> From the bourgeois perspective, the historical and cultural origins of the nation were nowhere to be found. After belittling and adulterating her roots, the pseudobourgeoisie attempted a formidable feat: to declare them nonexistent.[7]

Though national culture was by no means "nonexistent," the upper-class indifference toward Cuban culture (which we have examined in detail in the nineteenth century) continued into the twentieth. Yet the absence of a publishing *industry* in no way implies that no one *writes*, and the absence of official mechanisms to facilitate the expression of national culture does not mean that it has ceased to exist:

> The short-sighted thesis, absurd in its simplism, that after thirty years of fighting for independence we had only gained a flag and a coat of arms, completely dispenses with the historical process which had culminated in the formation of a nation-state. The democratic and egalitarian

---

[5]Luis Toledo Sande, *Tres narradores agonizantes* (Havana: Editorial Arte y Literatura 1974): 15.

[6]Ambrosio Fornet, *En blanco y negro* (Havana: Instituto del Libro, 1967): 60.

[7]Fornet, *En blanco y negro*, 49.

traditions, forged over the course of the struggle for national liberation, had consolidated bonds of social solidarity in the hearts of the people which could not be dissolved by the divisionary politics of the dependent bourgeoisie and North American imperialism. Nevertheless, the subjugation of national political leadership to the dictates of foreign interests would complete the process destined to deprive the nation-state of organs capable of expressing her will and sovereignty.[8]

Literature constitutes one of the most powerful and effective vehicles for the expression of national culture. A propos of the "moribund generation," the first generation of novelists and short-story writers in the Republic, Cuban cultural historian Jorge Ibarra, in his socioliterary critique, poses the following questions concerning the relationship between dependency and literary production:

> Was the Cuban intellectual community really a community of neocolonized intellectuals? Did they believe that foreign domination constituted an irreversible social process to which our nationality would eventually succumb?[9]

As the complex cultural history of nineteenth-century Cuba reveals, it was not the official "organs of expression"—the legal and permissible channels—but the unofficial and spontaneously formed institutions and groups that voiced the will and cultural dynamic of the age. Spain, a military and economic empire in decline, used the official channels to repress cultural manifestations, in literature and the arts, that distinguished themselves from those of the metropolis; to propose "things Cuban" in literature, over the course of the 19th century was a seditious act. Heavy-handed censorship practices in the Antillean colonies, particularly toward the end of the 19th century, force one to seek popular cultural expression outside the official institutions and salons, in muralist painting, campaign diaries, chronicles and unpublished or clandestinely distributed texts. When Cuba emerged from Spain's orbit in 1898, the writer's lot did not significantly improve. Immediately following the postwar transition on both Antillean islands, the stream of rhetoric unleashed by the accommodationist upper class foretold

---

[8]Jorge Ibarra, *Nación y cultura nacional* (Havana: Letras Cubanas, 1981): 15-16.

[9]Ibarra, *Nación y cultura nacional*, 49.

optimum possibilities for economic, cultural and political development. Those with keener sensibilities predicted further aggravation of existing problems, as evidenced by the growing indifference of the interim government toward matters which did not advance its strategic interests. Writers such as Manuel Zeno Gandía in Puerto Rico and Jesús Castellanos in Cuba were erroneously characterized as "pessimistic." Far from symptomatic of an obliging, colonized mentality, their somber tone was in reality a denunciation of the neocolonial condition. Spain's open hostility in the late nineteenth century gave way to U.S. indifference toward the cultural, educational and scientific development of Cuban society. This becomes apparent when we trace the evolution of those cultural institutions established in the colony under a license granted by the crown through the first decades of the Republic.

The cornerstone of all such development is the printing press. The first printing press arrived in Cuba in 1720 under the control of the government and *Capitanía General.* For the next century and a half it would operate solely with the "express license" of His Majesty. Although restrictions were removed upon independence, the Republic did not have any presses subsidized or encouraged by state agencies. In addition, ninety-nine percent of the owners of printing presses were foreigners, whereas ninety-nine percent of the workers were Cuban:

> The Republic's indifference toward all the current expressions of our culture, holding us to the partial view we have been given, that is, their indifference toward the development of our press is, in that sense, a colonial legacy. It is not that there are no printing presses because there is nothing to publish, on the contrary, there is much to be published but no presses.[10]

When the bibliographer Peraza y Sarausa stated that there were no printing presses in the Republic, he was assessing the situation in cultural rather than commercial terms. The existence of a national printing press, supported by the State, would at that time have been the equivalent of a publishing house with cultural vision, capable of fostering Cuban culture and literary creation by allowing for moderate print-runs of works whose production costs were subsidized, and therefore free from commercial pressures in a limited market.

---

[10]Fermín Peraza y Sarausa, *La imprenta y el estado en Cuba* (Matanzas: Amigos de la Cultura Cubana, 1936): 24.

The raison d'être of the small press in the Republic was, quite to the contrary, that of charging the author fees high enough to assure the owners' profit above and beyond the cost of machinery, parts and all the other basic materials provided by the National Paper and Type Company whose U.S. offices handled the sale of most printer's materials on the island.

Most of the printing presses operating on the island in the early years of the Republic were the same presses that had been established under Spanish rule. In the early twentieth century, the U.S. printing industry became the chief supplier of parts and materials to Cuban printers due to proximity, accessibility and lower costs, while at the same time substituting U.S. exports for Cuban printed matter which had the effect of paralyzing the development of several branches of the local printing industry. The history of Cuban postage stamps is a reflection of the setbacks experienced by the printing industry as a whole upon entering the twentieth century and the republican era. Printed in Spain from engravings in the colonial era after independence, Cuban stamps were produced by the privately held American Bank Note Company and sold to the island.

As we have seen, nineteenth-century Cuba had no scarcity of excellent printers and typographers experienced in the elaborate process of hand-printing limited editions. In the early twentieth century, books and pamphlets continued to be produced in the same manner, even as technologically advanced equipment was being introduced and installed in the larger Havana print shops by U.S. commercial interests, though not essentially for the purposes of literary production.

As far as authors were concerned, Cuban literature continued to be produced, in the Republic, as it had been in the colony: through the tedious and costly process of limited, and usually hand-printed, editions of no more than 500.[11] The continued cost and difficulties of publishing, even among the literary élite, combined with its marginal channels (the reading public constituted only 47 percent of the total population in 1919), caused Cuban literature to exist in near oblivion both domestically and, to a lesser degree, internationally. Intellectual circles and prominent journals voiced the urgent need to bring to light literary works that illuminated national reality at every stage of the republican period:

---

[11]Renée Méndez Capote, like so many writers who had had one or none of their works published prior to 1959, paid the sum of 1,000 *pesos* to Hermes García and Co., printers, to prepare an edition of 500 copies of her work in 1927.

> A people without vernacular literature is unknown even to itself....
> Novels, legends, biographies, short stories, are bonds to unite us, eyes
> with which to see ourselves, sentiments through which we come to
> know and value ourselves; that is, *to be*, to exist for ourselves and for
> others.[12]

That was how the writer Montenegro expressed his concerns in the 1930s,
with sound yet partial criteria; partial in the sense that the *we* which would gain
a clearer consciousness of being and existence in the nation and the world, of the
Cuban identity through literature, excluded all but the literate minority.

Twenty years later poet, novelist and critic José Lezama Lima expressed
similar sentiments with regard to the need to nurture and bring out into the open
a contemporary Cuban literature; Lezama's outcry is at once denunciation, exhor-
tation and hope for the future:

> If one of our poems attained the kind of texture which, in its litheness,
> presents an untouched reality, anxious to be made incarnate, it would
> enter historic time, and we would recover the clarity and sharpness that
> awakens a faithful warning. The vortex of an image becomes incarnate
> when it dominates the matter shaped by the symbol. We have already
> said that, among us, we must create a tradition of the future, an image
> which seeks incarnation, fulfillment, in historic time.[13]

Literature, always an intimate expression of the human condition, whether
evasive or defiant, situates itself and the reader within the dynamics of history.
The history of Cuban literature in the Republic is, to a large degree, the history
of the efforts of its creators to see their works in print. It is also the story of
their attempts, on diverse fronts, to create conditions that would allow for the
emergence of a national literary movement. Individual writers in the Republic,
as a rule socially marginal and isolated from the crises that affected the majority,
too often failed to recognize that in order for literature to assume a social func-

---

[12]Carlos Montenegro, cited in *En blanco y negro*, 62.

[13]José Lezama Lima, *Imagen y posibilidad* (Havana: Letras Cubanas, 1981):
196. See pp. 57-61 of chapter 5 for an outline of the role played by the journal
and publishing ventures of the "Orígenes" Group under Lezama Lima's direction
in the 1940s and 1950s.

tion that extended beyond narrow circles, society itself would have to be transformed,

> while the sugar mills produced rivers of sugar and mountains of gold, and the social climbers of the capital boasted of their march to the rhythm of modern times, the highest intellects, the most sensitive souls, in a gesture of disgust and abhorrence, fell back upon the voluntary ostracism of their book-lined studies.[14]

How was a book, any book, published in the Republic? What was the complete process, in the first half of the twentieth century, from manuscript to printed volume; the circuit that led from manuscript to printer to reader? With the exception of textbooks, the procedure had not varied from the late 1800s and early 1900s to the inauguration of the National Printing House in 1961. Each writer raised funds, by whatever means at his or her disposal, or signed a contract with a printer on an installment or subscription basis, and the printing process was not initiated until payment in full had been made to the printer. Usually the author designed, edited and proofread his or her own original in the process.

Epistolary archives chronicle the writer's lot in the prerevolutionary decades. For the poet, Julián del Casal, in 1889, at the close of the colonial period, "earning a living from literature" meant a series of jobs as proofreader and journalist for the weeklies of his day:

> Although this may surprise you, I must tell you that I work very hard...and earn very little. But I am so happy because I make my living from literature! Making one's living from literature in a country like ours where everyone lives by commerce, industry, robbery, and...worse, is extremely important and constitutes an event which you should be aware of.[15]

---

[14]Raúl Roa, cited in Salvador Bueno, *Medio siglo de literatura cubana (1902-1952)* (Havana: Publications of the Cuban National Commission of UNESCO, 1953): 14-15.

[15]Unpublished letter, Julián del Casal, January 6, 1889, [Cuban] National Archives, Box 574, No. 33.

Journalism in Cuba, as in most of Latin America, though it often drained their energies, supported countless writers through the 1940s and the advent of mass-media which turned scores of fiction writers into script writers for radio novellas, slogan writers for the soap companies that sponsored the radio programming and script writers for cinema.

The text of one of Virgilio Piñera's unpublished letters, from 1944, describes the process of publication by public subscription for his book *Poesía y prosa*:

> My dear sister, we just received your letter. I hope you do marry Infante. But I am writing to tell you that my book will be out any day and I need money. You must send me 5 *pesos* before the 23rd, the date by which I must pay the printer. It will be published through public subscription, and you should contribute as well. I am short 50 *pesos* and must raise them at any cost. Vinicio has already sent me 5.... Consider the importance of my request, and do all that you can.[16]

From the end of the nineteenth century to the 1940s is a long stretch in the history of Cuban literature; its production and reception. The conditions we have outlined prevailed, without major changes, for over five decades: the lack of official support or subsidies for book production, the absence of publishing houses, a high illiteracy index, and the growing ascendency of sugar in the nation's economy to the detriment of other industries. Add to this the periodic persecution and incarceration of socially active writers and thinkers during those decades and a general picture of literary life in the Republic emerges. Against these odds, in the isolated efforts of the groups and individuals who forged the literary history of the Republic, we find the seeds of all that constitutes literary, artistic and intellectual production, unmistakably Cuban in its full-blown expression. The experiences of the first half of the twentieth century allowed for a clearer definition of literary and cultural goals, as well as the development of alternative

---

[16]Virgilio Piñera, unpublished letter referring to the publication of *Poesía y prosa* (Havana: Serafín García, 1944), from the archives of Letras Cubanas. It is a final irony that Virgilio Piñera's ambiguous and difficult relationship with printers, publishers and cultural institutions throughout his life continued even after his death in 1979. Cuban houses have only recently, since 1987 and a full six years after his death, begun to publish his works again after a hiatus of nearly twenty years.

means for disseminating popular culture such as the multitude of literary journals and other periodicals which would appear briefly and disappear, often resurfacing years later under a new name. In the repressive 1930s even the prisonhouse served as alternate forum, classroom and powerful cohesive element for the intelligentsia of the Republic. It was during this period that a number of important literary works, as well as translations into Spanish of universal literature, were produced in the nation's prisons.

The lack of publishing houses, public libraries and a broad-based educational system in the twentieth century stemmed from the, in many respects, incomplete transition from colony to Republic, with a one-crop economy based on sugar cane. In studying the relationship between economics and cultural production, between literature and society, particularly in a nonindustrialized, dependent nation, statistics on illiteracy, the educational system and the cost of producing and purchasing books often speak more eloquently than the most impassioned essay. It may be argued that the emergence of the market economy, internationally, had a decisive influence on the arts at the end of the last century. In the transition from the nineteenth to the twentieth century and the shift from patronage—limited but secure—to the market, many writers found themselves in a no man's land:

> Cuban poets and novelists confronted a literary marketplace which could not guarantee them independent means of subsistence. In this regard, the poets seem to have drawn the worst lot. Whereas the naturalist novelists, Carrión and Loveira, had some success in publishing, Boti and Poveda barely managed to distribute copies of their books among their middle-class friends and acquaintances. In the end, none of them grew rich or were able to capitalize on their literary fame in politics, to which some of them turned as a means of survival. Carrión, Boti and Poveda failed in their electoral aspirations, while Loveira was content with a high-level bureaucratic appointment. Lacking a sufficiently developed, solid, literary market, neither the cultural institutions nor the State were willing to step in as patron to the literary intelligentsia.[17]

All societies, past and present, lacking an infrastructure for literary culture, create alternative mechanisms to outwit the censors, overcome official hostilities and attempt to fill the void, although they never take its place. The radius within

---

[17]Ibarra, *Nación y cultura nacional*, 219.

which they must operate is too narrow. The oldest literary institution in Latin America, the *tertulia*, or literary circle, often coexisted alongside the official colonial press:

> [I]n the realm of intellectual and cultural production, the circumstances under which the printing press was introduced in Latin America, owned and controlled by the Spaniards, were those of commodity production and the development of early capitalist relations.
>
> [I]t can be argued that only through deliberately subversive use of the press, taking a calculated risk by obviating its official purpose, did national culture and policy, clearly differentiated from that of Spain, emerge.[18]

One of the principal aims of this study, and of the developing tradition of social critique of literature and literary culture, has been to argue that "things literary" cannot be divorced from the ensemble of factors and forces that give rise to book production, that literary creation cannot be viewed in isolation from the publication and distribution of literary works.

From 1959 on, Cuba developed its publishing industry, in terms of available technology and expertise, on a *tabula rasa*, though this was far from true of the Cuban literary tradition that had been evolving and redefining itself from the mid-1800s on. The factors that inhibited the development of a solid infrastructure for literary creation are, historically, all too evident; more to the point, and relatively unstudied are those factors which made an incisive contribution to the rise of Cuban letters in the difficult decades from 1900 to 1959. Without recourse to publishing houses or patrons, the literary intelligentsia developed the alternatives studied so far in this chapter: literary groups, circles and societies. Literary circles of the nineteenth and twentieth centuries were of two basic types: those that lacked wealthy sponsors or editors and thus circulated their works by means other than periodicals and printed volumes (organizing conferences, meetings and public readings), and those that formed a nucleus around a journal or small press, or were backed by a political party.

In one form or another, the *tertulia* has been a constant in Cuban literary history from the nineteenth century to the present; in the colony, the Republic

---

[18]Juan Flores, *Insularismo e ideología burguesa en Antonio Pedreira* (Havana: Ediciones Casa, 1979): 35-36.

and the Revolution. The *tertulia* formed in the Alhambra Theater in the late 1800s remained active until 1935, spanning two historical periods. But it was in the first decade of the twentieth century, perhaps as a safeguard against the uncertainty of what the demise of the colony and the birth of the Republic would bring, that impromptu literary circles proliferated all over the island. At the turn of the century prominent young writers such as Max Henríquez Ureña and Jesús Castellanos, among others, would gather in the restaurants and cafés of Havana, and Juana and Dulce María Borrero transformed their home in the Marianao district into the "House of Poets." In the suburbs, the Bohemian Areopagus of Matanzas attracted poets, essayists and men and women of letters from 1910 to 1915. And in Santiago, the other provincial capital, the "Palo Hueco" group organized by José Manuel Poveda in the home of Dominican writer Sócrates Nolasco met from 1911 to 1913. In 1912, the journal *Orto* was founded to promote and disseminate literary production in Oriente province.

In the 1920s the Manzanillo Literary Group was formed and its activities revolved around the journal *Orto*, founded a decade earlier. The Manzanillo Group, and its journal, became a motive force in the cultural development of the nation's interior thanks, in part, to the considerable resources of its founder who placed his two printing presses at the group's disposal. Unlike most of the literary circles born in the first decades of republican life, the Manzanillo Group remained active and continued to publish until 1957. Short-lived but enormously influential in Cuban literary history was the Minorista Group, formed in 1923 and active until 1928 when it disbanded under pressure by the Machado administration. The Minoristas spearheaded a movement which changed the nature of the literary world, redefining the role of the writer in society and the function of literary culture.

In an atmosphere of increasing political tensions, the *tertulias* began to disperse, diminishing in number and visibility from the 1920s on. The last of the Havana *tertulias* of the republican period, headed by Fernando Ortiz, was founded in 1931, in the Hotel Ambos Mundos, later frequented by Hemingway. Ortiz's group survived only four short years, disbanding in 1935.

The *tertulias* served the same basic function, consistently, from the midnineteenth century to the 1930s; to bring writers into contact with one another and with a limited public in the absence of established publishing and distribution networks. Like their colonial predecessors, the Machado and Batista regimes worked to suppress the *tertulia* which they regarded as a center for conspiracy by their opponents.

Other cultural institutions lent indirect support to writers; these did not boost national literary production in an editorial sense but did offer employment and subsidies, within their means, to individual writers. The oldest of these is the Sociedad Económica de Amigos del País, established in 1792 by royal decree. With its far-sighted and comprehensive vision, the Sociedad Económica de Amigos del País was one of the first institutions of its kind to grant equal importance to economic, industrial and cultural problems, creating permanent commissions on education, economic and literary studies, history, fine arts, science, agriculture, popular industry and others. In order to strengthen national culture, the Amigos del País drew up a plan for overcoming colonial "backwardness" by addressing specific problems of overall development. Upon cessation of Spanish colonial domination, new institutions were established in place of the commissions created by the Sociedad, and its activities were then restricted to cultural affairs: conferences, publications, courses and literary contests.

The journal founded by the Sociedad Económica de Amigos del País, the *Revista bimestre cubana*, (published in two phases, 1831-34 and 1910-59) played an important role among the first generation of writers in the Republic. The introduction to the first issue of the periodical, in the 1800s, underlined the cultural lag suffered in the colony and announced its intent to serve as a literary organ:

> It is truly astonishing that in this fortunate land, a land in which culture and elegance reside, a periodical devoted to disseminating and promoting knowledge of the most worthy of our own and foreign literary works, to criticizing and judging them, has not emerged. These publications, which have given such impetus to and served as a great incentive for other nations, are, with few exceptions, unknown among us.[19]

In its second phase, under the direction of Fernando Ortiz, the journal continued to promote literary creation, publishing texts, articles, speeches and criticism, and incorporated a new, permanent section, "Cuban Poetry," open to the nation's unpublished poets. The Sociedad did not have its own press, other than the journal, but it did invite numerous writers and intellectuals to hold courses and conferences, thus providing them with an income, time to write and an atmosphere conducive to their work—the Sociedad was housed in its own building with a research center and a library, the first library in the nation.

---

[19]Instituto de Literatura y Lingüística de la Academia de Ciencias de Cuba, *Diccionario de la literatura cubana* (Havana: Editorial Letras Cubanas, 1984): II.888-91.

In the twentieth century, the Sociedad Económica de Amigos del País, contributed, through its work, to the establishment of two new institutions specializing in Cuban literature and culture: The Hispano-Cuban Cultural Institute (1926-48) and the Society for Cuban Folklore (1936-47). The former put out *Ultra* (1936-47), a journal that published translations and articles by international authors and the latter, *Annals of Folklore* (1924-31), which had as its goal "to gather, classify and compare traditional components of national popular life" including short stories, fables, legends from the oral tradition, *romances*, *décimas*, folk songs, *boleros*, and other poetic forms within the troubador tradition, as well as a variety of nonliterary expressions of popular culture. Both journals eventually folded, lacking institutional support, like most of the literary and cultural publications of the period.

The major literary journals born in the first two decades of the Republic, where most Cuban writers published their work, were *Chic* (1917-27, 1933-59?), the *Revista bimestre cubana* (1910-59), *Cuba contemporánea* (1913-27) and *Social* (1916-33, 1935-38?), the most influential of the four. Dozens of literary journals sprang up in cities all over the country but since they generally lasted only one or two years, none of these periodicals ever bridged the gap from intent to literary institution. In the first decade of the twentieth century

> there was hardly a village that did not have its own periodical or journal, and in many cities the printers took great pains to produce books and pamphlets of the highest quality.[20]

Aside from its literary significance, *Social* is a milestone in the development of the Cuban graphics industry and the history of print culture in general. The brothers Conrado and Oscar Massaguer founded *Social* in 1916, the same year that the first Institute for Graphic Arts opened in Havana. It was there that *Social* would make its mark on the history of printing with the 1919 issue that carried the following inscription: "The first publication in the world printed entirely by offset."

Like *Orto* of Manzanillo, *Social* had a sturdier base of support than the majority of equivalent journals; its founders enjoyed the fortunate combination of literary ideals, practical typographical experience and considerable economic resources.

---

[20]José G. Ricardo, *La imprenta en Cuba* (Havana: Letras Cubanas, 1989): 133.

Book publishing for the same period experienced erratic swings that reflect-ed the instability of the nation's economy. The following table indicates a drastic reduction in literary titles published immediately after the crisis of 1920 which came on the heels of the boom years referred to as the "dance of millions."

Year	Titles or Works Published[21]
1917	517
1918	503
1919	528
1920	326

After 1920, the year of the bank crash and the economic crisis, literary produc-tion increased incrementally, as the nation recovered.

1921	423
1922	495
1923	529
1924	561

While this table offers graphic representation, a more sensitive gauge is required to get to the heart of the phenomena suggested in the statistics. The birth, demise and rebirth of a seemingly endless succession of literary journals and societies from 1900 to 1958 is a tribute to the ongoing collective efforts of the intelligentsia to wed literary and social ideals, against difficult odds. It was the *tertulias* and their literary journals, much more than the private presses, that served as the principal literary institution throughout the nineteenth and early twentieth centuries. In a nation without publishers, the literary journal may be considered the true precursor to the present mode of literary production, leaving aside a handful of culturally significant though not necessarily commercially viable publishing experiments.

---

[21]Table based on the Bibliografía Cubana (1917-20), (1921-36), José Martí National Library, from *La imprenta en Cuba*, José G. Ricardo, 151.

CHAPTER 3. THE REPUBLIC: 1900 TO 1958

1920-30: The Minorista Movement and Periodical Literature

During this time a revolution occurs in the university, the José Martí People's University is organized, publications like *Venezuela Libre, Alma Mater* and *Revista de Avance* appear on the scene; the content of *Social* undergoes a change, the Manifesto of the Minorista Group appears and—cardinal events—the Communist Party of Cuba and the National Workers Confederation are formed. Never before over the course of our history have such varied and profound concerns been articulated, and in ten short years. Nothing pointed to a final decision, but everything was building up in an intense and often anxious concern.[1]

The decade from 1920 to 1930 was a period of prolonged social and political upheaval, precipitated by an irreversible crisis of government, which gave rise to a new national consciousness. The generalized crisis was to have profound repercussions in all sectors of society including the literary milieu, causing a small but influential group of intellectuals to question the very foundations of national culture. From 1921 to 1925 Alfredo Zayas Alonso governed the nation; from 1925-33, Gerardo Machado. Neither could stem the economic crisis or the increasing politicization of workers, students, and intellectuals. It was at this historical juncture that the Protest of Thirteen took place, "the first manifestation of dissatisfaction, on the part of intellectuals, with the customs and political practices which had taken root, like a cancer, in national life."[2]

In reality, one could speak of a series of interrelated phenomena resonating in intellectual and cultural spheres. Led by Rubén Martínez Villena, a group of

---

[1] Juan Marinello, cited in Ana Cairo, *El Grupo Minorista y su tiempo* (Havana: Editorial de Ciencias Sociales, 1978): 9-10.

[2] Cairo, *El Grupo Minorista y su tiempo*: 55.

young intellectuals raised their voices to publicly denounce an illicit transaction by the Zayas government involving state funds.[3] It is not the event itself which concerns us but its historical significance in the political and cultural life of the nation and the series of actions it unleashed. On the first of April of that year, the Falange de Acción Cubana was constituted, as a continuation of the efforts of the Protest of Thirteen, whose founding members had participated in that protest. The Falange never launched its program of political and cultural reform or published its manifesto and was dissolved four months later when all of its members joined the Movement of Veterans and Patriots. After the Falange's aborted attempt to initiate a program of political action, the Minorista Group was formed which, "independent of any political party or organization, would constitute a cultural and political entity."[4] The same nucleus of intellectuals had participated in the Protest of Thirteen, founded the Falange and joined forces with the Movement of Veterans and Patriots. They continued to gather over the years, redefining their purpose, and the ad hoc association became official in the February, 1924, issue of *Social*. It was not until 1927 that the group composed a "Declaration" in which they defined themselves as

> a group with no regulations, no president, no secretary, no monthly dues, in short, without pomp and ceremony; but that is precisely the most viable organization for a group of intellectuals: all over, the regulation of analogous groups has failed, groups in which the "backbone" formed by the unity of criteria on substantive matters is more important and thus has none of the inconvenience of a formal, adjectival, external structure.[5]

Unlike other groups from the same period, the Minoristas did not have their own journal when they began their cultural and political trajectory as a group. All of the members wrote but none was a published author. The greater part of their literary production was to be found in periodicals, in the established magazines and journals with wide circulation like *Social* and *Carteles*. The Minoristas

---

[3]The incident that sparked the protest was the purchase of the Santa Clara convent for the sum of $2,350,000.

[4]Cairo, *El Grupo Minorista y su tiempo*, 55.

[5]Cairo, *El Grupo Minorista y su tiempo*, 66.

later founded the *Revista de Avance*, typical of the journals which voiced the social and artistic concerns of the progressive intelligentsia of the 1920s and 1930s.

These journals, like those that preceded them, are loosely divided into two groups: those that functioned as commercial enterprises, accepting all sorts of advertisements and social announcements for publication without excluding literary pieces, articles and essays; and the noncommercial type, sponsored and subsidized by the founders and collaborators, existing precariously and on limited resources. Those of the first type, resembling *Social,* enjoyed much greater economic stability resulting from the revenue brought in by the advertisements and society pages. Like the commercial presses, they published a bit of everything, indiscriminately; wedged between advertisements and notices of high society weddings, appeared essays and literary texts by members of the vanguard, both Cuban and international. The second type of periodical, though "precarious," exerted a much greater influence on cultural and literary currents in the republican era.

Social, established in 1916 exclusively for its entertainment value, and "devoted solely to describing in its pages, with pen and paper or camera lens, our grand social events, artistic notes and fashion trends..." was radically transformed, assuming a new and far from frivolous attitude toward the social, economic and cultural problems of the nation and the world, from the moment that *minorista* Emilio Roig de Leuchsenring joined the team of editors as director of the literary section:

> When I assumed directorship of the Literary Section in 1923, I proposed to assemble, through the magazine, elements of the new Cuban intelligentsia, who, although for the most part extremely talented, were broken up and dispersed, as were all the other figures in our literary and artistic world. And I have seen these objectives realized, beyond my expectations. *Social* owes its rise to literary and artistic splendor to the Minorista Group, all its worth and significance.... Because of the Minoristas, *Social* was able to carry out the task of selection and refinement of literary and artistic values which I, as director, had proposed; because of the Minoristas, *Social* was able to offer in its pages the most current work available in literature and the arts, and introduced the newest and

most advanced figures, doctrines and schools to have emerged in Europe and America in the last few years.[6]

Social's permanent sections included "Costumbristas cubanos" (from the nineteenth century), "Poetisas cubanas," "Acotaciones literarias," "Indice de lecturas" (reviews of books recently published), "Escritores latinoamericanos," "Recuerdos de La Habana" (articles on the history of the capital), along with the pages devoted to introducing short stories, poems, literary criticism, chapters from unpublished novels and historical texts, the selection of which varied from issue to issue.

Juan Marinello, in an editorial appearing in the magazine in 1925, observed that "*Social*'s work is, in many respects, still to be done." Having brought together, in *Social*, a group of isolated intellectuals, the Minoristas now sought a vehicle more appropriate to their literary and social aims so they created their own publication, the *Revista de avance*:

> *Revista de avance* considered itself, in the first place, a companion to *Social*. Yet it distinguished itself from *Social* in its future projection. *Social*, by definition a publication for the entertainment of the petite and grande bourgeoisie, could not become an experimental workshop for the intellectual minority; the nature of its reading public was a limiting factor.[7]

The history of *Revista de avance*, representative of the noncommercial journals of the time, offers insight into the significance and function of such periodicals vis-à-vis the Cuban writer in a society without publishers. *Avance* served multiple purposes: operating as a miniature publishing house, distribution channel for literary works, and point of contact for Latin American intellectuals. *Avance* editor, Martín Casanovas' eloquent testimony, in hindsight, sums up what the journal represented in its day as well as its legacy for the publishing and literary movement of the 1960s:

---

[6]Emilio Roig de Leuchensring, "Diez años de labor," *Social*, Jan. 1926, cited in *Diccionario de la literatura cubana* (Havana: Letras Cubanas, 1980): II.973.

[7]Cairo, *El Grupo Minorista y su tiempo*, 142.

In 1965, fully from within the Revolution, perhaps an opportune moment has arrived to review those events, with true dialectical rigor.

In a wider context, the exchange with other Latin Americans obliged the magazine's editors and collaborators, perhaps subconsciously, to accentuate and strengthen all that brought out more clearly their Cuban identity, far superior to the anecdotal and trivial form, and to establish, as plainly as possible, an intellectual meridian for Cuba, a goal which took hold among the writers in those years.[8]

Traditionally, writers and other intellectuals in the colonies and newly formed republics of Latin America, have sprung from society's elite. However, the most interesting aspect of the Minorista movement revolves precisely around the writer's *status*, and how he or she defines him or herself in relation to the immediate social context. Those writers who remained faithful to the ideals and political-cultural program of the Minorista Group, renounced the social status granted to writers as guardians of culture *en petit*, in order to assume the greater responsibility of defending the cause of culture *en grand*. Opposition to the rise of imperialism, and the perceived threat of a denationalization process, would in the long run create fertile ground for the task of redefining national culture, even if it meant postponing the completion of literary projects and the fulfillment of individual goals. By signing the Minorista Declaration in defense of the economic independence of Cuba, the active participation of the people in government, as well as opposition to imperialism, a relatively large group of Cuban writers and artists "tacitly renounced accommodation with and favoritism from the officials."[9]

The "communist trial" of 1927—following a roundup of the opposition to the Machado regime, all accused of communism—the year that *Avance* was founded, directly affected the editors of the journal. Three of its editors, Martín Casanovas, José Z. Tallet and Alejo Carpentier, and several collaborators were among the fifty accused and tried by the Machado government. Juan Marinello, the central force behind the publication and all its projects, was jailed in 1930,

---

[8]Martín Casanovas, ed., *Revista de avance*, Colección Orbita (Havana: Instituto del Libro Cubano, 1972), from the prologue by Martín Casanovas, 7-8, 16-17.

[9]Casanovas, ed., *Revista de avance*, 10.

accused of having instigated the student protest of September 30 of that year. *Avance*'s last issue came out on September 15, 1930, giving notice that the journal would cease publication before it would submit to government censorship.[10]

During its three-year history, *Revista de Avance* had accomplished more than the nation's small presses in promoting literary culture. *Avance* had successfully disseminated the work of new writers who would otherwise have remained in the shadows and set up its own press whose editions carried the most significant literary production of the day.[11]

The journal's Latin American collaborators included Miguel Angel Asturias, Mariano Azuela, José Carlos Mariátegui, Horacio Quiroga, César Vallejo and others, as well as the current writers from Europe and the United States whose work appeared in translation. Having broken new ground in Cuban literary history, *Avance* "died when its time came, without having cause to be ashamed of what it undertook and accomplished in its three years."[12] Like the struggling literary journals of the nineteenth century's "Golden Age," journals from the 1920s on subsisted on the initiative of their founding members, against the prevailing social and political tides, until 1952 and Batista's coup d'état. A glance at the list of editors of each of the serious, independent journals reveals a conti-

---

[10]Government censorship under Machado and Batista was more stringent than that applied by the colonial administration which was constantly undermined by the "blank page." In the colony, any article suppressed by the censors of the monarchy appeared in the publication as a blank column. The blank page signaled to the reader the existence of movements of opposition to official policy. The first newspaper to attempt to revive the tradition of the blank page was immediately shut down by Batista.

[11]The following list of titles indicates the spectrum of books published by *Avance*'s press: *Juventud y vejez,* Juan Marinello; *Tres temas sobre la nueva poesía*, Regino Boti; *Goya*, Jorge Mañach; *La poesía moderna en Cuba* (anthology), Félix Lizaso and José Antonio Fernández de Castro; *Molde, imagen*, Rafael Suárez Solís; *Indagación del choteo*, Jorge Mañach; *El renuevo y otros cuentos*, Carlos Montenegro; *El latifundismo en la economía cubana*, Raúl Mestri; *El documento y la reconstrucción histórica*, José María Chacón y Calvo; *Kodak-ensueño*, Regino Boti; *La torre de Babel*, Luis Cardoza y Aragón; *Trópico*, Eugenio Florit; *Sobre la inquietud cubana*, Juan Marinello and *Viaje a la Rusia roja*, Sergio Carbó.

[12]Casanovas, *Revista de avance* 26.

nuity of effort, in spite of the many lacunae; journals were born and folded only to be reconstituted with a new name and format, by a single core of intellectuals.

By 1935, *Social* had fallen into decadence. Suppression of its cultural and literary material had reduced it to what it had been before the Minorista movement: a publication for the *divertissement* of the "high lifers." But the 1930s brought forth other journals which, like *Avance*, wedded literary concerns to social commitment. Of these, *Grafos* (1933-46), made the greatest contribution to the advancement of print culture, and enjoyed the longest life, due to its solid financing. Resembling *Social*, in its early period, in both composition and content, in *Grafos* society chronicles peacefully coexisted with serious experiments in literature: one subsidized the other. María Radelat Fontanills, a wealthy widow with business acumen, placed the literary and art critic, Guy Pérez Cisneros, at the head of productions and relations, and he was responsible for the cultural content of the journal as well as its layout and presentation, while she took care of cultivating sponsors and fundraising. It was printed on the best chromium paper, imported from Europe, Canada or the U.S., like all of Cuban paper, and production costs were covered by advertisers. In addition to selected poems, short stories and theater reviews, *Grafos* had three permanent sections written by prominent intellectuals: "Miniaturas literarias" (prose poems), "Del pasado" (Cuban history) and "Antología poética del siglo XIX."

Baraguá, Islas. Al servicio de los intereses cubanos and *Mediodía*, were among the other shortlived, noncommercial publications, in the tradition of *Avance*. *Islas* (Havana, 1936), with a varied content, proposed to examine "national problems with absolute objectivity, with a view to practical solutions useful to the majority," through analysis of political, cultural, economic and social issues. Its pages contained literary criticism, poetry and bibliographical notes on recently published works as well as its "Documentos cubanos," a permanent section addressed to the situation and concerns of Cuban workers. The principal collaborators were Carlos Rafael Rodríguez, Camila Henríquez Ureña, Jorge Mañach and Emilio Ballagas. *Islas* ceased publication that same year. In 1937, *Baraguá* (Havana, 1937-38?) was founded under the direction of José Antonio Potuondo, with the following declaration: "*Baraguá* was born as an organ for free thought, with no limitations other than that of exclusive service to the national majority in a time of utmost confusion of ideas and values, neither for the first nor the last time, among the Cuban people." *Baraguá* combined analysis of political issues with the dissemination of poetry and criticism, receiving contributions from members of the Cuban and Spanish vanguards. None of these publications expressed with greater force than *Mediodía*, in its declaration, the desire to forge a new collectivist culture, not on the margins of history, but squarely at the center of the crucial issues of the time:

> *Mediodía* is not a vehicle for entertainment in the arts. Its editors are well aware of the social role played by all the arts, even when this effect is not perceived. In recognition of this, they propose that the public function of art fulfill, in the pages of this journal, a profoundly human destiny, loyal to the peculiar circumstances prevailing in Cuba. *Mediodía* believes that thought must inexorably contribute to life and participate in the historical struggles of our time. Since the will to place art in the service of humanity is in no way at variance with aesthetic rigor, *Mediodía* will strive, in its vigilance over collaborators' work, to maintain a standard of literary and artistic excellence for the journal. Pulchritude without narcissism, outreach to the greatest possible number of readers, but without vulgar flattery, which is unnecessary yet often employed by us.[13]

The editorial board of the magazine included Nicolás Guillén, Aurora Villar Buceta, Carlos Rafael Rodríguez, Angel Augier, Edith García Buchaca, Jorge Rigol, José Antonio Portuondo and, from the second issue on, Juan Marinello. Those who edited and wrote for the magazine were also responsible for manuscript editing, layout, design and proofreading; every phase of its production. As a result, poets became overnight typographers and proofreaders in the collective preparation of the magazine.

The first four issues were devoted almost entirely to literature: poems, short stories, literary criticism, history and art in addition to the regular columns: "Noticias" (on cultural activities), "Libros" (review of recent titles, foreign and national) and "Revistas" (on the new national and international publications). In January 1937, the magazine began to incorporate articles on global and domestic politics as well.

In its first year of publication, *Mediodía* came up against police surveillance and censorship. After including a chapter of Carlos Montenegro's unpublished novel *Hombres sin mujer*, on prison life, the editorial board was accused of "pornography and subversive propaganda" and an order of detention was brought

---

[13]*Diccionario de la literatura cubana* (Havana: Instituto de Literatura y Lingüística de la Academia de Ciencias de Cuba; Editorial Letras Cubanas, 1984): II.589.

against all of its members. The only one actually detained and incarcerated was the poet, Guillén. This incident brought about change in format along with the new emphasis on national and global politics. After a three-month hiatus, due to the persecution of its editors, *Mediodía* resumed publication, having substituted newsprint for the costly antique paper. It appeared regularly until 1939, when its editors decided to abandon the project in favor of the recently consolidated daily *Hoy*, published by the Partido Socialista Popular.[14] Its literary supplement, *Magazine de Hoy*, put out the greater part of the literary production of the 1940s, publishing many of the writers and thinkers that had founded the series of journals, now defunct, of the preceding decade.

A comparison of literary journals of the nineteenth- and twentieth-centuries reveals a common denominator in the persistent efforts of editors and contributors. The limitations remained the same for nineteenth-and twentieth-century journals: lack of a stable, broad-based reading public able to afford, if not books, at least the more accessible periodicals, on a regular basis.

Books in Prison

In the Cuban Republic, government regulations protected the bookseller's right to trade even when such liberties were in direct conflict with policy on content. All of the major booksellers, including the most prestigious such as "Cultural," whose print shop was under government contract to produce textbooks for the nation's schools, ordered, displayed and sold the works of major European communists in their shops. The business of buying and selling "subversive" titles in an age of fierce repression was lawful; the transgression lay in *reading* them. A single copy of any of the "red list" books that adorned the display windows of the most elegant bookstores and stands of the capital, if found in the library of a private home, was grounds for the arrest and possible incarceration of the reader:

> I learned to read Marx and Engels in prison, I still have the books with the seal "Authorized by so and so."

---

[14]One of the various names assumed by the Communist Party in the Republic.

So-called communist books were sold in all the bookstores. Even "Cultural" sold books published by Cénit, along with translations arriving from Spain of Trotsky, Zinoviev, of all the Bolshevik old guard whom we were first introduced to. When they arrived from Spain they were sold here in all the bookstores. But if the police found one in your home, in a search, it constituted a crime. It was not a crime for the bookseller to sell the books, but it was a crime to have one in your home. [15]

Selling "red" books was a lucrative business which the government did not wish to prohibit. The booskseller remained untainted by the transaction; it was only the reader who purchased the books for his or her own use that ran the risk of arrest. The only place such titles could be read with impunity was in prison where they were read freely by the inmates, after receiving permission from the authorities. Once they had been stamped and signed by the warden, they circulated openly throughout the prisonhouse and study circles formed to analyze the works of major thinkers of the twentieth century. It was there that many important works in political science were translated into Spanish.

The inherent ironies of the prohibition of so-called communist works are quite telling: banned from the home to safeguard "bourgeois morality" and "domestic tranquility," the government showed a blatant lack of concern that such works were readily available to the "tainted intellectuals" who found themselves imprisoned, to the "betrayers of the patriotic ideal," presumed to be a minority without influence outside itself. Meanwhile, the presence of these volumes in the prisonhouse turned the months of confinement into a valuable lesson in political action and a rigorous intellectual and literary education for many.

Experiments in Publishing

Literary journals, despite limited readership, proved the most effective means of dissemination throughout the nineteenth century and up to the early 1950s. Once the uneasy transition from colony to Republic had been made, over the course of the first two decades of this century, the literary community sought

---

[15]From an interview with Enrique de la Osa, journalist for 57 years, Director of *Bohemia* (1960-71) where he had been editor in chief in the Republican period. Havana, December 8, 1984.

other means of publication and dissemination in addition to the journals, among them, a series of experiments in both commercial and nonprofit book publishing. One of the earliest of these was the Book Institute, founded in 1935 by Antonio Bustamante and other men of letters, and dedicated to promoting the production of Cuban intellectuals.[16]

This was a noble experiment doomed to fail for it was modelled after the structure of a commercial publishing house, with no sizeable market to sustain it. Operating funds for the Institute would be drawn from royalties, and the rather symbolic dues payment of one *peso* a month from each of its members who, in return, would be entitled to receive twelve books a year:

> The Institute solicited unpublished works for their editions, and stipulated that only 10% of the revenue produced by any edition would go to the Institute. The rest would go to the author, who would also be given one hundred copies of his or her book.[17]

A structure of this type, in order to survive, presupposed the existence of a consumer market for books able to support—with only 10% of the income from each edition—a publishing house with eight departments *and* a periodical. The founders of the Book Institute had not taken into account illiteracy rates, the cultural level or standard of living of its potential reading public. "Promoting Cuban intellectual production" through the establishment of a sophisticated literary/book publishing institute, dependent upon income from the sale of its editions in a nation with an insignificant market for their product was an exercise in building castles in the air. Literature, under the conditions outlined, should not have been viewed as a revenue-generating activity for individual authors. The Book Institute's founders would have been better served by the more modest and realistic goal of perhaps breaking even and introducing unknown or little known authors through their editions. The experiment never got off the ground or published a single book.

Another publishing experiment from the first decades of the Republic, distinct in nature from the Book Institute, was the printing press "El Ideal." Its founders did not set unreasonable goals; instead, they drew up a feasible plan

---

[16]José G. Ricardo, *La imprenta en Cuba* (Havana: Letras Cubanas, 1989): 186.

[17]Ricardo, *La imprenta en Cuba*, 187.

which, because it was based on existing conditions, did not overreach the parameters of national literary life:

> Workers in the tobacco industry, members of the Federation of Cigar Makers, achieved more than all of the government administrations managed to do when they founded their own printing press, "El Ideal"....[18]

The fact that a group of tobacco workers decided to found their own printing press is consistent with the long tradition of scientific and cultural inquiry in that sector. Books have been a constant presence and catalyst among cigar makers since the mid-1800s. The practice of public reading was common in the workshops of Havana and environs by 1866 and the tradition remains in force today. The workers paid the reader out of their own salaries and elected one of the group to be in charge of the reading sessions.

In the shops, literary and philosophical, as well as scientific works were read and discussed by the workers, along with newspapers, manifestoes and other proclamations from the workers' movement, in an effort to keep up with intellectual and artistic developments, at home and abroad. In establishing their own press, the tobacco workers benefitted themselves socially and culturally, and aided the development of Cuban publishing.[19]

Commercial presses—the majority, in Cuba—were notorious for underpaying their workers whereas El Ideal distinguished itself by offering salaries agreed upon by the guilds and distributed a third of all profits among the employees. The press' list was primarily cultural rather than commercial, yet El Ideal proved, for the first time, that with modest objectives and sound administration, a publishing enterprise could attempt to meet cultural and intellectual expectations and survive, without having to appeal to the advertisers that propped up the commercial small presses:

---

[18]Ricardo, *La imprenta en Cuba*, 172-73.

[19]El Ideal published books and pamphlets of which the following is a partial list: *El imperialismo americano*, Scott Nearing and *La esclavitud del bono*, H. Davis, in translation; *Cuba, un pueblo que jamás ha sido libre*, Julio Antonio Mella (1925), *Los problemas sociales de Cuba*, Emilio Roig de Leuchsenring (1927); *Alma Mater*, "official organ of Cuban students," and *Juventud*, a journal put out by the students of the University of Havana, and several workers' newspapers.

In the month of August, 1925, El Ideal made $3,509.11; paid out, for materials, electricity and rent, $1,089.71; the employees received a total of $1,225.93, and the press kept $1,193.47 for operating expenses.[20]

Mass-Media and Literary Production in the 1940s and 1950s

What was the dominant culture before now, why and for whom?

In the last years of the neocolonial period—especially from the introduction of television in 1950 on—a subcultural industry began to develop, managed by the advertising agencies and the U.S.-based transnational corporations which were testing their strategies for commercialization of the continent on Cuba. (Enrique González Manet, *Cultura y comunicación*)

The conditions outlined thus far were hardly conducive to a second "literary renaissance" in the post-independence period, but this in no way deterred the literati from redoubling their efforts to build readership and give Cuban letters a place in society. By striving to get current literature into print and circulating among the public, they sought to guaranty the continuity of a beleaguered tradition. The history of Cuban literary production in the Republic has its most reliable sources not in the bibliographies of the period but in the *tertulia*, the cultural societies and groups, the journals and publishing experiments which together served as the only viable, although fragile, literary infrastructure in an inhospitable environment.

The "decisive decade" from 1920 to 1930 which brought a critical focus to problems of national culture and forced readers and writers to address them with greater urgency, reexamining their role in the social process, drew to a close and the 1940s bore witness to the global reach of mass-media which ushered in a new era.

Uncovering the historical roots of the burgeoning mass-media network of the 1940s and 1950s, and the impending global "mass culture," would mean going back to the 16th century and the confrontation between "old" and "new" worlds. In the more immediate context of the late 20th century, the present day

---

[20]Ricardo, *La imprenta en Cuba*, 172-73.

"crisis of culture" which has drawn cries of alarm from diverse sectors of the international community is the culmination of an ongoing process which gained momentum in the 1940s, with the emergence of the televised image, and the potential for international transmission and marketing.

In 1960, the United Nations drafted the first declaration on "Freedom of Information" in order to protect the "free flow of information," but by the 1980s many member nations had spoken out against a doctrine which they believed only served to perpetuate dependent structures within a new global market, conquered with the aid of mass-media.

According to a 1973 study of the influence of nongovernmental mass-media based in the United States:

> The U.S. news agencies manage 80% of the international news in Latin America, and in many countries a significant percent of national and regional news as well is controlled by these agencies.

> U.S. programming dominates an average of 31.4% of television programming in the region, including both U.S. commercial and educational programming. In addition, U.S. recorded music is heavily used in radio and U.S. comic strips almost completely monopolize the newspapers.

> *Reader's Digest*...has nine editions in Latin America, eight in Spanish and one in Portuguese. Ninety-five percent of the material of all nine magazines, which is rarely from Latin America, is the same for all editions.

> *Films*. Of films shown in Latin America, an average of 55% are U.S. originated, ranging from 46% in film producer Mexico to 70 and 73% respectively in Bolivia and Guatemala.... In many countries international film companies also directly own the theatres to which their films are distributed.[21]

---

[21]Luis Ramiro Beltrán, and Elizabeth Fox de Cardona, "Latin America and the United States: Flaws in the Free Flow of Information," in *National Sovereignty and International Communication*, Kaarle Nordenstreng and Herbert I. Schiller, eds. (Norwood, N.J.: Ablex Publishing Corporation, 1979): 39-42.

Cuban literary critic Fernández Retamar reflects on the long-range effects of export products from the mass-media industry on aesthetics and cultural development in prerevolutionary Cuba, recalling the legacy of cultural colonialism:

> Half of the population was illiterate. Had they not been illiterate, they would have read *Selecciones del Reader's Digest*, and they would now have to "unlearn" one thing in order to learn another; since we want above all to teach them, we would not teach *Reader's Digest* but Homer, Aeschylus and Shakespeare.[22]

The implantation, in the twentieth century, of an international mass-media network, inundating the planet with editions of *Reader's Digest* and Walt Disney creations, is a product of the present phase of transnational marketing, with its assembly-line style "art for the masses" to be consumed by a "global village." In the 1940s and 1950s, the Cuban magazines with the largest circulation, such as *Bohemia*, began to incorporate comics, detective tales and feature articles supplied by U.S. syndicates, and prominent firms like Cuban ESSO began to put out their own magazines.

This was the dawn of a new kind of cultural and artistic production designed for *strangers*. The creators recognized, and worked on the premise of, a total absence of experience, history, social and cultural traditions common to both producers and consumers, and thus the new "mass culture" grew, removed from, incompatible with and perhaps even detrimental to the social fabric and life of the community in which it took hold. There are nine separate editions of *Reader's Digest* in Spanish and Portuguese, for nine Latin American nations; and each of the nine editions contains the same articles with only the slightest variation. "Mass art" thrives on the progessive fragmentation of communities once founded on shared history. The development of a transnational mass-media network has had the effect of creating a global chain of lone individuals, unknown to one another, united electronically by a common consumerist campaign. The "mass art" of the twentieth century has little tolerance for popular art forms that struggle against the tide, emerging from within a margin of vulnerability which the global industry would rather did not exist.

Mass art arises, in industrial society, in contradiction to and confrontation with traditional literary, artistic and cultural production, understood to be an act

---

[22]Roberto Fernández Retamar, et al., "Conversación sobre arte y literatura," *Casa de las Américas* 22-23 (January-April 1964): 132.

of conscious communication, by and for a specific community or group, which responds to collective concerns and desires, at a particular historical juncture: "Books are like bread. Throughout the world, the production of grain and basic foodstuff derived from it was primitive man's greatest victory over hunger."[23]

The printed volume was humanity's victory over spiritual hunger and isolation, multiplying human potential for communication and mitigating the immediacy of the spoken word by widening the sphere once defined by the limited reach of oral communication. Viewed as a commodity, the literary product will be less and less prone to satisfy vital intellectual and spiritual needs. The book-as-commodity or "social hieroglyphic" appears before us as a mysterious object, one whose origins and development (from idea to manuscript to printed volume), are rarely considered or examined.

From the moment the foundations were laid for market-based literary production, editorial decisions, market analyses, publisher's timetables and, more recently, priorities established by the corporations that own publishing houses have affected the creative process. It was not, however, so much the publishers as the unfolding of a mass-media cultural industry which hastened the transformation of literary and artistic products into market commodities by eliminating alternate channels for production and dissemination. Small presses and publishing houses around the globe exist under a potential threat of takeover by large conglomerates; independent bookstores with ties to communities, neighborhoods and university life are disappearing, with the warehouse-like outlets of national book chains taking their place; movies, television and videocassettes are now the primary source of information for many. A significant and related aspect of the "revolution" orchestrated by the transnational communications industry is the growing use of information as global currency; shared, withheld and manipulated through exclusive, often unilateral and strictly controlled channels. No longer content with merely increasing distribution networks on an international scale, each of the major media conglomerates now hopes "to gather under its control every step of the information process, from the creation of the 'product' to all the various means by which modern technology delivers media messages to the

---

[23]Robert Escarpit, *The Book Revolution* (London: George G. Harrap; Paris: UNESCO, 1966): 158.

public. 'The product' is news, information, ideas, entertainment and popular culture; the public is the whole world."[24]

Production of a variety of "mass art" forms has been consolidated in the second half of the twentieth century, and the fast pace and outreach of the mass communications industry has homogenized and standardized consumers' tastes and preferences the world over. By the 1990s, half a dozen publishing and other media corporations such as Hachette, Bertelsmann AG and Time-Warner, hope to control both production and distribution of most of the world's books, periodicals, movies, videos, radio broadcasting and recordings. The "corporate battle to dominate the international market" was renewed, ironically, on the eve of 1992 when "the twelve nations of the European Community are scheduled to meld into a single economic unit of 320 million consumers."[25] Five hundred years after the Conquest, the European Community attempts a reconquest of Latin American markets, with Spain, once again, at the helm of the public relations enterprise.

Exercising a limited degree of control over mass-media is now unthinkable, if we apply the old truism that the only way to obtain freedom of the press is to own the press, whereas a modicum of influence over the press was once a feasible ambition for those who sought to promote literary movements and reach the public. The printing press is being displaced by electronic communications technology; an advanced technology under the control of multinationals whose sphere of influence, no longer limited to the press, encompasses international publishing, news agencies and wire services, cinema, and periodical publications with global circulation.

There is evidence of a cultural decline when Batman and Superman are more popular and better known, in many regions and among ethnic communities of the United Sates, than William Faulkner or Langston Hughes. When Batman, Superman, Ninja Turtles, or the latest Hollywood creation, eclipse indigenous artists and writers in Latin America, it is not a measured decline but a crisis of national culture that is taking place.

The displacement of popular cultural forms by mass culture responds to the requirements of the modern global industry and depends on the degree of passive receptivity of the audience. When the meaning and content of mass art and mass literature do not correspond to the historical concerns and social reality of the

---

[24]Ben Bagdikian, "The Lords of the Global Village," *The Nation* 23.248 (June 12, 1989): 805.

[25]Bagdikian, "Lords of the Global Village," *The Nation*, 807.

target public, when none of its points of departure have roots in national culture, assimilation will occur to the extent that local cultural traditions and forms of expression of the community have been broken down.

The isolation that resulted from the U.S. trade embargo, and more limited exchange with Western Europe as well, was initially a double-edged sword, sheltering Cuba from the negative effects of the "global village" and the erosion of local culture while at the same time undeniably limiting the intelligentsia's exposure to the channels of communication with Western Europe that traditionally influenced Cuban thought. Peter T. Johnson chronicles this shift in his study of Cuban academic publishing, taking into account both the benefits and intellectual costs of nationalistic policy at all levels of publishing. Whereas Cuba shared the status of most Latin American nations as importer rather than producer within the transnational media and cultural industry up until 1959, developments through 1989 made Cuba atypical of contemporary Latin America and the Caribbean in that they occurred outside the parameters of the "global village." In his monograph, Peter Johnson analyzes the effects of the shift on specialized, scholarly publishing in the social sciences and humanities as follows:

> The intended audience has at least some university education, and in many cases readers include those whose responsibilities require advanced education. The range of subjects at this level is perhaps the widest of all because of the diversity of readers' needs. The increasing emphasis on technology, medicine, and science requires the substantial use of non-Cuban sources, which means a heavy reliance on translations of socialist-bloc publications and a few imprints from Western countries. Books by Cuban authors are in the minority, except for works about sugar. In the social sciences and the humanities, the opposite is true. While works by foreign authors certainly exist, they no longer constitute the dominant share of the market. The maturing of the Cuban state and its emphasis on higher education are responsible for this change.[26]

---

[26]Peter T. Johnson, "Cuban Academic Publishing and Self-Perceptions," *Cuban Studies* 18 (1988): 107. The fact that the years since this article came out have witnessed the dissolution of the Socialist bloc in no way alters the accuracy of the author's observations on readers, writers and the structure of contemporary Cuban publishing.

The contrary was true of the decades immediately preceding the Revolution. Events of the 1940s and 1950s, the Machado and Batista years, which also coincided with the rise of U.S.-based mass-media programming on the island, brought Cuba's political, economic and cultural crisis to a head. It was not a passing phase but a permanent impasse which could only be resolved through social revolt. The influence of commercial radio and Hollywood-type fantasies had reached its apex in an atmosphere of terror that extended beyond the labor unions to the general population. The pseudocultural industry of soap operas, radio novellas, and Hollywood superproductions, mostly U.S. exports, put all mechanisms for reality-swapping into high gear, fomenting disdain for national culture while offering the allure of an exotic and dazzling media world capable of distancing the population from dismal conditions within the country, closing their eyes to what was going on around them.

In 1900, the interim government of occupation took the overtly racist measure of prohibiting "the use of drums of African origin at all public and private gatherings,"[27] and by the 1940s almost any manifestation of national culture that went beyond the stereotypical would come to be considered an outrage, if not a criminal act. Soap operas unfolded against the exotic backdrop of Europe or New York, almost never Cuba.[28] Radio novellas were, like their print counterparts, the pocketbook novels imported from the U.S., in the detective, romance or "realist" genres (if "realist" can be used to classify the Cuban characters and scenarios of radio novellas which, like *Los tres Villalobos*, were based on those of Hollywood films such as Tarzan and Superman).[29] In fact, official publications and guidelines for radio script-writers stipulated that the characters be based on the Tarzan and son model if, for example, it was a family drama.[30] The formulas were extremely rigid, the recommendations to be followed left no room for creativity or autonomy on the part of the writer under contract: "This is scientific. It never

---

[27]Oscar Luis López, *La radio en Cuba* (Havana: Letras Cubanas, 1981): 374.

[28]Reynaldo González, *Llorar es un placer* (Havana: Letras Cubanas, 1988): 272.

[29]Cited in Reynaldo Gonzáles, *Llorar es un placer*, 266.

[30]López, *La radio en Cuba*, 353.

fails. It is based on an analysis the Americans did of the most successful newspaper serials of the nineteenth century."[31]

Formulas for writing serial newspaper fiction in the United States of the nineteenth century governed the structure and production of radio soap operas in the 1940s and 1950s in Havana. With all its disadvantages, radio had become much more influential than the press, so writers turned to radio, as they once had to journalism, for economic survival that would also allow them time for their own writing. According to several scriptwriters for radio whose testimony appears in *Llorar es un placer*, a study of the Cuban radio industry, the greatest aspiration for a writer was to be hired by one of the major soap companies, such as Gravi, Crusellas and Sabatás.[32] Once the contract had been signed, despite ambition and good intentions, all hopes of reconciling the two *métiers*, that of salaried script-writer and novelist or poet, were rapidly shattered for numerous writers. A close reading of a typical contract offered by Crusellas and Co., Manufacturers of Soaps and Perfumes, makes clear there would be little *free* time for the personal literary pursuits of the freelancer. In the event that the script-writer did produce a literary work on his or her own time, the author would then have to dispute rights to intellectual property with the soap company.[33]

In addition to retaining exclusive rights to the intellectual property of its "authors," the company reserved the right to change words, phrases, plot and story line, without the author's prior consent. Scriptwriting tended to dull and drain the writers involved. The magazines and journals born in the heat of the 1920s and 1930s were long dead; radio was the primary means of communication in the 1940s and presented one of the few options for many writers who found themselves in a cultural vacuum, at loose ends. Yet, in time, adversity strengthened writers' resolve, and they redoubled their efforts in defense of national culture. Throughout Cuba's cultural history, from the colonial writers like Villa-

---

[31]González, *Llorar es un placer*, 276.

[32]See "Los autores, ¿culpables?" in González, *Llorar es un placer*, 244-82.

[33]Standard contract, reproduced in *Llorar es un placer*, 245-51. Clauses in one contract on intellectual property for the period of employment were ambiguously worded to the employer's advantage: "To insure the good quality, emotion and interest of the works THE AUTHOR hereby sells to THE COMPANY, she voluntarily swears not to work on any other projects for radio and/or television, for any entity, person or company other than Crusellas and Company, Inc., during the period in which this contract is in force."

verde and Martí who risked imprisonment for merely positing the existence of a *Cuban* literature and continued to produce in exile, the most troubled periods often bear the most interesting fruit. The final decades of the precarious Republic are no exception. At the height of the crisis, in the face of a campaign against national culture, three notable experiments were carried out in the erratic but unbroken chain of independent actions by Cuban intellectuals so often under siege: the "Orígenes" group, "Páginas" and "Manigua."

The "Orígenes" Group: Publications and Periodical

The "Orígenes" chapter in the history of Cuban letters has elicited a wide gamut of opinions, from the most exhorbitant praise—as if Cuban literary creation in the Republic, and for some, in the twentieth century as a whole, began and ended with the production of Orígenes—to accusations of aestheticism, hermeticism and frivolous escapism in art.

Julio E. Miranda, in his survey, *Nueva literatura cubana,* offers an overview of literary tendencies in the decades prior to the Revolution, placing special emphasis on the *origenistas* work:

> Any attempt to criticize Orígenes, as someone once did, on the basis of having evaded the concrete realities facing the nation in those years, is to ignore the state of literature within that reality.[34]

Just as the Orígenes group and their movement have been misunderstood and subject to wildly divergent interpretations, so has the figure and *oeuvre* of its leading member, José Lezama Lima. The publication of the correspondence between Rodríguez Feo and Lezama Lima in the 1940s, framed by the astute commentaries of Rodríguez Feo himself decades later, has done much toward setting the record straight by placing the group and its principal figures in context. This and preceding chapters have, in the same spirit, sought to study the role of writers and readers and examine literary life by revisiting the latter part of the nineteenth and the first half of the twentieth centuries.

Following the activism of the politically charged decade from 1920 to 1930, the failed revolt against Machado, increased repressive measures in all arenas of

---

[34]Julio E. Miranda, *Nueva literatura cubana* (Madrid: Taurus Ediciones, 1971): 25.

national political life, and the mass-media onslaught of movie producers, radio producers and advertisers; the general state of affairs in the 1940s, when the Orígenes Group was formed, offered few inducements to or outlets for literary creation.

The first anthology of contemporary Cuban short stories appeared in 1937 (*Cuentos contemporáneos*, Federico Ibarzábal, ed., Havana: Editorial Trópico), but by 1947, only a decade later, "of the twenty-three surviving short story writers from Ibarzábal's anthology, sixteen had given up literature for good."[35]

Gone was the cohesion of the 1930s, and writers found themselves once again alone, facing official corruption and disdain for national culture. It was against these odds that the Orígenes periodical and publishing venture, without the support of a political party or any of the government-backed academic or cultural institutions, brought together prominent Cuban writers[36] who proved their adherence to literary ideals in a ten-year effort—through the worst of the nation's economic and political crisis—to reaffirm cultural values and traditions that were breaking down; to capture, create and re-create the essence of Cuban reality in literature and art.

While the nation appeared submerged in a superficial cosmopolitanism, a world of imported cultural values, the Orígenes Group created its own channels for the literary efforts of a minority, but a minority with a far-reaching aesthetic and cultural program.

Nowhere is the asphyxiating atmosphere in which they wrote examined more closely or captured with greater immediacy than in the correspondence of the two founders, and Rodríguez Feo's later reflections on the period in *Mi correspondencia con Lezama*. This important text bears further testimony to the unrelenting efforts of the Orígenes group in a cultural vacuum which would, as Rodríguez Feo observes, inevitably take its toll on Lezama:

> Nevertheless, the solitude and tedium, the indifference with which all artistic manifestations were met, the apathy and pessimism which para-

---

[35] Ambrosio Fornet, *En blanco y negro*, 89.

[36] Founded in Havana in 1944 by José Lezama Lima and José Rodríguez Feo, the Orígenes Group and journal brought together the writers Gastón Baquero, Eliseo Diego, Samuel Feijóo, Pablo Armando Fernández, Fina García Marruz, Lorenzo García, Angel Gaztelú, Fayad Jamís, José Lezama Lima, Luis Marré, Pedro de Oráa, Virgilio Piñera, José Rodríguez Feo, Justo Rodríguez Santo, Octavio Smith.

lyzed all efforts to overcome the circumstances, wore away at his creative vitality. By the end of the 1950s, Lezama had already produced his major works.[37]

The Orígenes journal went on to earn international acclaim. By accepting only unpublished poems, short stories, essays on the philosophy of art, aesthetic theory and the plastic arts by Cubans and foreigners, Orígenes provided an invaluable stimulus, both intellectual and material, for literary and artistic production with few outlets to society at large.

On its tenth anniversary, Orígenes assessed the situation and future as follows:

> If we have carried on for ten years in spite of your indifference, do not now offer us, we beg you, the fetid fruit of your admiration. We thank you kindly, but we much prefer your indifference. Your indifference has been beneficial, we would not know what to do with your admiration. It would confuse us all, since there is nothing more noxious than an admiration that is rotten to the core. You are totally incapable of admiration....[38]

With justifiable irony, Lezama Lima, director of the journal, lashed out at the government officials and respectable academic institutions which, after turning their backs on all of Orígenes' projects and pursuits, sent congratulatory messages, *a posteriori*, on the occasion of their tenth anniversary. His was a reaction not only to the immediate situation of Cuban letters and the vociferous hypocrisy of the reigning cultural institutions at home but to an age enthralled by spectacle, against which Lezama, throughout, maintained a quiet independence:

> Our epoch tends to turn everything into a spectacle. Gide and Eliot receive prizes, their purses are fattened and the King, under the footlights, hands over the check and the parchment. If Lautréamant had lived in

---

[37]José Rodríguez Feo, *Mi correspondencia con Lezama* (Havana: Unión, 1989): 31.

[38]José Lezama Lima, *Orígenes*, 35, cited in *Los poetas del Grupo de Orígenes,* Félix Cruz-Alvarez, Ph.D. thesis, University of Miami, 1975, p. 2.

our time, we would give him the Nobel prize too and the right not to wait on line to get into the movies.[39]

Orígenes made no pretense of being a literary-cultural movement for the general public, although they had earned the respect of literary groups with close ties to popular mass movements by virtue of their honest and independent stance. They had accomplished what they set out to do; remaining together through ten years of active literary life while publishing a journal that maintained absolute independence from "sinister officialdom," constitutes a remarkable record of endurance when compared with the precarious existence of most independent literary journals. In addition to the journal, Orígenes Editions put out a total of 23 titles between 1945 and 1955.[40]

Orígenes was a major force in Cuba's cultural process, both for the independent stance and productivity of its members. Although they never achieved a broad following, the participants remained faithful to the goals they had set for themselves as well as the aesthetic ideals which inspired them:

> Trapped within their own hermeticism, Orígenes, nevertheless, did not go about offering their literature as merchandise; while the high priests of Cuban letters wrote on consignment and divvied up the honors

---

[39]Letter from Lezama Lima to Rodríguez Feo, November 10, 1948, in *Mi correspondencia con Lezama*, 103.

[40]The following is a complete list of titles published by the Orígenes Group: *Aventuras sigilosas* (1945), José Lezama Lima; *De mi provincia* (1945), Cintio Vitier; *Divertimientos* (1946), Eliseo Diego; *Del furtivo destierro* (1946), Octavio Smith; *Transfiguración de Jesús en el Monte* (1947), Fina García Marruz; *Suite para la espera* (1948), Lorenzo García Vega; *Diez poetas cubanos* (1948), Cintio Vitier; *La joven parca* (1949), Paul Valery, trans., Mariano Brull; *En la Calzada de Jesús del Monte* (1949), Eliseo Diego; *El hogar y el olvido* (1949), Cintio Vitier; *La fijeza* (1949), José Lezama Lima; *La belleza del cielo no amortaja* (1950), Justo Rodríguez Santos; *Espirales del Cuje* (1951), Lorenzo García Vega; *El teatro de O'Neill* (1952), Mario Parajón; *Tiburón y otros cuentos* (1952), Ramón Ferreira; *Vísperas* (1953), Cintio Vitier; *Magia y realidad del teatro* (1953), Mario Parajón; *La poesía contemporánea en Cuba* (1954), Roberto Fernández Retamar; *Los párpados y el polvo* (1954), Fayad Jamís; *Gradual de laudes* (1955), Angel Gatzelú; *Asonante final y otros poemas* (1954), Eugenio Florit; *Canto llano* (1956), Cintio Vitier.

among themselves, the members of Orígenes, practically in a vacuum, never lost faith in poetry and produced an *oeuvre*.[41]

The Páginas Publishing House

As we have indicated, the most enduring publishing experiments in the republican period were either financed by their founding members or relied on the support of the Party. "Páginas" was the publishing operation of the first Socialist Party of Cuba, headed, from its founding in the early 1940s to its dissolution in the early 1950s, by Carlos Rafael Rodríguez.

The Party of Revolutionary Unity, as it was then called, decided to set up a publishing house, bookstore and radio station (One-Thousand-Ten) in the early 1940s, taking advantage of the legal status granted the Party by the Constitution of 1940, in order to bring the latest developments and currents of national and international art, literature and culture to the population in general, and facilitate distribution of literary works to the reading public. All of Páginas' editions were mass editions; prices were kept very low, on principle, but also because Páginas could afford to and had in fact been set up to do so by the Party.

The publishing operation was housed in the same building as the bookstore, in a top-floor apartment. Their printing press belonged not to the publishing wing but to the Party itself; Arrow Press printed all the titles on the publisher's list. Páginas' editorial program was to publish works with a political focus: criticism, scientific studies, essays, Cuban and universal literature, all with a progressive outlook and at prices that made them highly accessible.

Páginas prepared a massive Cuban edition of the *Communist Manifesto*, as well as the first Cuban edition of Darwin's *Descent of Man*. In general, Páginas used existing Spanish-language translations and the bookstore bought its stock from Argentine, Mexican and Spanish houses. When necessary, they had Spanish translations prepared on contract. Novelist Alejo Carpentier's mother occasionally translated for Páginas. Their Cuban editions ranged from anthropology and political science to literary criticism, including such titles as: *El engaño de las razas*, Fernando Ortiz, *En torno a la novela detectivesca*, José Antonio Portuondo and *Fundamentos del Socialismo*, Blas Roca.

Páginas' bookstore served as cultural center and meeting place for progressive writers and intellectuals of the 1940s. Their editorial projects attracted, and

---

[41]Ambrosio Fornet, *En blanco y negro*, 93.

welcomed, the collaboration of many writers with no ties to the Party, assuming the posture of a "united front" and lending financial support to all Cuban writers who shared a cultural vision. When it was not prudent for a writer's work to be published by Páginas, the editorial board took up a collection to finance the edition with a commercial press. Aware that most Cuban writers subsidized the publication of their own works, Páginas took every measure within their means, which were considerable for that time, to remedy the situation. The consistent quality, both in presentation and selection, of their editions, along with massive print-runs, made Páginas, together with Orígenes, one of the most significant publishing projects of the republican decades, with its own printing press, two journals (*Dialéctica* and *Fundamentos*), a team of translators and frequent contributors.

The efficiency of Páginas, both organizational and financial, was unique among literary groups. In spite of the low price of its editions, Páginas' publishing operation broke even. Like the tobacco workers' press, El Ideal, Páginas was a prototype of sound administration, proof that a noncommercial, cultural press could be a feasible undertaking.

The Manigua Publishing Group

Another influential publishing experiment, born a decade later, voiced the concerns of writers from the provinces. Manigua Publishers was founded in Santiago de Cuba around 1953; the first title was published under the Manigua label in 1954. Manigua was not a publishing house in the strict sense of the term; it was the brainchild of a group of writers from Santiago who got together to publish their works as a collection, under a common label. They had no journal, no money to speak of, only a common desire to project themselves nationally as a literary movement, which they hoped would incorporate new writers as it gained strength and presence. It is important to note that in Santiago de Cuba where the Manigua experiment was born there were no other publishers at that time, and presumably no culture or civilization, hence the ironic name, "Manigua"—"jungle"—adopted by the group. The notion that the western region of the island was a cultural wasteland, or worse, the barbaric counterpoint to Havana's "refinement," developed, as we have seen, in the nineteenth century, in the postwar years when reconstruction monies flowed into the capital and Havana's refurbished industries held a monopoly on goods. It mattered little that the western provinces, particularly Santiago, had had their own thriving cultural centers before the war. The postwar Havana print shops were soon supplying the whole island, doing away with local production. Journals, newspapers and cultural centers in the provinces fell by the wayside as well, unable to compete, and the myth of Havana's cultural superiority was reinforced:

> In the first place, we got the idea of forming a publishing house when Dr. Mañach published an article in *Bohemia* in which he referred in a disdainful tone to "jungle" culture. That, naturally, wounded writers from the provinces, and their first reaction was to write an article, to put out a call, in response to Mañach, or an open letter in *Bohemia* itself, but we all finally agreed that the best response to Mañach was to publish our works. If we hadn't done so up until then it was simply because we had no money with which to do so and besides, there were no publishers in the province.[42]

Radio and film messages had set the tone for the 1940s and 1950s; culture was something that existed *elsewhere*. If one admitted that a degree of culture existed on the homefront, it was to be found in the capital, never in the provinces. Manigua's founders were right in believing that the best way to promote the literature that was being written in the provinces was not by placing articles in magazines to denounce Havana's chauvinistic views on literature and culture but by actually getting their books published, at any cost. The Manigua Group published their works the same way writers had been publishing and distributing their works for a century, with the difference that theirs was a collective effort. Their first step was to contact the best printer in Santiago de Cuba, Mario San Román, who printed all the publications of the University of Oriente. San Román agreed to print limited editions, at cost, averaging 500 copies per title. Each member of the collective financed, individually, the edition of his or her own work, as writers had always done and when funds were short, they took out loans.[43] All of the members functioned as editors, copy editors and proofreaders, correcting each other's work. Economically, the publishing process was the same

---

[42]José Antonio Portuondo. From an interview with Portuondo on the origin and modus operandi of Manigua Publishers, Havana, January 24, 1985.

[43]The third title in the collection, *Presencia*, by Lino Horruitinier was published only because each of the members chipped in toward the cost of printing. Lino Horruitinier did not have a regular job, "he did occasional administrative work in offices." *Presencia* was the only book he published, leaving behind several manuscipts of poetry when he died.

same for the group as it was for individual writers, but the idea behind the effort, the motivation, was unique. It is one thing when an individual publishes and distributes his or her own work as a lone venture and quite another for a group of writers to project themselves nationally as a literary movement with a publishing program. Their efforts and approach were groundbreaking and helped overcome ingrained prejudice and contempt for provincial writers. After the first two volumes by members from Santiago were published, two Havana writers joined the collective. "Manigua Publishers" was never, and in fact never became, a publishing house in its own right but it was an influential group, making readers and writers aware, by example, of new possibilities for the transmission of literary culture on a national scale. Manigua, like Orígenes, never aspired to become a mass movement; their literary efforts were strictly by and for the "guild," a select group of writers and intellectuals aware that the reading public was a minority. The books published by Manigua were, for the most part, read by other writers and distributed by the Santiago bookseller who had donated his services as agent for the group.

Manigua inaugurated its collection in 1954 with *Aquelarre*, a book of short stories with an unusual format, by Ezequiel Vieta. Vieta wanted the book's typography to reflect its expressionist content, so every available typeface was employed in its composition. The collective published roughly a book a year. In 1955 *Tierra y nación* by Jorge Castellanos and *Presencia* by Lino Horruitinier were published; in 1956, *Son de otros* by Rosario Antuña, followed by an anthology of essays on *La vorágine* by students of one of Manigua's members; the professor, Hilda Pereira. The last book to be published by the group was *La historia y las generaciones* by José Antonio Portuondo, in 1958.

Manigua Publishers put out a total of five books between 1954 and 1958. In a parallel effort, the artists and writers that had founded Manigua developed other vehicles to promote literature and the arts, among them, *Galería, Bulletin of the Gallery of Plastic Arts in Santiago de Cuba* (1955-60), with the stated purpose of

> offering our creative personalities, renowned or unpublished, the exposure and stimulus needed to keep their heads held high in an atmosphere that considers serious artistic efforts to be the most frivolous of pursuits.

The principal literary movement to come out of Santiago and Oriente in the 1950s revolved around the journal *Galería,* which attracted many writers not native to Santiago. José Antonio Portuondo, Nicolás Guillén, José Soler Puig,

Rosario Antuña, Electo Silva, Raúl Pomares, Nereida Neira Fernández and Guillermo Orozco Sierra were frequent contributors.

The magazine's distribution, relying on the personal initiative of editors and contributors, proved very effective:

> The magazine enjoyed wide circulation. If we define circulation as distribution by an agency, no, that is, you rarely ever found the magazine in kiosks. There were very few kiosks around; there were a few places where magazines were sold in Santiago de Cuba and we saw to it that they stocked our magazine. In Havana, in general, distribution was primarily person to person. We sent groups to cultural centers and libraries with the magazine. Besides, we printed a limited number of each issue.[44]

Those who took part in the literary activities of Manigua and *Galería* worked in universities, schools and offices. They received neither income nor royalties from their literary and publishing work, only the satisfaction of having boosted recognition of literature, the arts, and culture in general in Santiago and Oriente, and built a bridge which strengthened ties with intellectual and cultural circles in Havana:

> Those were the five books we wrote and published. We would have published others and had many other projects in mind but in 1958 the Revolution reached its climax and we abandoned our own adventure for another, much more important.[45]

Literary Contests and Contraband Silk in the Cuban Republic

The first literary contest was held in Cuba in 1793, sponsored by the Patriotic Society of Havana and its publication, *El papel periódico de La Havana*, with prizes for a variety of themes and genres. The tradition of literary contests continued through the nineteenth and twentieth centuries. In the republican period, cultural institutions and periodicals founded in the colony along with those

---

[44]Interview with José Antonio Portuondo, January 24, 1985.

[45]Interview with José Antonio Portuondo, January 24, 1985.

that had emerged in the Republic, held contests for patriotic, historical, journalistic and literary works.

In a country with a small army of unpublished writers and no publishers, contests can be a very effective means to stimulate literary production. Neither small press nor publishing house, the literary contest, as institution, falls somewhere in between, using existing periodicals as a vehicle for disseminating the award-winning works among magazine readers. Contest winners were thus spared the expense of printing and the labor of distribution; the sponsoring institution arranged for publication in a magazine or journal. Available space was the only limiting factor; works submitted could not be lengthy, which automatically eliminated genres other than the short story, article, or essay.

There were three major literary contests in the Republic: "Hernández Catá," initiated in 1942; "Justo de Lara" (1934-57),[46] and the National Contest held by the Cultural Council of the Board of Education for unpublished works in history, philosophy, criticism, biography, economics, science, journalism and literature, including novels, plays, short stories and essays. The Cultural Council, in principle, published the award-winning works by arrangement with private presses and thus admitted lengthier works in a variety of genres.

The history of state-sponsored literary contests in the Republic cannot be told without touching on the systemic administrative corruption that characterized government institutions. Loló de la Torriente, after winning the contest held by the Cultural Council, had to publish the book herself, taking up a collection among friends and colleagues. The Board of Education had failed to comply with the statutes of its own literary contest.

Winners of the literary contests sponsored by private institutions suffered a similar fate; on occasion, the cash prize was simply never received and the manuscript was not published. Along with the prize money awarded to the author, his or her story or article was reviewed in the press by leading journalists and writers. "Hernández Catá" was open to national and international authors. Juan Marinello, Fernando Ortiz and Jorge Mañach were among the judges. In the national contest, Félix Pita Rodríguez, Onelio Jorge Cardoso, Dora Alonso and

---

[46]Alfonso Hernández Catá (1885-1940). Born in Spain and raised in Cuba, Hernández Catá began as a reader in tobacco factories before joining the diplomatic service. He is the author of short stories, novels, zarzuelas, plays and poems published in Cuba and Spain. Justo de Lara was the pen name of José de Armas y Cárdenas (1866-1919), well-known Cuban journalist, translator, critic and novelist.

Ernesto García Alzola won the short story prize; in the international, Juan Bosch. "Justo de Lara" was a national contest with a 1,000 *peso* cash prize. Of the three, "Justo de Lara" was the most coveted, sponsored by El Encanto, the most glamorous shop in Cuba, then known as "the pearl of the Caribbean" to the international set. El Encanto used the literary contest as one more form of advertising, and the panel of judges varied from year to year.

El Encanto's "Justo de Lara" literary contest was more prestigious than that sponsored by the Cultural Council for the simple and obvious reason that the department store had more money to spend and could offer greater incentives to writers: 1,000 *pesos* was more than enough for a 500-copy edition, prepared by the best printer in Havana.

El Encanto dealt in contraband goods, silks, for the most part. As local police chiefs looked the other way, contraband trade flourished, and El Encanto built a reputation by offering "only the best" and reaped substantial rewards. In the complex relationship between literature and society, even contraband silk may play a part: if it were not for contraband goods, El Encanto would not have become influential enough to sponsor a literary contest with cash prizes sufficient to cover the average cost of a modest edition, and in which pillars of the Cuban literary community, such as Raúl Roa, ironically, were honored.

El Encanto had a book section which stocked literary novelties, though not necessarily works by its award-winning Cuban authors. An advertisement appearing in the Cuban magazine *La feria del libro*, in 1943, invites consumers to practice "the social elegance of gift-giving," recommending books or *objets d'art* for this purpose. The fact that a book produced and marketed as a book-object or a gift-book bears the El Encanto label, or that the edition was financed by the company, or offered to its public as merchandise does not, in itself, impugn or negate the work's literary and intellectual merits. As we have seen, committed Cuban intellectuals viewed the "Justo de Lara" and other contests as one of the few channels open to them to gain exposure for their works. This said, the context in which the literary work was presented to the public—which is what is under scrutiny here—is a blatantly consumerist context in which *all* merchandise, from a silk handkerchief to a volume of poems is indiscriminately sold to the public on the weight of the prestige conferred by El Encanto's label. It is difficult to imagine a more artful exposé of the book-commodity, the "coffee table book," valued for the prestige of a label, independent of content, than the 1943 advertisement for the book section of El Encanto, when viewed with a critical eye. From the seller's point of view, and in the context in which the literary work is sold, it is indistinguishable from and interchangeable with the "suggestive" *objet d'art*.

Another ironic twist in the relationship between El Encanto and Cuban letters has to do with the publication, in 1933, of a book of poems, *Nosotros,* by Regino Pedroso, whose themes were suggested by the lives of factory workers. The cover design depicted an imposing cogwheel. This was one of the "subversive" books, later to appear on the list of officially banned titles, primarily on the basis of its cover. Anyone accused of reading it, or having it in their possession, would be condemned to six months in prison:

> A group of intellectual workers—schoolteachers who often met at La Propagandística bookstore and press...a few writers and a pianist—made small contributions toward the cost of printing Pedroso's book. The edition of *Nosotros* carried another printer's label as camouflage, copies were taken out of the print shop under a cloak of secrecy, and no one knows whose idea it was to send a few copies to the aristocratic El Encanto on Galiano Street. An ignorant manager had the book placed in the display window; seeing the cogwheel on the cover, he believed it to be a Rotary Club publication.[47]

On that note, we close the chapter on the first century and a half of Cuban literary production and the evolving relationship between literature and society, between infrastructure and literary culture in the colony and the Republic.

Perhaps Cuban literary history would have taken a very different turn if the editors, scholars and writers of the Spanish Republic, those who contributed so much to the growth of publishing in Argentina and Mexico, had found refuge in Cuba. The decade of 1930, and its generation, in many ways, hastened Cuba's belated entry into the twentieth century. The intense political and cultural activism of the 1930s opened Cuba up to the world, through the cultural exchange and dialogue of ideas that took place in the nation's periodicals. Cuban participation in the Spanish Civil War accelerated the process, yet after the war Cuba did not reap the benefits enjoyed by those Latin American nations that gave asylum to the intelligentsia of the Spanish Republic. The political climate did not allow the Spanish intellectuals expelled from their homeland to put down roots in Cuba. When they reached the island's shores they encountered such hostility that most continued on to Mexico. The statutes of the major universities, traditional refuge and source of employment for the uprooted intellectual, required all pro-

---

[47]José G. Ricardo, *La imprenta en Cuba* (Havana: Letras Cubanas, 1989): 180.

fessors to be Cuban either by birth or naturalization, and the naturalization process took a full five years. The Spaniards' presence on the island posed both practical and political problems. The government feared the influx of intellectual activists, and in pragmatic terms, apart from the university, the cultural infrastructure of Cuban society in the 1930s and 1940s was not sufficiently developed to accommodate and support those who wished to remain. Mexico welcomed the Spanish intellectuals seeking asylum, and their arrival in 1938 spurred tremendous growth in publishing; they were undoubtedly instrumental in advancing the cause and state of the Mexican publishing industry. The same initiative in Cuban society would have made an invaluable contribution toward building a literary infrastructure. At the same time, history has shown that the growth of book publishing and the extension of literary culture to the broadest strata are two aspects of literature's social existence that do not necessarily go hand in hand. The development of Mexican book publishing, and the direction it took, was not based, from the start, on the achievement of full literacy among the citizenry nor was it followed—save a brief period in Mexican history—by a conscientious and constant campaign to raise the cultural level of the majority toward the goal of creating a society of readers and thinkers. Mexico's publishing industry grew to meet the demand of supplying books to the continent. Nations can become book producers, industrially, without spreading literary culture. The jarring testimony, given in the early 1980s, by an editor from Siglo XXI Publishers in Mexico underscores this fundamental difference:

> A visitor's first impression in Cuba is to note the great extent to which such a small country, in such a short time, has made the book an instrument of knowledge and an item enjoying mass consumption. It is equally astonishing that while we publish 4 or 5 thousand copies of one title for the entire population of Latin America and Spain, Cuban editors never know how many readers a new title will have; it is admirable that a reading public of 10 million inhabitants absorbs ten times more books than the Latin American continent.[48]

Though conditions have changed greatly in both Mexico and Cuba from the mid-1980s to the mid-1990s, the logic behind the observations remains the same.

---

[48] Alejandro Ríos, "El libro en Cuba," published by CERLAL (Mexico City: Centro Regional para el Fomento de la Literatura y el Libro en Mexico, 1984): 48.

The remaining chapters of this study will address questions raised by the development of Cuban literary culture from 1959 through the 1980s, primarily literature's role in the democratization of culture. Yet an analysis of the new relations between literature and society being forged in Cuba over three decades, from 1959 to 1989, would be incomplete if it did not first seek to understand the historical process of building on the vernacular literature born in and against the Spanish colony, and redefined in the process of nation-building in the first half of the twentieth century. A social history of literature is an inquiry into literature's meaning and function in society, over time, by and for whom; it is an examination of literary creation as a social and historical process. The history of Cuban letters from the dawn of the nineteenth century to the present is a complex history of upheaval and rupture within the continuity of a struggle to assert nationhood and define national culture. One hundred years of Cuban history, in the periods encompassed by this study, experienced the transition from Spanish colonial possession, to Republic within the U.S. sphere of influence, to socialist state. Cuba is again, as I write, in a state of transition. In cultural terms, from the late 1800s to the late 1980s, Cuba struggled against the Spanish colonial doctrine of "national unity" and the influence of the U.S. mass media and embarked upon a campaign to realize the full potential of its literary tradition through universal education and the development of its publishing industry. And now Cuba is attempting a delicate balancing act, trying to hold on to many of the state-sponsored gains in education, health and culture, while building new, and rebuilding old, ties to the global market economy.

CHAPTER 4. THE CULTURAL POLICY OF THE REVOLUTION AND THE LITERARY SPHERE: AN OVERVIEW

I began research confident that primary sources for a study of Cuban literary production for the period dating from 1959 and the onset of the Revolution to the foundation of the Ministry of Culture in 1977 could be found in archives. Data compiled by others would serve as a springboard for my own research. I found, however, that in the initial years of the Revolution when an infrastructure for literature was being laid, problem-solving and the urgent need *to do, to act, to create*, was so great it left no room or resources for the meticulous and far less exhilarating task of documentation; there was no time for systematically chronicling all the educational, literary and cultural initiatives while they were underway. It was a question of establishing priorities: documentation can be done *a posteriori*, reconstructing events in retrospect. Consequently, I was faced with the task of creating the archives I had hoped to find ready-made and at my disposal, gathering the material that would enable research to follow developments in the literary/editorial dynamic of the initial phase of the Revolution, from the inauguration of the National Printing Press to the creation of the Ministry of Culture, and serve as a point of departure for further studies.

When I began to develop the ideas that would culminate in this project, not yet clearly defined, one of them centered on a literary "renaissance," an avalanche of literary creation unleashed by profound social change. This was to be the main thesis for a chapter on the early revolutionary years. It is a splendid concept—the victorious *guerrilleros* march into Havana and a literary "renaissance" occurs in their wake—as concepts go, but it proved to be a distorted and somewhat simplistic notion of how literary creation responds to a radical transformation of society. I discarded that thesis, and later abandoned all "theses" which freed me to examine the *process* of creating conditions favorable to literary creation and of laying the foundations for a new literary culture.

That first year, 1959, was witness to a cultural explosion and catharsis which cleared the air and opened the way for a renewed, less fettered expression of Cuban culture. From that moment on, "culture" would no longer be a "given," something presumed to have the kind of common and simple definition one need not give a second thought to. "Culture" and all that it implies would by definition envelop the lives of all Cubans, and be broadened and enhanced by the contribution of every member of society, from those just learning to read and write to the celebrated intellectuals returning from exile.

A study of the *Casa de las Américas* review, as a barometer of the situation and response of the intelligentsia over several decades, posits Cuba in the revolutionary period as a classic example of national culture, both forming and redefining itself:

> It is seeking out the roots of its nationhood and attracting technical, scientific and artistic resources of other nations, making them accessible through large-scale educational programs to the masses, who are ultimately responsible for the creation of a new national culture.[1]

Cultural policy, as theoretical guide and framework for this study,[2] was one of the major achievements of the Revolution and an integral part of the historical moment when the old gave way to the new, and suddenly nothing could be taken for granted. The essential elements of the cultural policy born of the events of January 1959 have evolved, yet each step in the process has brought new contributions. From 1959 to the mid-sixties, Cuba looked to existing elements—machinery, human resources, *savoir faire*—rediscovering them in light of the new functions they would assume, particularly in the task of consolidating an editorial base and philosophy for literary creation.

There was no "avalanche" of literary production in those years, not even a minor landslide; conditions were not yet ripe for that to occur. In the early 1960s, Cuban society was forced to take a long, hard look at material conditions and existing resources to determine if and how they might be combined to forge modest but solid foundations for the development of a graphics and book publishing industry. As a part of this ongoing effort, machinery installed by entrepreneurs for diverse purposes was adapted for book production. These were not machines designed to produce books but produce books they did, in vast quanti-

---

[1] Judith A. Weiss, *Casa de las Américas: An Intellectual Review in the Cuban Revolution* (Chapel Hill: Estudios de Hispanófila, 1977): 27.

[2] See *Política cultural de la Revolución Cubana: documentos* (Havana: Editorial de las Ciencias Sociales, 1977); *Tesis y resoluciones*, Primer Congreso del Partido Comunista de Cuba (Havana: Editorial de Ciencias Sociales, 1978); and *II Congreso del Partido Comunista de Cuba* (Havana: Editora Política, 1981), among others, for the basic tenets of the cultural policy of the Cuban Revolution.

ties. A Cuban *Quijote* was the first to emerge from the rotary presses and find its way to every corner of the island. The compelling force behind the arduous and complex task of building a publishing industry was a cultural policy made up of the compound aspirations and desires of many generations, and the determination to see them realized. It was a far-reaching cultural policy

> contained in Fidel's words to the intellectuals, pronounced in 1961; in the conclusions of the Congress on Education and Culture in 1971; the precepts of the Constitution of the Republic that refer to national culture and, especially, the Thesis and Resolutions on Artistic and Literary Culture of the First Party Congress.

> But to apply this policy, we needed to clarify certain concepts and place emphasis on certain aspects. And the first thing to be made clear was that art and literature are the means or forms through which culture expresses itself, but the content of culture is much broader and deeper than what the words "art" and "literature" bring to mind. Art and literature cannot develop if we don't go to the very heart of the matter.[3]

The heart of the matter is the Revolution itself, its survival, "its right to exist, its right to develop, its right to prevail."[4]

These are not new concerns; they can be found in "History Will Absolve Me," "Words to the Intellectuals," and the documents that formed and guided cultural policy at every step of its implementation. They all spring from the same source: Cuba's recurrent need to reshape itself. Without the Revolution, even the skeletal structure for book publishing, providing an industrial base for literary creation, would not have taken shape when it did. In that sense, the Revolution is the primary cultural act which predates all others. Without a radical transformation and reorganization of society's resources, literary and artistic culture would have remained, as it was in the 1940s and 1950s, within isolated enclaves, in the fragmented efforts that contained the seeds of a cultural renaissance that would eventually coalesce as a result of the events of 1959.

---

[3] Armando Hart Dávalos, *Política cultural de la Revolución Cubana: documentos* (Havana: Editorial de Ciencias Sociales, 1977): 1.

[4] Fidel Castro, "Palabras a los intelectuales," in *Política cultural de la Revolución Cubana*, 18.

Immediately following the Revolution, palpable changes in the world of literature and book publishing were, as one would expect, modest. The machinery, the print shops, supplies of paper and ink, and the printers and writers themselves functioned, for the most part, as they had the year before; except for an increase in volume, books were also produced just as they had been the year before. But a definitive change of spirit was manifest as well as a change in the reader for whom literature was now being written and published. As a result, the availability of books, channels for their distribution and all the mechanisms that bring readers, old and new, and books together, are directly tied to the cultural policy of the Revolution.

The declarations, documents and texts which define cultural policy are essential tools for reconstructing the world of literary production and dissemination in the early 1960s, in conjunction with the testimony offered by the architects of the first graphics and editorial initiatives upon which the Cuban publishing network was built. No written records exist for those years, but much can be gathered from the testimony of those who took an active part in the process. It is only through the tenacity of memory that we are able to "gather data and information on how things were, what took place and how we lived"[5] in the complex world of Cuban book publishing in the first phase of the Revolution.

It is not difficult to imagine the paucity of resources for turning out literary works, or books in general, in the spring of 1959. It was not a matter of reinventing the wheel, of beginning from degree zero, but still an enormous challenge if we consider the urgent demand for books created by the Revolution's ambitious educational campaign. Linotype printing, a laborious process, was the most common; existing offset equipment was not set up for book publishing, having been installed to print pamphlets and magazines for "offshore" distribution in Latin America. Advanced technology had, up until then, little to do with the needs of production for domestic consumption. In that sense, the offset print shops were much like the "turn-key" installations in other industries which contribute little to the development of the host country: foreign built, with imported machinery, replacement parts, technology and technicians, the turn-key factories produce primarily for export, leaving neither revenue nor expertise behind. Originally designed to produce 30- to 40-page magazines that required no binding or "finishing" (the last stage in book production: cover, dust jacket, title page, etcetera), Cuban offset equipment had to be overhauled to meet the demands of

---

[5]Fidel Castro, "Palabras a los intelectuales," in *Política cultural de la Revolución Cubana*, 47.

book production. The rotary presses were adapted for books as well, and all the binding was done by hand.

The modified rotary presses that once printed newspapers and the offset equipment at Omega, the shop that put out *Selecciones del Reader's Digest*, produced tens of thousands of books, among them classics of Cuban and world literature published for the first time in Cuba. The National Printing House launched the literary/editorial initiatives that would lead to the creation of the National Publishing House, "Edición Revolucionaria," primarily for textbooks, the Cuban Book Institute, and the founding of Casa de las Américas and the Writers and Artists Union, although these last two institutions arose more in response to problems posed by intellectual and artistic endeavor in a new social context than to material exigencies. In addition to the problems Batista left unresolved, a whole set of difficulties was engendered by the Revolution itself, both internal and external. Casa de las Américas was created as part of an effort to break out of the cultural isolation that came with the economic blockade which cordoned the island, by establishing direct artistic, cultural and intellectual dialogue with its Latin American and Caribbean counterparts, unhampered by governmental restrictions imposed by nations taking part in the trade embargo. Through the 1980s, Casa's journals and editions were still distributed largely on a courtesy basis or through exchange with other institutions in which no money changed hands in order not to run afoul of treasury laws which might prohibit trade with "enemy nations" and thus have the effect of restricting circulation of Cuban publications.[6]

The Writers and Artists Union was a direct response to tensions within Cuban society, particularly insecurity on the part of Cuban writers who, accustomed to "marginal" status, were now encouraged to participate fully in the social process. Many were unsure how they fit into the new scheme of things: the writer's *métier*, considered a frivolous and extravagant pastime, viewed with skepticism by the authorities before 1959, was now supported, officially, as a vehicle of change, communication, self-knowledge. At the crossroads, the writer's very existence became problematic. The Writers and Artists Union addressed

---

[6]Judith A. Weiss' study, *Casa de las Américas: An Intellectual Review in the Revolution*, stresses the Latin Americanist, internationalist orientation of the review *Casa*, conceived by many, from its inception as an alternative to Mexico's Fondo de Cultura Económica, in the continental arena: "The review *Casa de las Américas* would serve to coalesce the efforts of the cultural center as well as to spread its young ideas in the same area covered by the Fondo" (42).

the needs of many who felt bewildered and out of touch, bringing writers together and providing a forum in which they could communicate with one another and
begin to define their relationship to society at large. The Writers Union functioned as a cultural "united front" for all sectors of society; religious groups and
others, from which writers emerged—it should be noted that by this time the
Revolution had declared itself Marxist. The Writers Union arose not so much to
assuage the fear of writers who felt threatened by the Revolution—although there
were undoubtedly those who did—as to confront long-term effects of the margin-
alization and isolation writers had experienced in the last three decades of republican life. Resources were now made available to writers: by facilitating research
for and publication of their works, the Revolution had granted writers their
"citizenship," as such, the essence of which was recognition of their contribution
to society. In 1962 the Writers Union began to publish its members' books, along
with the magazines *Gaceta* and *Unión*. Prior to 1962 it had no publishing house;
its members, like most Cuban writers, were published in the collections of the
National Printing House.

Consciousness of the writer's craft and vocation, notions of what it meant
to be a writer, had not yet crystallized, and writers were, as a group, unsure of
their place, of their role as protagonists rather than outsiders. The Writers Union
attempted to address these problems, bringing writers together and putting them
in touch with the society to which they now perhaps more than ever, belonged:
a literate society which formed their reading public. Perhaps no single element
altered writers' status and self-perceptions, nor created greater confusion and
uncertainty, than the changes that were taking place in the Cuban reading public,
not only in sheer *quantity* but in *quality* as well: their interlocutor and partner in
the literary act was now a reading public both larger and more engaged and
demanding than the "circle of friends" of old. Cuban critic and literary historian
Ambrosio Fornet has spoken of an initial silence, like a catharsis, on the part of
writers in the first few months and years, while writers got their bearings, in
response to revolutionary change and the new reading public. Jacques Leenhardt,
a European theorist in the sociology of reading, has established how national
culture and social group impinge on the process of reading, the "transformational
processes undergone by textual materials as they are perceived, internalized, and
restated in the process of reading," in terms of 1) the ways in which the reading
process establishes a relationship from readers to social norms, 2) the relationship
readers build in their relations with the text, and 3) the ways in which readers

"perform" or actualize a text as a set of norms. [7] This has obvious relevance to the changes that occurred in Cuban literary culture after 1959 with the élite circle of readers of old broadened to potentially include the entire population following the literary and educational campaigns and the enormous influx to the universities. The transformation of Cuban readership, the changes in its composition, from narrow to broad-based, irrevocably altered the dialectics of both the production of literary works, and reception, with readers' "horizons of expectations" infinitely expanded as the result of an inclusionary cultural policy largely concerned with literature and print culture. All contemporary proponents of reader reception theory and the sociology of reading share an awareness of active readership as inseparable from the notion of the literary text, not unlike Montaigne's conviction that "speech belongs half to the speaker and half to the listener,"[8] both of whom are equal partners in the act of literary communication:

> [C]hanges in understanding are always functions of changes in the readers' horizon of expectations, changes which are themselves the result of both literary evolution and the evolution of cultural, political, and social conditions and norms of society at large.[9]

Nowhere is this dynamic more apparent than in the first two decades of postrevolutionary literary life which experienced the greatest impact resulting from changes in the production, reception and dissemination of literary texts.

The advances made by the National Printing House had gone a long way toward meeting the demand for books. Improvising as they went along, the staff made up for the parts and personnel they lacked and the Printing House functioned much like a clandestine print shop on a large scale. The history behind the

---

[7]"The Sociology of Reading," Seminar conducted by Jacques Leenhardt at the Dept. of Sociology, New York University, Nov., 1980. See also Jacques Leenhardt, "The Sociology of Reading," in *The Reader in the Text*, Susan Suleiman and Inge Crosman, eds. (Princeton: Princeton University Press, 1980).

[8]Michel de Montaigne, "De l'expérience," cited by Cathleen M. Bauschatz, "Montaigne's Conception of Reading in the Context of Renaissance Poetics and Modern Criticism," in *The Reader in the Text* (Princeton: Princeton University Press, 1980): 264.

[9]Susan R. Suleiman, "Introduction: Varieties of Audience-Oriented Criticism," in *The Reader in the Text*, 36.

first edition of *History Will Absolve Me* parallels the genesis of the Cuban publishing industry: with the capacity to print 500 copies, and the desire to print 100,000 they managed to put out 10,000 copies.[10] Like those who reconstructed the history of the underground press in the 1950s, for which there are no existing records, I have structured this chapter around the testimony, the first hand accounts, of those who designed and worked in the editorial and literary institutions of the 1960s and early '70s: the National Council on Culture and the National Printing and Publishing Houses. All attest to the fact that Cuba set its incipient publishing industry in motion in the face of a multitude of seemingly insoluble problems and deficiencies.

The National Printing House was the cornerstone of Cuban publishing, the basis for developing graphic and industrial design and consolidating human and material resources; the rotary presses left idle after nationalization of the newspaper companies in 1960 constituted its lifeline. No sooner had the most rudimentary conditions for book publishing been met, when the Missile Crisis took place, hostilities deepened and the trade embargo was imposed. In building an infrastructure for literature, for a broad-based print culture, Cuba had considerable handicaps to overcome. A nation without a publishing tradition, no editors by trade, and negligible quantities of wood for paper production, now had to make do in the face of a commercial blockade. Parts, chemicals, good quality paper and wood pulp grew scarce. Cut off from suppliers of the high quality paper traditionally used in the publication of literary works, a Cuban "semi-bond" was improvised and produced domestically in small quantities, from recycled magazines and newspapers. Limited paper supplies compelled editors to rethink the philosophy of book publishing, and establish their priorities, weighing the cultural and educational merits of each title to be published in accordance with the immediately available paper supply: "[W]e are now faced with the task of planning; and that poses a problem since up until now we have been the creative spirits of revolutionary initiatives and investments that must now be planned ahead."[11]

---

[10]See Adelina Vázquez, Gladies Egües, et al., *Apuntes de la prensa clandestina y guerrillera del período 1952-1958* (Havana: Unión de Periodistas de Cuba): 13-14.

[11]Fidel Castro, "Palabras a los intelectuales," in *Política cultural de la Revolución Cubana*, 35.

Limits on available material resources condition the realization of spiritual and creative potential; such were the dialectics of literary production from 1959 on, the repercussions of which could not be ignored. For economic, social and cultural, as well as literary development to take place, Cuban readership had to be built up and cultivated in a sustained and conscientious effort; that would prove impossible without further developing the book publishing industry. These were necessities brought to the foreground by the Revolution; growing needs that could only be met by revolutionizing the literary, cultural and educational institutions established prior to 1959. In retrospect, it is important to note the time frame within which initial measures were taken toward satisfying the needs and demands of the population:

> In truth, this is a revolution which grew swiftly and came to power in record time. In contrast to other revolutions, we had not resolved the major problems at that time.

> One of the characteristics of the Revolution has been, for that reason, the need to confront so many problems in such a short time.[12]

The Revolution confronted and worked to eradicate a host of problems inherent to the social structures that preceded it only to face, shortly thereafter, the blockade and the incidents of military and civilian aggression that accompanied it. As it went forward, and to the extent of its capabilities, the Revolution devised measures to combat both problems inherited from the Republican administration and those that arose from ongoing international tensions. These capabilities were strengthened by the need to contend with prolonged hostilities on the part of the nations participating in the U.S.-led embargo. By the 1980s Cubans made little reference to the blockade and all the difficulties it had engendered, and yet all could attest to the benefits, personal and institutional, of the blockade as an inevitable component of political education and catalyst for innovation in industry and cultural exchange. With the cut off of Soviet oil after 1989, things came to a sudden, devastating halt.

Few had anticipated the wave of aggression unleashed in the 1960s; or that children and young adults would lose their lives in the campaign to teach basic literacy skills to those in the rural areas who had never attended school, in fact, had no schools to attend. The literacy campaign began in the guerrilla camps,

---

[12]Fidel Castro, "Palabras a los intelectuales," 35.

initiated by the peasants themselves, as was noted in the guerrilla diaries of Ernesto Guevara, published in English as *Episodes of the Revolutionary War*:

> The uneducated peasant, the illiterate peasant who understood the enormous tasks the Revolution would face after the triumph and was preparing himself for them by learning the alphabet, would not be able to complete his labors.[13]

That peasant lost his life in the guerrilla war, others would lose theirs in the literacy campaign in the Escambray region, the Sierra Maestra, and other rural zones. It was not the first time in history that bloodshed was companion to the cultural process; events of the early 1960s demonstrated once again that the cultural field can suddenly and literally become a battlefield. Rapid cultural development in postrevolutionary Cuba, in the 1960s above all, brought repercussions and reprisals, both on and off the island. The foundation of the National Publishing House was due, for the most part, to the demand for books created by the massive literacy campaign concluded the year before. These interrelated events are essential to the understanding of the dynamics and trajectory of literary production in the Revolution; together they constituted the first and most important step in developing Cuban readership and publishing and left an indelible reminder of the price to be paid for cultural integrity, for the commitment to a national culture synonymous with the goals of the Revolution. A social history of Cuban literature would be incomplete if it failed to recognize the central role of literary culture in attaining those goals.

Silent dedication to the tasks at hand, disregarding the limitations imposed by the blockade, unlike the jaunty silence that often cloaks uncertainty, was a sign of endurance and of the confidence acquired in the course of overcoming historical obstacles. The blockade has contributed to a unique course of development, one in which industrial, technical and human problems posed by the publication and distribution of literature have been met according to the possibilities afforded by each stage of development. Publishing has evolved as the nations' resources developed, grappling with setbacks and limitations, yet through the 1980s Cuban book production surpassed that of most Latin American nations. With fewer trade restrictions, and the ability to import as much advanced technology as their finances permit, these book-producing nations, for the most part,

---

[13]Ernesto Che Guevara, *Pasajes de la guerra revolucionaria* (Havana: UNEAC, 1963): 34.

have not enjoyed sustained growth. In Cuba, the opposite occurred: with limited access to parts, materials and equipment, little or no personnel with publishing experience, vast quantities of books were produced to meet rising demands. When technicians emigrated and the shops where they once printed magazines and newspapers were left idle, the equipment was adapted for book production and incorporated into the National Printing House; when a shortage of college textbooks, due to copyright problems occasioned by the blockade, threatened to paralyze the educational campaign, "Edición Revolucionaria"[14] was born.

Accustomed to solving technical problems with one phone call to New York or Massachusetts which summoned a team of engineers in the company plane, what characterized the initial phase was an absence of the easy options that had, in the long run, done more harm than good. Newspaper vendors were learning to bind books, print shop workers were mastering the overall operations of systems and equipment that had been the exclusive domain of highly specialized, if not foreign, technicians. The Revolution's responses to the needs of the population overall and the solutions to practical problems that arose in those years, defined an epoch, laying groundwork in preparation for the future.

We began with the basic premise that a social history of literature, an analysis of literature *within* society, must define the social function of writer, reader and print culture. A new definition of the role of the Cuban writer, reader and literature itself, from 1959 to 1962, had grown out of the literacy campaign, the efforts of the National Printing House, Casa de las Américas and the Writers and Artists Union. The basis for a new relationship between text—for those who read, write and produce literature—and context had been established. As we have seen, it was not so much a change in the way literary works were produced as a radical change in the way literary creation was approached and assimilated that marked the transition from the last decade of the Republic to the first decade of the Revolution, transforming the relationship between the reader and the writer, the reader and the text, as well as the means of distribution for literary works. In four years, two historical challenges were met: illiteracy was all but eradicated and scattered resources for book publishing were consolidated in the formation of the National Printing and Publishing Houses. Cultural institutions, municipal libraries, writers' workshops and bookshops began to spring up all over the island, reinforcing the literacy and postliteracy campaigns.

---

[14]Edición Revolucionaria was a project for rapid, offset publication and free distribution of specialized, college textbooks on which no royalties or copyright fees were paid.

It is only by placing literary production within a broad-based program for cultural development, itself an integral part of the overall development of the nation, that we begin to understand the literary and cultural process of these critical, transitional years.

CHAPTER 5. READERSHIP AND REVOLUTION: RESTRUCTURING PRINT CULTURE

The Early Years: Needs and Responses (1959-62)

"Words to the Intellectuals," the product of a conference by and for artists and writers, in June of 1961, considered the earliest formulation of cultural policy, addressed the concerns of intellectuals in the process of gaining their bearings in a new social context, of defining their place within the Revolution, while at the same time, the Revolution sought to define its position on literary and artistic production. Shortly thereafter, in August of that year, the Writers and Artists Union was constituted as a network for its members in each community, much the same way that Casa de las Américas has, since 1959, helped to break the cultural isolation of the Revolution, resulting from the embargo, by establishing direct links to the international, intellectual and artistic community.

After outlining the goals proposed by the new society in the cultural, literary and artistic spheres, we will examine the material underpinnings of the process, the utilization of existing resources to create new institutions; the evolution of the tripod on which literary production rests: the publishing system, the graphics industry and distribution mechanisms. Law 187, of March, 1959, governed the foundation and organization of the National Printing House for the purpose of stimulating literary and scientific production:

> Article Two. The General Directorship of the National Printing House will be in charge of printing:
>
> a) school books for the Public Schools and other schools annexed to the Ministry of Education.
>
> b) for those enterprises necessary to the administrative functioning of the Ministry.
>
> c) all books published by the Cultural Council.

d) all other works contributing to the education and culture of the people, published by the Ministry of Education.

Article Four. The General Directorship will be in charge of the Cuban Graphic Arts School, annexed to the National Printing House.

Article Nine. Technical managers at the National Printing House will be responsible for organizing the work of and inspecting all shops as well as the School of Typography.[1]

Law 187 defines the gamut of interrelated activities involved in producing textbooks and literary works, setting standards for an editorial policy that integrates cultural, educational and technical development in the graphic arts industry. This law was in reality a blueprint for the national publishing industry which would, for the first time, place cultural priorities in the forefront, even though resources for implementing the plan were not yet in hand.

The small private presses coexisted with the National Printing House for some time; several lent their services to state-sponsored publishing projects although they did not necessarily subscribe to their editorial philosophy or share their cultural focus.

In between the shoeshine, fritters and cheap costume jewelry stands, there are now rows of books for sale. The last remains of a breed almost extinct: romance novels that recount the edifying life of Sisi, northern style adventure novels, pseudotreatises on the most extravagant topics. Next to these, in greater numbers, the new books: Marx, Engels, Lenin. Gorki's autobiographical trilogy, current Soviet novelists, progressive literature from all around the world.[2]

Such works were, in fact, not "new" to Cuba; classics of world literature had made the rounds before, along with the romance novels and potboilers, however the former were only within the reach of a minority who, in most cases, ordered them directly from European and Latin American publishers. The new

---

[1]Law 187, Legal Archives of the National Center for Authors' Fees, Havana.

[2]Jesús Izacaray, *Reportaje a Cuba* (Havana: Ediciones Venceremos, 1962): 163.

component of Cuban literary culture is the broad-based, majority, reading public with access to the classics of international literature through the affordable editions of the National Printing House, and a distribution system which, although still somewhat chaotic, took great pains to bring books and readers together.

When the law was passed governing the creation of a National Printing House in 1959, it existed on paper only; the state-run, centralized production units did not have the wherewithal to set up a printing house, and the same law allotted a time frame of fourteen months within which to acquire the necessary equipment and shops. In March of 1960 (one year later, two months short of the deadline) the National Printing House had the shops it needed, and the presses began to roll. "In March, Fidel proposed the creation of a National Printing House; a National Printing House with the potential to become a *publishing system*. In 1959, the creation of a National Printing House was proposed—a National Printing House with no printing press."[3]

After the fall of Batista, the first books in postrevolutionary Cuba to be published by the state, under the supervision of the Council on National Culture's Department of Literature and Publications,[4] run by writer José Lezama Lima, were produced in the following manner:

> What did Lezama, his predecessors and successors, do? He would put four or five books, or perhaps seven or eight, on the list of publications scheduled for that year, then farm them out to small private presses under contract for a one or two thousand copy edition, pay the printer and then give them all away. A small quantity might go to the bookstores. The small presses continued to function as they had in the past.

---

[3]Interview with Rolando Rodríguez, advisor to the Secretariat of the Cabinet; he directed Edición Revolucionaria and has been president of the Cuban Book Institute and Vice-Minister for the Ministry of Culture. Havana, January 30, 1985.

[4]Founded in 1961, and annexed to the Ministry of Education, the Department later became a central organism responsible for orienting and overseeing all of the cultural activities of official institutions.

The real basis for developing the Cuban graphics industry at that time were the rotary presses employed by the dailies.[5]

The key to expanding the possibilities for literary production, at that time, was adaptation and incorporation of the presses once used by the major dailies into the Revolution's fledgling book publishing network. Until those presses became available, books continued to be produced in costly, limited editions.

Details on literary and publishing developments in the early 1960s were provided by Rolando Rodríguez, Luis Suardíaz and Marcos Llanos.[6] Combining their testimony with existing documents, I am able to trace the evolution of the major literary, cultural and editorial institutions founded in the first decade: The Department of Literature and Publications of the National Council on Culture (1959-62), The National Printing House (1959-62), The National Publishing House (1962-67), Edición Revolucionaria (1965-67), The Cuban Book Institute (1967-76).

The process of incorporating small private presses into the Revolution's book publishing program was as follows:

In Cuba, there were several large presses linked to North American capital and interests, such as Omega where *Selecciones del Reader's Digest* was printed which, at that time, had relatively modern equipment with severe limitations. For example, the man who was formerly second in the chain of operators for one of the Omega machines told me that his only function was restricted to pressing buttons.

When the Revolution began to utilize the original cameras and offset equipment, it became clear that the press' capacity was extremely limited. Where were the negatives prepared? Industrial negatives had always been shipped from the United States.

---

[5]Interview with Luis Suardíaz, director of the magazines *Cuba internacional* and *Prisma latinoamericano.* He has been director of the Department of Literature and Publications of the National Council on Culture, the José Martí National Library and Editora Política publishers. Havana, January 30, 1985.

[6]Marcos Llanos, journalist and essayist, participated in the creation of Edición Revolucionaria.

It was only half of a complete process, the process by which underdevelopment is linked to development. We were manufacturers of intermediate products. Here, at this end, the process was limited to one or two phases. There were offset presses used for other types of commercial production; product labels and soap boxes, for example. That was what they were used for, not for books and magazines.

The North American magazines printed here arrived as a "prefab" product, only the last two phases were executed in Cuba: printing and distribution to Latin America. Cuba had the advantage of language and security. Because of our dependency, Cuba was a very "safe" country for the United States.

There were printers who turned out high quality editions, but the books were produced practically *by hand*. Several shops in Old Havana were famous for their work, but editions were restricted to two or three thousand copies, very limited editions.[7]

The small presses continued to operate until 1968, yet their influence was greatly diminished, and their days as literary presses were over, eclipsed by the collections of the National Printing House and the National Council on Culture, collections of nineteenth-century Cuban and Spanish literature, international poetry, drama, dance, classical and contemporary fiction. Unión, the publishing house linked to the Writers and Artists Union, began putting out its own editions in 1962.

As Luis Suardíaz explains:

The small presses were dying, as publishers of significant literary titles, not as all-purpose print shops. Books published by all the organisms under the National Council on Culture which had previously been put out by several private presses were now being printed by the Graphics Section of the Ministry of Industry.

The Revolution brought with it a demand for books. Books continued to be produced for Havana bookstores and stalls that sold newspapers and magazines, often with large print runs, which were passed on to

---

[7]Interview with Rolando Rodríguez, Havana, January 30, 1985.

vendors.... There was a reading public and a demand for books. Books were good business....

But after the blockade, in 1963 and 1964, matters were complicated by a shortage of plates, chemicals and paper; machinery began to break-down. Book production depended on an outlay of dollars, which were scarce, for raw materials, and since, in any event, the private editions were chaotic, hard to keep track of, we [the National Council on Culture] proposed that all the printers submit a list of the titles they planned to publish to our Editorial Board. A private press might, for example, publish an illustrated edition of *Madame Bovary*, badly translated, on poor quality paper, and sell it on the street corners. We had preference, in the first place because we had a say in such matters, and in the second place because our editions were culturally and typographically superior, the others were commercial.

From 1962 on, Cuban authors chose to publish with the Artists and Writers Union rather than with the small private presses, or with the Ministry of Education, the National Council on Culture or Samuel Feijóo's press in Las Villas.

Cuban authors no longer had to pay, out of pocket, to publish their own works with a private printer. The state publishing houses paid royalties, and their editions were generally prepared with greater care:

What did the private presses do? It's very simple. What printers the world over have done: sell envelopes, ruled paper, notebooks and secretarial supplies. The complex world beginning with the sweet sixteen card through the wedding invitation, along with the office supplies, traditionally produced in print shops, and it was a good, solid, business. But it no longer had anything to do with the book phenomenon. Little by little, the private press withered away, for the reasons we have mentioned, and due to the concentration of resources. Authors now enjoyed royalty payments, and a variety of options within the cultural collections and editions of the State publishers.[8]

---

[8]Interview with Luis Suardíaz, January 30, 1985.

When we look at the statistics on national literary production, it becomes clear that private "publishers" or presses (they supplied no editors or proofreaders, the author performed those tasks in addition to layout and design) only "had a significant output for the first four years of this period, when they accounted for 43.5 percent of production." They gradually lost their book-publishing function and began to atrophy, long before 1968 when small private industry was nationalized. "From 1963 on their influence began to decline, and by 1966 and 1967, when private presses published three, then one title, respectively, they had all but disappeared."[9]

Historically, the publishing industry's growth has been spurred by the implementation of free and universal education. Cuba is not an exception to this rule. As we cited earlier, in the industrialized nations of Europe and the United States, this took place in the mid-1800s whereas in Cuba, it wasn't until 1959 that conditions began to favor book production. In September of 1959, "ten thousand new classrooms were created throughout the nation, and within months of the triumph of the Revolution there were more schoolteachers in the rural areas than there had been in the entire history of [Cuban] capitalism."[10] In June of 1961 a law was passed nationalizing educational facilities, with free admission to all students. In the spring of 1960, the rotary presses of the nationalized newspapers began to turn out books for the National Printing House and in August, the literacy campaign was launched. That these events came in quick succession of one another is not accidental. Education and culture, increases in literacy and literary production, go hand in hand. When labor conflicts erupted in the newspapers *Excelsior* and *El país* in March of 1960, it led to the fulfillment of one of the dreams of the organizers of the educational campaign: a National Printing House able to meet the demand for more than a million primers for the literacy campaign, texts for primary, secondary and adult education, and the hundreds of literary titles that would be printed there from 1960 to 1962. Paralyzed by the conflicts that culminated in an irresolvable labor crisis, the presses of *Excelsior* and *El país* lay dormant:

---

[9]Cuban Authors Published from 1959-1986," from the archives of Letras Cubanas publishers.

[10]*Informe del Comité Central del PCC al Primer Congreso* (Havana: Imprenta Federico Engels, 1975): 117.

What a waste of paper!, we repeated. And we knew we had to put it to use, but how? With an eye to the future, to education. With whom? With the Ministry of Education where this initiative of the Revolution was born. We could use that paper to publish, for example, 60 works of universal literature, Martí, works that aren't in the libraries, that aren't accessible to the people. To print all of the classics, with a special title page for each, with the input of the people, with the support of the Revolution.[11]

The first step toward the dream of a library in every home and culture accessible to all was the literacy campaign; the goal of one hundred percent adult literacy was the stimulus and cornerstone for building a national publishing industry. Guarantying access to culture through literacy is an integral part of the same initiative that led to the creation of an infrastructure for literary production as well as the strengthening of a literary tradition rooted in majority culture.

The Literacy Campaign and Literary Production

> What is inconceivable is that anyone should go to bed hungry while there is a single inch of unproductive land; that children should die for lack of medical attention; what is inconceivable is that 30 percent of our farm people cannot write and that 99 percent of them know nothing of Cuba's history. (Fidel Castro, *History Will Absolve Me*)

Hunger, natural resources squandered and human potential gone to waste before it could be realized: their intimate correlation has been laid bare in this depiction of conditions in the 1950s. The first resolutions on national illiteracy date from March of 1959, when commissions on the literacy project and basic adult education were formed. The eradication of illiteracy was, in addition to meeting educational goals for and developing critical faculties in the overall population, central to the long-range program of balanced development of society's resources, "the beginning of cultural development, technical and social im-

---

[11]Fidel Castro, speech to the assembly of workers from the newspapers *Excelsior* and *El país*, March 15, 1960.

provements, political and ideological awareness, and the involvement of the masses in further economic development of the nation."[12] The educational campaign bridged the historical chasm separating city and countryside, by uniting distant sectors of the population in the task of eradicating illiteracy, and the existential isolation it imposes. The Revolution had inherited an overall illiteracy rate of 23.6%, rising to 42% in rural areas as compared with only 11% in the cities, which was the result of a short-sighted educational policy that considered textbooks primarily a business venture, all other books an extravagance and schooling a privilege. In the early decades of the Cuban Republic, daughters of the best of families were, for the most part, not deemed deserving of instruction beyond the primary level, after which they might resume their education in the more "practical" arts of botany, embroidery and crochet. The linen sheets, intricately hand embroidered by great aunts and grandmothers, hung to dry in the sun on patio clotheslines or stored away with other family keepsakes, still bear eloquent testimony to this phenomenon. They are carefully preserved like Dupont's beachfront home and library, now a museum and restaurant favored for Sunday outings, as a historical reminder of days gone by. It is well documented that in nineteenth and early twentieth century Spain and Cuba "education represented for women an instrument that taught them to accept a social system that imposed upon them the role of submission."[13] The beauty that came of women's labor, of hands that had long toiled on the margins of history, within the asphyxiating confinement of privilege, therefore gave way, in the catharsis of revolution, to the charged, dynamic, more humane aesthetic of a culture that lost its fear of encounter with the world at large. It had become a looser, idiosyncratic culture that now sought contributions from all sectors. Economic privilege offered women little protection against cultural ignorance and prejudice in the history of Cuba before 1959; it merely had the dubious advantage of keeping them out of the labor force. Cuban critic and women's studies scholar, Luisa Campuzano, in one of the few existing studies of genre in contemporary literature, confronts gender issues in Cuban literary production on three levels: women's access to education and the labor force, women as protagonists in Cuban literature, and women as

---

[12]Ana Núñez Machín, *La epopeya* (Havana: Editorial de Ciencias Sociales, 1983): 2.

[13]Brígida Pastor, "Una feminista cubano-española: Gertrudis Gómez de Avellanada ante la sociedad de su tiempo" *Association for Contemporary Iberian Studies* 8.1 (Spring 1995): 57.

authors of literary works, stressing their interrelatedness. As reflected in census figures from 1903 to 1953, Campuzano notes that

> in 1903, seventy percent of the female population active in the labor force worked as domestic servants; sixteen years later, fifty percent of working women were still maids and domestics, and in 1953, domestic workers were a full third of the female labor force.[14]

During the same period, "housewives" devoted themselves to embroidery, crocheting or sewing, either for themselves and family or on consignment. Unrestricted access to education on all levels from 1959 on would produce enormous changes in how women invested their time and energies.

> In 1979, seventy-two percent of young adults enrolled in higher education were women who did not constitute the overwhelming majority in courses of study that had traditionally been favored by females, such as humanities and education, but showed high indexes of enrollment in other fields of specialization such as the natural and hard sciences (72%), medicine (66%), agriculture and animal husbandry (51%). Only in technological fields (40%) was women's enrollment below that of men.[15]

While noting women's major advances in higher education and as active members of the labor force beyond traditional roles, Campuzano admits that by 1983, when research for her study was carried out, these gains had not yet been translated into a greater presence of women authors on the contemporary literary scene. Taking stock of the novels of the Revolution, she cites

---

[14]Luisa Campuzano, "La mujer en la narrativa de la Revolución: ponencia sobre una carencia," in *Quirón o del ensayo y otros eventos* (Havana: Editorial Letras Cubanas, 1988): 71.

[15]Campuzano, "La mujer en la narrativa de la Revolución," 76.

twelve novels in twenty-four years, only twelve novels written by women as opposed to more than one hundred and sixty written by men.[16]

Division by gender of Cuban short story writers reflects a similar disproportion. Yet in contemporary Cuban poetry there are as many female voices of note as male. The social history of Latin American literature in general, and Cuban literature, in particular, has shown that poetry, the short story and brief article or essay tend to predominate in societies without a long publishing tradition and that poetry, the world over, reflects epic events in the life of a nation or community and contemporary reality with greater immediacy than other genres. This, in part, explains the origins of many of the gender issues, by genre, taken up in Campuzano's study, the most pressing being the relative absence, as yet, of contemporary female novelists. Campuzano herself attests, after studying the phenomenon in detail, to the difficulty of getting a solid grasp on its complex and varied root causes, from Virginia Woolf's *A Room of One's Own* on: "The reasons, the causes, do not escape anyone, yet it is difficult to enunciate them clearly."[17] Campuzano concludes her study on the "shortage" of women narrators in contemporary Cuban fiction with an "epilogue on abundance," referring to a swelling of the ranks of women working in and around the world of letters, at that time, as

> Typists, acquisitions editors, manuscript and copy editors of texts they do not write and in which they often don't appear; participants in the industrial process of their transformation into books, women are not only those who sell, classify and catalogue books, stick labels on them, place them on shelves and guide them toward the curiosity of an almost always feminine reader, but also, on many occasions, it is women who scrutinize and ponder over texts, and it is almost always women who instill in children and young people, with their example and skill as educators, lifelong reading habits.[18]

---

[16]Campuzano, "La mujer en la narrativa," 82.

[17]Campuzano, "La mujer en la narrativa," 91.

[18]Campuzano, "La mujer en la narrativa," 103.

In attempting to explain women's absence as protagonists on the contemporary literary scene, with the exception of poetry, Campuzano takes stock of the extent to which women were denied access to education and excluded from all spheres of the active, productive social life of the nation in its first fifty years, while at the same time documenting the inroads made by Cuban women since 1959. Throughout the world, women's integration, as professionals of all stripes, into the social space in which literature comes to exist, will inevitably tip the scales of authorship and gender, historically weighted in favor of men; it is a matter of time. In this sense, then, Campuzano's study of gender and contemporary Cuban narrative bears witness to a slow but inevitable transformation, chronicling the origins of "a deficiency that will soon cease to be"[19] in a society in which women constitute the majority in universities and have gained a leading edge in traditional and nontraditional professions.

The resources society invests in education, the degree to which it allows citizens access to educational institutions, reveals the strength of its leaders' commitment to social, political and economic justice, to human dignity and development. It is significant that in *History Will Absolve Me*, Fidel Castro juxtaposes the inability to sign one's own name and the most abject ignorance of one's own history, origins, people and culture that can result from a lifetime of illiteracy. The men and women who learned to read and write in the literacy campaign of 1960, through conscientious follow-up and adult education classes, quickly advanced to a sixth-grade reading level and are now striving to attain a ninth-grade level. It is not inconceivable that the Cuban population will have acquired reading skills equivalent to those required to enter university by the close of the century.

"We must be learned in order to be free," declared José Martí. The author of a recent study on the legacy of the Cuban literacy campaign seconded, astutely, "We must be free in order to become learned."[20] Literary production is stagnating in the U.S. and the western European nations, which is not to imply that no one is writing or that new works are not being produced. We mean only to suggest that such works cannot enjoy a full literary and social existence if they do not reach the reading public. This relative standstill is not, at base, due to a lack of "creative impulse," but rather to the result of social and economic prob-

---

[19]Campuzano, "La mujer en la narrativa," 103.

[20]Núñez Machín, *La epopeya*, 13.

lems that reverberate within the structure of the educational system and the publishing industry of the market economies, as we have argued, and to the concentration of publishing houses chronicled in the *Wall Street Journal*, and other financial and trade publications, in recent years.[21]

In Havana in the early 1980s there was talk of putting together a research team to compile a list of the titles read by adults who participated in the Cuban literacy campaign of 1960, tracing their history as readers from the first primer to their current habits and preferences. If we go back a quarter of a century, to the campaign itself, it would not be unreasonable to presume that, along with the primers and basic texts, the men and women just learning to read tested the limits of their new found power on the poster and street art of their immediate surroundings. The content of Cuban poster art—text and image, intellect and imagination—held the intrigue of an idea, evoked collective history or projected into the future. Phrases such as "You are civil defense" or "We are one" evoke a very different response than that elicited by "Drink Pepsi and smile" or "Coke is it." Cuban poster art has much in common with literacy practices in that it demands reflection, analysis and invites the free play of the imagination.

---

[21]It may be of some value to refer here to some interesting statistics not published in UNESCO's tables. One of the nations of the world, where education is by law free and universal, is experiencing a crisis: by conservative estimate *one* out of every *three* citizens is illiterate or functionally illiterate (Jonathan Kozol, *Illiterate America*, 1985). It is not difficult to come to the conclusion that the most vital, rich and varied literature is being produced today in Latin America, Africa and Asia, in the so-called "Third World" nations, while literary production in Europe and the U.S. lies dormant. Yet there is a kind of Third World within the U.S., an underdeveloped region that lies within its own borders, from which new voices, a vibrant and energetic literature could emerge, but those voices are silenced by illiteracy and semi-literacy. Booksellers meet to analyze the consumer crisis, the slow-moving stocks; editors gather, seeking ways to increase production and sales. Yet who is analyzing the crisis of readership, the squandered human potential of the growing numbers submerged in illiteracy and unemployment? Who dares mention the taboo topic of growing illiteracy which most are unwilling to mention or come to terms with? On illiteracy in the U.S. and related problems see Jonathan Kozol, *Illiterate America* (New York: Doubleday, Anchor Press, 1985). On the crisis in U.S. book publishing, see Leonard Shatzkin, *In Cold Type: Overcoming the Book Crisis* (Boston: Houghton Mifflin, 1982).

The following section will examine the historical relationship between literature and the graphic arts, and how it is expressed in the poster art of the Cuban Revolution.

Cuban Poster Art: Concept and Praxis

> The far-reaching influence of the written word broadens infinitely the primitive, family horizon of the former "man of the spoken word." (Sergei Tretiakov)

Before the invention of the written word, man used images to convey ideas, concepts, to transmit knowledge and experience. Long after the advent of the written word, we have continued to communicate through images: images drawn with charcoal, chalk or ink; etched or carved in wood and stone; sketched in watercolors or portrayed in oils. There are no linguistic barriers for visual language; communication is immediate and direct. It is only accessibility or location that determine its power to communicate: *who* will come across an image and *where*.

Word and image, visual and written language, have joined forces consistently if not harmoniously, throughout history. Communities within the oral tradition have relied on the pictorial image both as artistic expression and medium of communication, in part because they lacked a written language. The masters of the written, and later printed word, found an even greater communicative force in the alliance of word and image. Yet this alliance has not always constituted a creative synthesis, a vehicle for new forms of communication. Words have been tamed by association with a single, dominant image, erasing all other possible associations; the infinite play of possible interpretations of an image may be reduced to one by wedding it to a single word or phrase that serves as label.

In the twentieth century, the posters used in the Soviet literacy campaign are the first significant example of the union of word and image on a grand scale, in public spaces, realizing the increased potential of word and deed joined together to expand and illuminate perceived realities.

Word and image have often worked together—one supporting the other, adding new dimensions—in brush-stroked or pen and ink manuscripts, in the painstaking craftsmanship of limited editions of illustrated books and pamphlets. El Lissitsky describes the rise of a new, synthetic form that combines the creative force of the literary and plastic arts, in an experimental artisans' movement in which poets and painters worked together on manuscripts, in the decades preceding the explosive debut of poster art in public spaces:

> The new movement which began in Russia in 1908 bound painter and poet together from the very first day; hardly a poetry book has appeared since then without the collaboration of a painter. Poems have been written with the lithographic crayon and signed. They have been cut in wood. Poets themselves have set whole pages. Thus the poets Khlebnikov, Kruchenich, Mayakovski, Asseeyeev, have worked with the painters Rosanova, Goncharova, Malevich, Popova, Burlyuk, etc. They did not produce select, numbered, deluxe editions, but cheap unlimited volumes, which today we must treat as popular art despite their sophistication.

> In the Revolutionary period a latent energy has concentrated in the younger generation of our artists, which can only find release in large-scale commissions. The audience has become the masses, the semiliterate masses. With our work the Revolution has achieved a colossal labour of propaganda and enlightenment. We ripped up the traditional book into single pages, magnified these a hundred times, printed them in colour and stuck them up as posters, in the streets. Unlike American posters, ours were not designed for rapid perception from a passing motorcar, but to be read and to enlighten from a short distance. If a series of posters were today to be set in the size of a manageable book, in an order corresponding to some theme, the result would be most curious.[22]

The book, broken down into its component parts, assumes a new and plastic form in order to move out into the streets and engage passersby, transforming the individual and personal practice of reading into a massive, public spectacle. If the poster-size pages were scaled down once again to manageable size and bound, the resulting book would never quite be the same; transformed by the

---

[22]El Lissitsky, "The Future of the Book," in *Communication and Class Struggle*, Armand Mattelart and Seth Sieglaub, eds. (New York: International General, France: International Mass Media Center, 1983): II.268-69.

gaze of the spectator, it would retain the aura and dimension of the public space, the exposure to the masses.

Public posters are the ultimate symbol of the two-way track on which cultural, literary and artistic creation take place. Cuban posters seem to emerge from their surroundings, inspired by popular sentiment and collective concerns, taking their cue from current events, all of this distilled in a graphic image by the team of artists and designers involved in the process of poster design and production. The poster will, in turn, return to the public spaces under the collective gaze of those who inspired it. Poster art was made for open spaces—streets, parks, public squares, exterior walls and palisades—where the creative process comes full circle upon receiving "the gaze of the other, of the thousands of individuals who give it meaning and function within its surroundings,"[23] enriching that meaning through their participation.

Adelaida de Juan, in her "Notes on Contemporary Cuban Graphics," refers us to the nineteenth century in order to trace the origins and development of modern graphics:

> Those odd figures that bore no resemblance to anything in heaven, on earth or in the rivers of the underworld, were the muralist paintings that covered Cuban buildings in the early nineteenth century.... [B]y the end of the century the paintings had been implacably destroyed, or, in the best of cases, painted over with lime. We have learned, from existing documentation, that they were works of popular origin, by mulatto and black artisans, for the most part, whose identities remain unknown; we also know that their works were considered worthless. And that academic painting, from the second decade of the century on, would establish itself and remain dominant. We also know that although few saw the framed paintings that hung in churches and residences, all retain, even today, the mention if not the image of the muralist paintings meant to be viewed by the vast public, out walking around in the streets.[24]

---

[23]Edmundo Desnoes, "Los carteles de la Revolución Cubana," *Casa de las Américas* 51-52 (November 1968-Febuary 1969): 228.

[24]Adelaida de Juan, *Unión* 14.3 (September 1975): 28-29.

Edmundo Desnoes refers back to the early 1950s and the worst years of the Batista dictatorship, seeking the origins of contemporary Cuban poster art in the slogans and graffiti of the period. In the previously cited article, Desnoes recalls:

> It all began at dawn; it was the tenth of March, 1953: the sun beat down violently on the facade and walls of the University of Havana, here and there could be read, in uneven, black letters, still dripping paint: DOWN WITH BATISTA, DEATH TO THE DICTATOR, CONSTITUTION OF 1940. Those improvised slogans were, in more than one sense, the first revolutionary posters.[25]

Both essayists underscore the social function of poster art, its improvisational nature, and its historic links to the longstanding traditions of both muralism (image) and popular graffiti (word), which serve as a counterbalance to street advertisement and populist political sloganeering. They analyze the emergence and development of commercial poster art, of the poster as advertisement for a product—whether it be a politician or a brand of toothpaste—as a practice that has tended to isolate and alienate the viewer, since the earliest combinations of text and image served a commercial purpose. It is not our intent to expand on the origins and earliest history of poster art, studied at length in the essays cited, but to examine Cuban poster art of the revolutionary period, as concept and praxis, as well as its points of intersection with literary production.

The Bolshevik Revolution took apart the printed volume in order to transform its loose pages into poster art. The Cuban Revolution broke open the closed structure of newspaper formatting in order to turn the front page into a poster:

> In the early years, the newspaper *Revolución* instigated a revolution in graphic design by transforming the front page into a poster on significant occasions—demonstrations, nationalization, threats and victories. Many of *Revolución*'s front pages from that time were hung as posters. Currently, the tradition has been adopted and enhanced by *Juventud Rebelde*: its first pages transformed into bright, four color posters dedicated to Che or Céspedes in commemoration of One Hundred Years of Struggle.[26]

---

[25]Edmundo Desnoes, "Los carteles de la Revolución Cubana," 224.

[26]Desnoes, "Los carteles de la Revolución," 226.

In both cases the direct relationship between printed volume and poster art, between literary and graphic production is laid bare. What was once a privileged mode of communication in both prerevolutionary Cuba and czarist Russia—the printed volume—has become accessible to all. In their new social context, both the printed volume and the poster are directed toward the broadest strata. Absent the classist divisions which kept all things in their "place"—muralist and academicist painting, the former appropriate for the street, the latter for the salon—poster art fulfills a function which is at once multifaceted and extremely specific within the spheres of culture, education, ethics, political formation and the dissemination of information. Cuban poster art mediates between oral or visual culture and print culture, borrowing from both traditions in order to create a new language and form of communication.

Unlike mural art and political graffiti, the poster is an industrial product; the possibilities for production and reproduction are infinitely greater than those created by artisans. Poster art came of age with the Revolution and owes its existence to the graphics industry which developed, in turn, as an integral part of the publishing system, whose rapid growth would have been inconceivable without the literacy campaign.

Cuban posters are masters at the art of synthesis, demanding of the viewer an active, mental process capable of constructing the whole from the existing parts. They can be found in the streets, classrooms, workplaces or parks, and even on the beach, engaging the intellect of the spectator in all three spheres of daily life: study, work and leisure. Cuban poster art provides a lesson, practical training in the art of critical thinking, "placing us face to face, through the magnification of a single detail, with the totality."[27] Poster art assumes its place within the literary practices that demand active, critical participation on the part of the reader. Cubans are exposed to dozens of posters each day and must assimilate them, form and content, quickly; each poster invites further development of those same critical and creative faculties used in reading a novel, a poem or an essay, or in the analysis of a film.

There was a concerted effort under way to cultivate the free play of the senses and creative faculties. The artificial division between street and salon had been swept away, although neither ceased to exist as a specific cultural and social zone. The popular murals of the nineteenth century, like the political graffiti of the 1950s which voiced the aspirations, morale and dignity of the people in the public sphere, were reborn in contemporary poster art. Like posters in public

---

[27]Desnoes, "Los carteles de la Revolución," 226.

spaces, the *Sábado del Libro*[28] was an outgrowth of the cultural policy formulated in 1959. *Sábado*'s purpose was to remove books from the often stuffy atmosphere of libraries, bookstores and archives, and move them out into the street so that they might occasionally occupy open, public space along with the Cuban poster. The *Sábado del Libro* recognized literature's new function within a culture oriented toward the majority, bringing books, new titles, to potential readers in public spaces rather than waiting for readers to seek them out.

A revolution tends to send shock waves through the creative world, through the arts, in all their forms, both as concept and social practice. Julio García Espinosa, the Cuban film producer, sums up art's destiny as social practice—in painting, graphics, music and literature—which is to fuse with or be dispersed into all the other spheres of daily life and work, in a powerful synthesis: "Art will not disappear into nothingness. It will disappear into everything."[29]

The first years of the Revolution, with the rise of poster art and the literacy campaign, changed the nature of print culture in society, creating a climate which fostered the reading of books as a universal vocation. It was in this climate that the process of building an infrastructure equipped to respond to the growing material and cultural needs of literacy volunteers and their students, as well as readers and writers in general, began.

In the Republic, writers could count on the readership of an educated minority, a *literati* conversant with the latest trends and works, who kept up with international literary currents and also read each other's works. The educational programs underway from 1959 to 1962 were designed to develop and cultivate a broad-based Cuban readership, encompassing the entire population. The literacy campaign created a social conglomerate of new and potential readers who, as they attained greater cultural levels and acquired reading habits, required greater and greater quantities of books. It is important to bear in mind that "at that time we had a total population of six million, not ten as we have today, and ten million people today who study and read is a far cry from a population of six million with a million illiterates who were just beginning to study and more than a

---

[28]An activity designed to promote literary culture and awareness, initiated in 1977, in which new titles are sold out of doors, in parks or other public spaces close to bookstores, with authors and editors present to engage in a dialogue with the reading public.

[29]Julio García Espinosa, *Una imagen recorre el mundo* (Havana: Editorial Letras Cubanas, 1979): 16.

million who were not in the habit of reading."[30] The National Printing House was established to respond to the immediate needs of Cuban readers, both established readers and adult literacy students, but also to anticipate and meet future needs by providing the basis for a publishing network capable of addressing, industrially, technologically and culturally, the needs of ten million. Many of those writers who had been discouraged after publication of their first volume or had never been able to get any of their works into print due to the lack of an industrial infrastructure, a publishing tradition and a broad public with consistent reading habits, joined in to help get the National Printing House set up and rolling. The greatest emphasis was placed on educational texts, for children and adults, with massive print runs. In terms of the literary output of Cuban authors for those early years, what was published was for the most part "the content of their desk drawers, file cabinets and closets. Writers producing new works at that time were still a minority."[31]

Books had become a necessity and all attention was centered on the task of producing, editing, and distributing them, with limited resources and a lack of skilled professionals in these areas. From year to year, the ability to produce, in the broadest sense of the term, works that would raise the cultural level and political awareness of the Cuban population, increased incrementally. Soon the literary output of Cuban writers would increase in volume as well.

The National Printing House

The history of the National Printing House's first publication, the 100,000 copies of *Don Quijote*, is well known, but few are aware of the colossal effort that went into it. Rotary presses accept sheets of two to four pages in length. The rest of the process had to be completed by hand; each of the sheets had to be folded into book-size pages by hand. One hundred thousand copies of *Don Quijote* were produced this way, and all the other titles that followed, from 1960

---

[30]Interview with Luis Suardíaz, January 30, 1985.

[31]Interview with Luis Suardíaz, January 30, 1935.

when the National Printing House was founded until its closing in 1962 to make way for the Cuban National Publishing House, which opened that year.[32]

The poems of Neruda, Vallejo and Darío, the works of Gorky and Brecht, essays by Aníbal Ponce and Jean Paul Sartre, were among the first titles published, in massive editions. The educational campaign had generated the creation of new research centers and educational facilities, in general, each with its own library. It was hoped that each Cuban home would have its own private library and each town, a public library. The first National Library, headquartered in the ancient, damp fort, El Castillo de la Fuerza, exposed to the salt air, was founded in 1901 by decree of the U.S. government of military intervention, with only three thousand volumes. The massive print runs were designed, in part, to support the effort to establish a public library in each municipality, and partly the result of machinery which dictated high volume: rotary presses can only be operated to produce twenty, forty, sixty, up to one hundred thousand copies at a time. That is how all the novels from the world literature series were published: using newsprint, with a six by nine format and a modest book jacket. The National Printing House's collections, designed to meet the most urgent and immediate needs of Cuban readers, included: The Basic Library for Elementary, Secondary and Workers and Peasants Education, for adults; The Popular Encyclopedia of Cuba whose editions included books for the general reader on history, art, anthropology and other disciplines, destined for the rural zones most in need of books; The People's Library, a collection of universal classics; The Basic Library of Cuban Culture, a collection of titles by Cuban authors, almost all from the nineteenth century, which had never been published in Cuba; and the Special Editions which published, among others, a massive edition of Arévalo's *The Shark and the Sardines*.

The National Printing House also undertook a number of ambitious related projects, among them opening bookstores all across the island where exhibitions and conferences on literature and the visual arts would also be held; they proposed increasing the production of scientific and technical texts and recruiting artists for book production in order to stimulate interest in the development of

---

[32]"In total, from all of its different sections, in twenty months, from August of 1960 to April of 1962, the National Printing House published: books (literary, political, ideological, scientific and educational): a total of 14,497,956 copies; pamphlets (for which the same genre and thematic classification applies): a total of 16,463,600 copies; magazines (news and current events, cultural, political, economic, and professional): 22,579,882." Jesús Izcaray, *Reportaje a Cuba*, 164.

Cuban book design. The Basic Library of Cuban Culture's editions disseminated the literary production of the eighteenth and nineteenth centuries. After publishing the eighteenth and nineteenth centuries, this Collection would eventually have moved on to the twentieth century and begun to publish contemporary authors. But the publishing industry, barely a skeleton at that time with ambitions and goals far beyond its capacity, continued to evolve and to branch out in new directions.

These were years of epic events: the year of the Educational Campaign was also that of the Bay of Pigs invasion; the following year, the October Missile Crisis unfolded. They also constituted a decisive period, one in which strengths would be put to the test, and the capacity to both create and solidify existing institutions and structures would be measured, not just within the publishing world. Those old enough to have lived through and recall those years, can also recall the works read in the trenches, titles published by the National Printing House: *Ten Days That Shook the World*, by John Reed; *The Road to Volokolamsk*, by Alexandre Beck; *Canción de gesta* by Pablo Neruda and chronicles of the Spanish Civil War, among others.

In the early 1960s when Cubans spent a lot of time in the trenches, the literature they read there, printed on the Revolution's presses, reflected the historic moment, the immediacy of history as it was experienced day by day. Poetry was, by its very nature, the only genre to capture episodes of the revolutionary epic while they were occurring and being experienced by the reader.[33] Poetry does not always require, as does the novel, a long period of gestation. Within this climate it is not surprising to encounter a "homeric" phenomenon, the fusion of life and art, of action and reflection. It was not by chance that the first Cuban edition of Homer's *Iliad* was published in those years.

The establishment of a National Publishing House in 1962 ushered in a new era; production of Cuban and world literature increased, and the publishing network was restructured: "the presses themselves were incorporated into the

---

[33]The best-known of the popular poets of that time was the Indio Naborí, pseudonym of poet and journalist Jesús Orta Ruiz. He wrote a series of poems from 1960 to 1967 for a section of the newspaper *Noticias de hoy* titled "Al son de la historia," and the poems offered a kind of running commentary of current and political events.

Ministry of Industry, and domestic book distribution and sales was subsumed under the Ministry of Interior Commerce."[34]

The first major project undertaken by the National Publishing House was an edition of the complete works of José Martí, which had never been published in Cuba in their entirety. The team under whose supervision this was to be carried out was composed of five people: only two had publishing experience and they taught the others as they went along. Book design, production and editing had been an ad hoc affair in Cuba, as we have seen, although the care and skill of printers and writers produced magnificent editions on a limited scale. The professional editor came into being with the Revolution and, as a result, there exist fewer prejudices and rivalries with regard to the role he or she plays in the contemporary literary and intellectual milieu.

Elemental material and graphic necessities having been met, the National Printing House was transformed into the National Publishing House, with a greater diversification of function and editorial policy. The National Printing House had six divisions when it was founded, the Editorial Board having been given the faculty to create as many as became necessary.[35]

The increasing latitude granted the fledgling industry reveals the projected force and importance of books and book production on a large scale as vehicle and instrument in educational, cultural, scientific and technological development, in the formation and cultivation of the imagination of the citizenry from infancy to full maturity.

From 1962 to 1966 the reorganization of Cuban publishing allowed for a degree of fine-tuning and adjusting that had not been possible before. Novels enjoyed more flexible print-runs, permitting a lower volume of 15 to 20 thousand copies per title. Production teams began to concentrate on the *format* of Cuban books, improving the tables of contents and indexes and incorporating prologues by well-known authors. Painters created book covers and graphic artists worked on their design. The diversity of editions, more modest and flexible print-runs, the acquisition of new equipment from what was then the German Democratic

---

[34]Rolando Rodríguez, "El libro cubano es obra de la Revolución" (Interview) *Granma*, March 31, 1979.

[35]The six divisions were: Publishers for the Ministry of Education, Publishers for the National Council on Culture, Publishers for the Council of Advanced University Study, Scientific Publishers, Technological and Labor Publishers, Juvenile Publishers.

Republic, principally to complement existing machinery for printing and finishing work, made it possible to pay more attention to the aesthetic aspects of format and design. Literary production was on the rise, and the publishing industry was growing in an attempt to satisfy the nation's demand for books. As we have indicated, those things that would seem to constitute a disadvantage—the lack of a publishing tradition with a core of trained professionals for each branch and phase of editing and production—have been enormously beneficial to the development of Cuban publishing.

Few nations are in a position to consider the possibility of developing and implementing curriculum at the university level for the publishing professions, and even fewer have had the foresight and sensibility to undertake the task of doing so. After three decades, the Cuban publishing industry is now ready to draw up, together with the departments of language and literature, a course of study for university students interested in applying their academic studies towards a career in publishing. For over thirty years, college professors have come into contact with the world of book publishing as consultants or specialized readers in their field of expertise; they have collaborated in the writing of the college texts to be used in their classrooms; writers have also collaborated enthusiastically on this project. Together, these editors, professors and writers constitute an "army of veterans" representative of different spheres of the book publishing industry with considerable experience to pass on to a new generation. This generation will have no lack of mentors; they will not have to build a publishing industry from the ground up but they will have to meet the growing needs of a society of readers and the challenges of increasing productivity in an industry not only providing for the national market but exporting, in all genres, to the Spanish-speaking world.

Arguably, the most important developments of the early 1960s for national literary production and the industry that supports it were the the birth of the Cuban editor and the Cuban publishing house, per se, and the rise of literary genres for children and adolescents.

Cuban Literature for Children: A Postrevolutionary Genre

By the time the first forum on Cuban literature for children and adolescents got underway, Editora Juvenil, publisher of children's literature founded in 1962—which later became the publishing group Gente Nueva—had already published seventeen titles by Cuban authors, an impressive statistic when you consider that national literary production aimed at young readers had been practically non-existent in the Republic. Achievements in the realm of literary creation for young people cannot be measured solely in terms of the number of books written and published; one must also take into account the quality and breadth of the movement to consolidate and disseminate the genre, with the input of a myriad of educational, cultural and social institutions, all intent on drawing up an editorial policy and creating a publishing base devoted to the literary formation of children and young people, quite apart from the classroom texts put out by the Ministry of Education.

In the Republic, textbooks were a lucrative business. A glance at Cuban bibliographies for the first half of the century reveals the same schoolbooks edited and reedited year after year—some even reaching the eleventh printing—while literary works generally did not make it past the first edition of only two to five hundred copies. Good literature, creative works of fiction appropriate for young readers, did not exist. In 1959, children's literature was uncharted territory, a blank page which posed an appealing challenge to writers, inducing novelists, short-story writers, poets and historians to adapt their craft to the formation and reading pleasure of children and adolescents. From 1959 on, all children attended school; there was a vast new social conglomerate of very young readers, and everything having to do with this genre had to be invented: writers, editors, librarians, and educators who would specialize in children's literature and study the problems peculiar to literary production for young readers. The same philosophy and determination that brought *Don Quijote*, the first Cuban edition and the first book to come off the refurbished rotary presses, to the new adult readers who had recently learned to read and write, also dictated that the first title in children's literature to be published by the Revolution be the classic *La edad de oro* by José Martí. In both cases, for children and adults, the printed volume was clearly meant to be a window opening on the world, history, the human condition and universal culture, the larger context within which national culture would assume its place.

The first juvenile books printed during the period corresponding to the Editora Juvenil, the first publisher of titles for young readers, were Mark Twain's *Tom Sawyer* and *Huckleberry Finn*, the fairy tales of Andersen and the brothers Grimm, Soviet science fiction, a biography of Lenin, *Cuentos de la selva* and *Cartas de la selva*, by Horacio Quiroga and anthologies of fables and folk tales from around the world. In terms of Cuban literature for children, the first titles published were *Navidades del niño cubano* (1959), an anthology of short stories; *Una niña bajo tres banderas*, by Flora Basulto de Montoya, and *Dos niños en la Cuba colonial* (1966), by Renée Méndez Capote, among others. During the period in which Editora Juvenil was functioning, approximately twenty titles of children's literature were published each year; fifty thousand copies constituted the smallest print run. Every year they did a double printing of José Martí's classic work for children, *La edad de oro*, and yet demand outran supply; Martí's prophecy was becoming reality, as well as the program explicitly outlined in *La edad de oro:* "so that American children will know how people lived, and how they live today, in America and all the other lands; and how so many things are made from iron and glass, and steam engines and suspension bridges and electric lights."[36] In the 1960s the first stands with books for sale began to appear in the most isolated rural zones—in the Sierra Maestra, the Escambray and the Ciénaga de Zapata—with book stands occupying a small area within the general store where food, utensils, clothing and other basic goods were sold. They began with a selection of ten or fifteen titles, primarily children's literature. Today, the same rural areas have bookstores and paved highways on which to transport the books—where once they could only be brought in by mule or airplane—and Gente Nueva, publishers of children's literature, puts out ten to twenty titles a year by Cuban authors alone, without counting annual publication of works by universal authors.

Renée Méndez Capote, who contributed to the process of creating a *corpus* of national literature for children from its inception, addressed her works both to young readers and adults with an average reading level equivalent to that of a sixth-grader. The fact that her works are read by adults as well reflects the intellectual climate that reigned in the years following the massive literary campaign, the combined effort not to lower standards, with paternalistic criteria, in order to "come down" to the level of the novice reader—child or adult—but to seek ways to constantly *raise* that level. Literary practice for the youngest readers, and the texts made available to them, should be decisive in their formation as human beings:

> For the topic we are focusing on, the question is this: human beings change, from one epoch to the next, with the constant changes in the world around them. Man is shaped by the period in which he lives, as he in turn influences that period and prepares for the dynamic changes that will be brought about by the next generation, creator of nuances characteristic of its own milieu. The epoch experienced by a generation, or that experienced by a child, is its natural and social landscape. In our epoch, there are no longer

---

[36]José Martí, *La edad de oro* (México: Edición Porrúa, 1982): 28.

enchanted princesses—there are very few left of any kind—and the mythical visions of fairies, basilisks and magic wands have disappeared. Do we aid in developing the imagination of today's children by immersing them in the ideas and plots of that world from the past? Authors of literature for children have fundamentally resorted to themes of the unreal to amuse readers; that is, to take them outside the confines of reality with the lure of an impertinently imaginative and outdated, moralistic evasion, as if reality were an undignified and vulgar substance. They have neglected two very rich veins which have not been sufficiently explored in the western world: life, which has only lost its charm for the disillusioned and skeptical adult, in addition to heroism on the world scene; humanity's conquest through work and effort, plot, scenario and principal motivation in our life. Writing for children and young people is an engaging and difficult task; and writing well for children and young people is a goal that has only been achieved by a few distinguished talents.[37]

In the literary production for young readers, the lines along which cultural, educational and publishing policies were developed converge. They are all aspects of a plan for development that projects into the future, anticipating the needs of generations to come. Education and culture form the backbone of a process initiated in 1959.

From all across the nation, organizations of every stripe converged on Havana to participate in the First Congress of Education and Culture in April of 1971:

[T]his Congress, initially conceived of as a strictly educational event, was planned and discussed on a local basis, from the municipal to the provincial to the national level, and as discussion progressed the problems posed went beyond the strictly educational. Topics having to do with aesthetics emerged, and the potential expanded to the point where upon reaching Havana, in the national

---

[37] Herminio Almendros. "La imaginación infantil y las lecturas para niños," in *Revolución, letras, arte* (Havana: Editorial Letras Cubanas, 1980): 477-79.

phase, the name had to be changed; it was no longer merely an Educational Congress but a Congress on Education and Culture.[38]

In theory and in practice, education and culture are inseparable. Cultural problems are central to the educational process, and books are central to the development of both education and culture, specifically Cuban book production and the publishing industry's ability to keep up with the cultural and educational advances of the population as a whole, to expand as cultural and educational levels rise. In the declarations made over the course of the Congress, the greatest concern revolved around book publishing and the editorial movement—the material foundations for producing all the books the educational and cultural initiatives required—along with highlighting the importance of literary creation for young readers. The following year, coinciding with celebrations in honor of the International Year of the Book, the first Forum on Children's and Juvenile Literature was organized, in response to the problems posed during the Congress on Education and Culture.

Among the topics presented in the Forum, the declarations on "editions and publications for children and adolescents" are worth examining more closely:

> Attention must be paid and incentives given to authors who write for children and adolescents; infantile and juvenile literature can be enriched through the incorporation of national and Latin American folklore; adaptations; respect for the authors; emphasis on quality and appreciation for the importance of typography, design and illustrations; magazines and periodicals for children and young readers.[39]

Until 1959, the children's literature titles available in Cuba were for the most part imported from Spain, Argentina and Mexico. Since the genre was incorporated into the prizes for literature offered by Casa de las Américas, the majority of the award-winning books for children have been by Cuban authors. Where there is a lack of schools, there will be little need for books. In the most

---

[38]José Antonio Portuondo, in *Memorias del Primer Congreso de Educación y Cultura. Referencias* 2.3 (1971): 48.

[39]"Memorias del Primer Fórum sobre Literatura Infantil y Juvenil." *Boletín para las bibliotecas escolares* 3.2-3 (March-June 1973): 17.

elemental sense, a society's educational structure and resources condition the possibility and potential for creative expression. The parameters for action in the other cultural mediums begin where the educator's work leaves off; a movement of literature and theatre for children can only be developed on a solid educational base. The educational premises of the Revolution—free access to education for the majority, at all levels—have given rise to the birth of a publishing industry and increased cultural levels in all sectors. The emergence of a national literature for children in a country which 30 years ago did not have enough schools for its population, and produced negligible quantities of books, is a significant indicator of overall development. The first Congress on Education and Culture was an attempt to channel energies into these areas, with analysis of past accomplishments and an eye to the future:

> [I]t seemed to us that this congress offered a glimpse of society in the future of our nation. It remains to be seen if an illiterate or an ignorant person could live in that world, and we have even begun to consider, for economic, scientific and other reasons, that education constitutes the fundamental condition of spiritual and moral life for the man and woman of the future. We believe that in a society attaining higher and higher levels of culture, life for the ignorant will be morally unbearable.[40]

Whereas reading was once a luxury, it had become a necessity, and the need to fulfill the demand for books all the more urgent. At the close of the 1960s, with the demand for textbooks for elementary, secondary and adult education being met, attention was focused at the university level.

Expensive Beer and Cheap Books: Edición Revolucionaria

> *Compañero:* This book is extremely valuable, and that is why you are receiving it at no cost. It is valuable for the years of work required to gather the knowledge held within it; for the many hours of effort involved in producing it; because it symbolizes a step forward in man-

---

[40]Fidel Castro, Closing Speech, *Primer Congreso Nacional de Educación y Cultura. Referencias*: II.3 (1971): 62.

> kind's struggle toward ever greater humanity. Its greatest
> value, however, lies in the use you make of it. Because
> we are confident you will put it to good use, and because
> of its great value, you receive it at no cost.

This text appeared on a note card that accompanied every college textbook published between 1965 and 1967. It sums up the spirit behind an editorial experiment carried out by a group of philosophers from the University of Havana: Edición Revolucionaria. None of them had any publishing experience when they undertook the enormous job of producing and distributing college texts for the entire country, and their experiment revolutionized concepts and techniques in book publishing that would later be applied to literary works as well. Their innovation was to utilize offset techniques to copy directly from printed texts, with a skeletal structure: minimal and centralized, and an operational mandate: to drastically reduce the time that elapsed between the decision to publish a given title and its completion, in order to carry the texts "hot off the press and directly to the classroom." All of this, together with the decision to eliminate copyrights, led to an overhaul of book publishing mechanisms across the board. If the gears set in motion by Edición Revolucionaria improved the output of college texts, couldn't the same technique, given existing capacity, be applied to literary production and other branches of the publishing industry? Edición Revolucionaria no longer exists, but it filled a great gap by taking the thorny and difficult decision to eliminate copyrights for national and foreign authors as well as patents in industry, principally within agriculture.

In the mid-1970s, in the midst of an ongoing blockade, the major impetus was directed toward agricultural and educational development. Hence, the overarching significance copyrights and patents acquired as factors restricting development. Children's education was viewed as the basis for all, the hope and future of society; it is for that reason that children's literature was cultivated with such care and zeal. Similarly, the formation of highly trained technicians was considered vital in order to emerge from underdevelopment, an educational premise that would have remained largely unfulfilled had the crisis in college textbooks continued.

In December of 1965, in the Philosophy Department of the university, Fidel Castro outlined the plan for Edición Revolucionaria. The critical problem was acquiring textbooks at all university levels. Numerous requests to foreign editors for the rights to reproduce college texts in Cuba had been denied. Up to that point, Cuba had respected and upheld its legal obligation to pay the authors' fees stipulated by copyrights, but the critical shortage of college textbooks was by all lights a direct consequence of the economic blockade. More than others, those books presented a complex and sensitive problem, since academic texts are the bearers of the latest currents and discoveries of the international scholarly community in scientific and technical fields. They must, of necessity, be up to date, and as such are highly susceptible to international pressures and monopolization. Schoolbooks are a domestic problem; at that level, pedagogical tools are, and should be, created by the nation's educators, according to the exigencies of the domestic student body. The interchange and flow of knowledge at the university level is international, as is the mechanism that regulates it: the institution of the copyright. Conflicts over authors' fees or copyrights were, in a blockaded island, extremely delicate and complicated. As Fidel Castro pointed out in his April 29, 1967 speech on intellectual property, authors' fees and copyrights are not necessarily one and the same, since in the case of copyrights the economic benefits do not always go to the author. Book publishing is a multinational industry; the "rights" to a work can be sold outright by the author and change hands several times. In the end, it is often hard to determine where they will end up and who they will benefit. The copyright law is a double-edged sword: a just, social recompense for the author or authors of a scientific, literary or other creative work, or a legal, commercial mechanism which converts knowledge and information into currency:

> To deny a country that had been dominated, exploited, underdeveloped, permission to reproduce college texts is as criminal as refusing to sell it medicine.

> Cuba had been erased from the map, condemned to civil death.

> We had no other alternative. A commission went before the Tricontinental Conference being held in Havana, and other forums, and proposed publicly, without any attempt at subterfuge, that we, at that time, denounced copyrights as a "right" that limited educational and cultural development in Cuba, the most basic, elemental project of the Revolution.[41]

Three weeks after the decision was made, Edición Revolucionaria began putting out its first books.

---

[41]Rolando Rodríguez, Interview, January 30, 1985.

The philosophy of Edición Revolucionaria corresponded to the educational demands of a society in transition and the significance of print culture for such a society, one in which books did not have a static but rather a dynamic value, conferred by the demands and needs of a changing reading public. Fidel Castro's speech of April 1967 sought a definition of intellectual property and outlined the pressures that led to the decision to eliminate the copyright which, at the height of the economic blockade, would have truncated the Revolution's educational, and by extension, cultural growth and development. That speech, as we indicated above, made official the policy of *reciprocity* with regard to the elimination of patents in industry and agriculture, and copyrights for Cuban works reproduced abroad. It also signalled the willingness and commitment on the part of the State to subsidize book production, it had been doing so for a year, as an integral part of the planned economy and an absolute priority in terms of working toward maximum cultural and educational development; beer would be expensive in order to keep the price of books easily within reach of all:

> From this year on, college textbooks will be free, and technical books will be sold to all who want or need them at cost. Why? In keeping with a principle that can be summed up in one phrase: "Expensive beer and cheap books." In this manner, those who drink a beer on a summer afternoon will not only experience a moment of pleasure but also the satisfaction of knowing that they are contributing to technological and cultural development.[42]

Cuba had respected international copyright law and paid authors' fees, domestic and foreign, up to and through the early 1960s. Following the events of January 1959, the publishing houses created by the State were the first to pay royalties to authors whose works were accepted for publication, whereas the private presses continued to charge authors for the edition of their works as they had done in the republican era. However, in the tensest moments of the blockade, respecting copyright regulations to the letter of the law would have resulted in cutting the nation off from the conceptual, educational and scientific tools desperately needed to prepare an entire generation. The State was aware of all that was involved in the decision to do away with the payments stipulated by copy-

---

[42]Fidel Castro. Speech, May 1st, 1966, in *Documentos políticos*, "Política Internacional de la Revolución Cubana" (Havana: Editora Política, 1966): II.38-39.

right law, and anticipated possible resentment on the part of some Cuban authors, none of whom would continue to receive royalties, as well as the imminent international repercussions which were, in fact, immediately felt. Yet Cuba remained faithful to a perceived social mandate to make print culture accessible to all. And in the face of refusal from many foreign editors to grant licensce, with or without copyright payment, to reproduce sorely needed texts, took the decision to conserve convertible currency.

The long view on writers and royalties in Cuba bears out the fact that doing away with the concept of authors' fees was not an inmutable philosophical premise but rather a historical decision arising from a particular set of circumstances. In 1977 the law stipulating the payment of authors' fees was in effect once again, although many foreign college and scientific texts continued to be pirated. The first pirated texts distributed by Edición Revolucionaria broke with the tradition of massive editions that had been the norm at both the National Printing House and the National Publishing House. For some very specialized texts, presses were set in motion—the same presses that were once used for *Selecciones del Reader's Digest*—whose optimum efficiency was attained in print runs of 10,000 to print one thousand copies of a college text. Such specialization represented an economic sacrifice for the nation, but at the same time, allowed the graphics industry to get off the ground and signalled a new direction for the editorial movement.

An overview of the pivotal events of those initial years yields the following outline: human and material resources were centralized in the creation and operation of the National Printing House, decentralized during the years of the National Publishing House, and regrouped on a much more solid base, in terms of resources and experience, as a result of the Edición Revolucionaria experiment, precursor to the Cuban Book Institute. By 1962, it was apparent that great strides could be made in book publishing by separating specifically editorial tasks from the other branches of the industry; graphics was relegated to the Ministry of Industry, distribution and sales abroad, to the Ministry of Foreign Commerce. The publishing houses Unión, tied to the Writers and Artists Union, and Casa de las Américas were autonomous, not linked to any ministry, and drew up their own publication lists, independent of the National Publishing House. In time, however, editors became aware of how difficult it was to coordinate their activities across the different houses and came to the conclusion that a certain degree of centralization would lead to greater efficency, as it had for Edición Revolucionaria, in meeting increasing demands:

We feel it is indispensable that each time a book is needed, we have a quick and easy method of acquisition.[43]

The Book Institute

The Edición Revolucionaria experiment signalled the direction Cuban book publishing was to take. In April of 1967, the Book Institute was founded; set up to organize into one more or less organic *system* all the diverse components of the publishing industry. In the same way that the National Printing House linked all the components of the material base for book publishing—existing print shops and presses—the Book Institute brought together all the publishing enterprises created by the Revolution. In its first year, the Book Institute placed on the market roughly nine million copies of diverse titles—more than one book per capita per year.[44] The basis for graphics and editorial functions was laid early on, but this was not the case for distribution. The same year that it was founded, the Book Institute proposed creating a bookstore in every province and coordinating under the supervision of one institution all book-related activities, not just the editorial but the global process, from production to mechanisms for getting books to readers. The Institute coordinated all the functions that had been carried out by the National Publishing House. All the divisions dependent on the National Publishing House disappeared, giving way to the publishing "series" or "groups" organized by genre and content or discipline; these were working groups responsible for editing, production and distribution of literary, scientific and educational texts, structured in the following manner: Arte y Literatura (Cuban and foreign literature), Ciencia y Técnica, Ciencias Sociales, Orbe (no longer in existence), Gente Nueva (children's and juvenile literature), Pueblo y Educación (school books and college texts), Ambito, Ediciones de Arte (no longer in existence). These "series" were the basis for what would become the Cuban publishing houses of the 1980s. Gente Nueva is, in turn, a continuation of the projects initiated by Editora Juvenil, and Arte y Literatura, an outgrowth of the collections of Cuban and international literature put out by the National

---

[43]Fidel Castro Ruz, Speech, XI Congreso Médico y Estomatológico, February 26, 1966.

[44]"En pos de nuevos triunfos," *Granma*, January 17, 1979.

Council on Culture, in addition to Casa de las Américas and the Writers and Artists Union (UNEAC).

The Book Institute laid the foundations for a radical restructuring of Cuban publishing to accommodate growth; allowing for a substantial increase in editions in the years to come. But from 1967 to 1970, the problem of college texts was overwhelming, absorbing time and energy that could have been devoted to other initiatives, so the publishing "series" continued to function as they had been set up, without major changes. Perhaps the most important and noteworthy trend in those years with regard to new directions in Cuban literature and publishing was the emergence of Arte y Literatura's "Huracán" collection, together with the efforts to stimulate the production of novice writers, Cuba's youngest literature, the literature of the Revolution. The Huracán collection was an offspring of the technological innovations of Edición Revolucionaria, going beyond the bounds of textbook production to suggest new possibilities for literature. The possibility of extending the technical prodedures employed by Edición Revolucionaria—direct photocopying of printed volumes—along with the ethical premise of reciprocity in eliminating copyrights for nontechnical or scientific works as well, was latent and foreseeable in the April 1967 speech which defined intellectual property as all that emanated from human intelligence, whether it be "a work of a technical nature or a novel":

> [Edición Revolucionaria] was a wonderful thing, but it was equally
> wonderful when I realized that we held in our hands the possibility
> of other editions, and that was how Huracán was born.[45]

There was equipment in the print shops that was not being used as well as available staff, machinery and cheap paper but paper that was nonetheless adequate. A preliminary list was drawn up for the new collection, not of typescripts or manuscripts but of published works to be "fusiladas,"[46] works it was felt the reading public should become familiar with: *Les misérables*, by Victor Hugo;

---

[45]Interview with Rolando Rodríguez, January 30, 1985.

[46]"Fusiladas" is a term coined by Cuban publishers in the 1960s referring to works photocopied directly from books published in Spain, the U.S. or other capitalist nations in cases where the fees requested for rights to reproduction exceeded Cuba's economic possibilities or the request for permission to reproduce such works on Cuban territory at the height of the blockade had been denied.

Man's Fate, by Malraux; *The Kingdom of This World*, by Carpentier. The procedure for these "pirated" editions was simple: simply show up at the shop with the
original edition in hand. In some cases linotypists were enlisted in the process,
and they would compose directly from the books they received, as there was
often no time to produce a typescript, and those originals were then sent to the
factory. Like the college texts put out by Edición Revolucionaria, titles in the
Huracán collection were reproductions of works published by foreign houses or
prerevolutionary Cuban presses. Painter and graphic designer Raúl Martínez,
considered the father of contemporary Cuban book design, took on cover design
for the Huracán project.

Another of Arte y Literatura's collections from those years was Pluma en
Ristre, for young, unpublished, Cuban authors. The impetus behind the emergence of this collection was to stimulate the literary production of novice Cuban
writers. The atmosphere, the climate of the literary and publishing milieu, was
oriented toward reaching out to the unpublished authors, both young and not so
young, who would usher in a new Cuban literature. UNEAC, the Writers and
Artists union, sponsor of various literary contests, sponsored yet another in 1967,
the "David," for unpublished works of poetry, theater and the short story. The
Hermanos Saíz Brigade, a division of the UNEAC for young people, offered
seminars, fellowships and exhibits to stimulate the production of novice writers.
Simultaneously, there was a growing movement which transcended the youthful
category to embrace all writers who had not been able to publish and disseminate
their works, giving voice to the silent, unpublished component of the Cuban
literary tradition up to 1959.

The dialectical relationship between "the universal" and "the Cuban" which
shaped the development of contemporary publishing can be traced in the evolution of the series "Arte y Literatura," from its earliest beginnings in the Instituto
del Libro to its existence as a full-blown publishing house in its own right today.
With a keen sense of cultural integrity, and without sacrificing plurality, the
Cuban publishing network has placed great emphasis on editing and disseminating the classics of Western literature, always taking pains to ensure that this
effort did not overshadow or hamper contemporary Cuban literary creation. The
literary/editorial sphere purposely opened itself up to the contributions and stimulus afforded not only by the classical Western literary tradition, but also the
contemporary cultures of Africa, Asia and Latin America—long before the so-
called boom—through a sustained and conscious effort which guided an editorial
policy of familiarization with and dissemination of, in Cuba, the literary expression of nations and peoples who had little or no presence within the major enterprises of the international cultural industry. Casa de las Américas' well-known

efforts to encourage and disseminate contemporary Latin American and Caribbean arts and letters is paralleled by those of Arte y Literatura on a global scale.

Cosmopolitanism and true universality in literature were the ideals of an editorial policy that applied inclusive, decolonized criteria to the selection process. Free from economic dependence on the U.S., Cuba embarked on a battle against cultural colonialism which consisted, principally, in broadening horizons. In terms of editorial policy, this translated into the publication of unpublished Cuban authors, European and U.S. classics, as well as an ambitious campaign to gather the most up to date information possible on everything of significance that was being written worldwide.

As qualified personnel, industrial capacity and stocks of paper and other necessary supplies grew, the number of titles that could be published on an annual basis increased. With publishing potential on the rise, the editors' job required greater vision and precision, in order to establish and define priorities in keeping with the cultural policy of the Revolution. In the early years of the Book Institute, Truman Capote's *In Cold Blood* was published in the United States, to immediate international acclaim; the history of the Cuban edition bears testimony to the importance of an editorial policy that reflects the cultural priorities of a society in transition. If a choice had to be made between publishing *In Cold Blood* in translation or the original manuscript of an important Cuban author, precious paper was reserved for the Cuban author. That was the immediate cultural imperative. Later, when the backlog decreased and industrial capacity opened up, there would also be room for a Cuban edition of Capote's work.

In the 1970s, the decision was made to give greater autonomy to the Book Institute's "groups" or "series." Titles and print-runs increased, and the thematic content grew more varied. Developments in the editorial, literary and intellectual spheres at that stage of the Revolution demanded further changes in book publishing that would assure continued growth. The "series" were transformed into autonomous publishing houses, each with its own headquarters and structure, as well as its own production, design and editing departments. Until 1976, Cuban publishing houses functioned, in all but the economic aspect, as independent entities, except that their financial resources were allotted from the overall budget of the Book Institute. A System of Economic Management and Planning for the cultural sector was adopted in 1975, in a resolution of the First Party Congress, although a de facto initiative had been underway for several years to integrate economic planning, cultural development and editorial policy.

The Juan Marinello Polygraphic Complex

In 1972, steps were taken to broaden the foundations of the publishing industry. Growing literary, scientific and educational demands on the industry led, as we have seen, to the creation of the publishing "groups" or "series"; smaller but with a greater degree of specialization. Plans were laid to renovate and enlarge the Havana print-shops and to install a polygraphic combine for book production in Guantánamo, a province with no history of printshops or printers and thus no tradition, handed down from generation to generation, from which to draw experienced personnel. All the printing and publishing activity had historically been concentrated in Havana; the commercial center for the book trade, the shops, the printers and publishers, as well the major literary institutions. The decision to produce books in rural Guantánamo was part of a push to develop the nation's less developed provinces, feeding in, ultimately, to a plan for equitable development of all the provinces. The rural zones presented the greatest challenge: that of transforming mountains and swamplands. Havana dispatched cinema-mobiles to show films where there were no theaters, helicopters to transport books and periodicals where there were no paved roads, and entire opera companies travelled to mountain villages on trucks and performed in the open air. When the Cuban Opera Company made its first tour of the Sierra Maestra, they performed for "the largest audience in Cuban history: two thousand spectators came down from the Sierra for the performance."[47] The initial challenge was that of bringing books, paintings, film, theater, dance and opera to the mountains and swamps; the *greatest* challenge lay in creating conditions for cultural expression in the plastic, literary and musical arts, to take root, grow and continue to develop in the rural zones, cultivated by the inhabitants themselves.

Up until the 1970s, the major campaign revolved around getting books to readers, even in the most isolated zones, with Havana as the operational base; from the 1970s on, books would be produced in one of the most abandoned backwaters of the country, neglected by all the administrations of the Republic. The famous public works projects of the early republican administrations at the turn of the century, and those designed to improve the quality of education and general services, never reached Guantánamo; it remained a relatively unpopulated and forgotten zone and thus became the site of the military base that remains to this day. In July of 1977, at a cost of more than fourteen million pesos, the Juan

---

[47]Jorge Garrido, "El reto de la cultura en las montañas," *Bohemia* (March 29, 1985): 26.

Marinello polygraphic combine opened in Guantánamo, with permanent double shifts and the capacity to produce twenty-two million books and a million magazines a year. The decision to install the complex in Guantánamo was foreshadowed in the theses and resolutions of the First Party Congress which stressed the right of all workers to participate in national culture, providing "the framework of a comprehensive plan for the development of national culture and, especially, material support for the National Council on Culture."[48] As a result, the enormous plant, one of the most modern in Latin America for the production of books and periodicals, was planned for Guantánamo.

In addition to the guarantee of continued technical and cultural development and the formation of trained personnel implied by the presence of an enormous, technologically sophisticated combine for book production, one must not lose sight of the implicit political challenge its location posed. Guantánamo is a physically and politically divided zone: on the one side, the imposing military presence of the United States; on the other, the presence of the book, with its potential to spread and multiply ideas. The political challenge suggested by the force of ideas incarnate in books is a continuation of the romantic tradition—the best of romanticism and the romantic movement that shaped the essence of Latin American consciousness as such—of pitting ideas, books, the force of knowledge, against weapons. The Juan Marinello complex of Guantánamo, producer of twenty thousand books a year, is symbolic and reminiscent of José Martí's "barricades of ideas" which, he argued, were ultimately more powerful than the "barricades of stone" a short distance away.

In the 1950s, all books were produced by linotypists, directly and by hand. In the 1960s, investment in offset complemented existing equipment. A number of printers began to acquire cameras, granulating and other equipment; the idea was to complement equipment in place since 1950 when it was installed to print magazines and cigar labels, both products for export. In the 1950s these shops printed everything *but* books.

The inauguration of the Marinello plant marks an important moment in the history of Cuban editions; important in terms of the social role of literature and intellectual production and its role in the global development of the nation. It was hoped that producing books in Guantánamo would strengthen many of the fragile new bonds that had been forming between writers and readers, the intelligentsia and industry, city and country, literature and society. Installing a techno-

---

[48]*Tesis y resoluciones*, Primer Congreso del Partido Comunista de Cuba (Havana: Editorial de Ciencias Sociales, 1978): 478.

logically sophisticated plant in a rural zone meant facing difficulties not present in Havana: problems of transportation and communication with publishing houses located in the capital. Book production in the countryside required a much greater effort at every step, but the effort involved also implied the promise of making the quality of life in the rural zones and provinces equal to that of the major cities, while at the same time providing new jobs in the region, and training editorial and graphics personnel. Book production, regardless of the phase or facet of the process, demands increasing cultural levels on the part of employees, and in that sense the Guantánamo plant would also help erode Havana's dominance as the center of all literary life. Literati and editors alike would now have to make occasional trips to the countryside, coming into contact with the alien world of rural life.

The combination of factors most favourable to literary creation, the optimimum conditions we have alluded to throughout this work, began to come together in the 1980s: a reading public made up of the majority of the population, with active participation in the cultural process; essential, social contact between writers and society at large; expansion of the capital's literary and cultural centers, stretching from Havana to the provinces—the establishment of a publishing house in Oriente, for example, or a combine for book production in Guantánamo—the convergence of educational, cultural and industrial development, and its effect on literary production.

CHAPTER 6. THE INSTITUTIONALIZATION OF LITERARY CULTURE

The Philosophy of Cuban Publishing

> The likelihood that exceptional artists will arise will be that much greater because of the enlargement of the cultural field and the possibilities for expression.... It is a process that requires time. (Ernesto Guevara, *Man and Socialism in Cuba*)

> Does writing have any meaning? The question lies heavily in my hand. (Eduardo Galeano, *Days and Nights of Love and War*)

If writing is an act of communication then it constitutes, by that very fact, an act of faith, when the writer feels powerless to make his words reach the vast public. Creative fulfillment on the part of writers and readers is not attained by cultural means alone, but the means of cultural expression are transformed by new relations of production. Many a concerned writer laments—and some even despair and cease to produce—that his or her published works never break out of the "elite" circuit. Eduardo Galeano describes the process as one of writing against solitude, the solitude of the writer and that of the other, the others, knowing that even a massive print run of a hundred thousand, five hundred thousand, a million copies, will not suffice, given the conditions in which the majority of humanity lives, to achieve massive readership. Massive readership cannot be arrived at through a policy of massive print runs; such readers must be created:

> I think it would be a midsummer night's dream to imagine that the creative potential of the people could be realized through cultural means alone—the people who were lulled to sleep long ago by harsh conditions of existence and the exigencies of life. How many talents have been extinguished in Latin America before they could reveal themselves? How many writers and artists have never had the opportunity to recognize themselves as such?[1]

The same could be said of any society which, having satisfied the basic material necessities of its citizens, did not strive to create a climate favorable to the cultivation of the creative impulses of all. Once these conditions are met, it is more likely that talent will reveal itself in the most unexpected places, if it meets with encouragement rather than obstacles.

Editorial policy is, in that sense, the end result of a process, not its point of departure. In understanding readership and the social process, it is important to bear in mind that Cuban publishers enjoyed, in the 1980s, approximately the same annual output in volume as Siglo Veintiuno Editores, in Mexico. The Mexican publishers' output supplied books to the entire continent, in addition to domestic demand, while the volume of Cuban editions was not enough to meet the requirements of the national public.

Few would dispute the fact that, sooner or later, such aspects as distribution, print-run, royalties and copyright law must be considered in an analysis of the relationship between literature and society. The concrete, material dimensions of intellectual production, manifest in the book industry, can be restricting factors in the marketplace of ideas. Yet Cuba's publishing industry was built and existed, until recently, in a context of relative freedom from commercial pressures. The whole world receives a best-seller[2] with open arms, yet the term itself is neutral; it only has meaning within the economic structure of the publishing industry within which the phenomenon occurs.

In Cuba, the axis upon which the whole, complex, "extraliterary" structure behind each printed volume has rested, since 1976, is the Ministry of Culture. The function which in a market economy is carried out by a complex of private enterprises that intervene in the edition and distribution of an author's work, is assumed, managed and coordinated, in Cuba, by the Ministry of Culture's three book-related branches: editorial, graphics and design, and promotion and distribution.

---

[1]Eduardo Galeano, trans. Bobbye Ortiz, "In Defense of the Word," in *Days and Nights of Love and War* (New York: Monthly Review Press, 1985): 189.

[2]We employ this term in its original sense; to designate those works with an initial printing of 100,000 or more.

The Dirección de Cultura already existed in 1959, as part of the Ministry of Education; it was, in truth, a virtually useless appendage with neither the resources nor the independence necessary for meaningful cultural work. With the new programs initiated after the Revolution: universal education, the literacy campaign and the intense educational and cultural work among the masses that followed, a mere "appendage" or office of cultural affairs within the Ministry of Education was not enough. An independent, cultural institution had to be created, without severing the direct link to education, and that was the premise on which the National Council on Culture was founded. When the Cuban Book Institute was created, it took over the editorial role, along with supervision and planning, that had been the responsibility of the Council.

Toward the end of 1976, initiating the period in Cuban literary history which concerns us here, the Ministry of Culture was created, and the publishing "groups" that had been part of the Book Institute, now dismantled, became autonomous publishing houses. The social function of the Ministry of Culture and that of the intellectual and artistic community often overlap but are not indistinguishable; their identities and responsibilities are clearly differentiated. The task of the artists and writers is to create, to produce a body of work; the role of the Ministry of Culture, to support their work. The Ministry of Culture claimed, in and of itself, no artistic identity or function, although it serves the needs of artists, creating conditions that stimulate artistic and literary production without any direct intervention in the creative process:

> The Ministry's responsibility is to develop the material bases for art, to address problems having to do with material resources, financing and technological development. It is also responsible for artistic education in the sense of establishing art schools and organizing an artistic network in accordance with the principles of the national educational system. In addition, the Ministry is responsible for everything related to cultural dissemination, directed toward creating a climate of receptivity to and participation in cultural activities...perhaps in developed countries, or those that have a lengthy tradition of supporting cultural work, all of this developed more organically but our country lacked, until now, a strong, systematic tradition of support for the arts.[3]

---

[3]Armando Hart Dávalos. *Cambiar las reglas del juego* (Havana: Editorial Letras Cubanas, 1983): 11-12.

All of the terms change, when removed from a commercial context, as well as the objectives. Although, apparently, no single element of the material foundations for literary culture has changed, there is, in this initial stage, a social movement toward new ways of conceiving of and producing literary culture.

No society can save itself, collectively, through cultural means alone; that is, quite simply, playing the violin while Rome burns. It is equally true that the existence and equitable distribution of resources adequate for the development of all spheres of human activity does not guarantee the sudden appearance on the scene of that society's literary or artistic opus magnus; however, under such conditions, wherever talent and or creative potential reveals itself, the basic social foundations are in place to allow for the continued development of potential and talent. It could well be argued, as Galeano has done, that the majority of potential artistic and literary talents have been snuffed out before they could reveal themselves.

The literary history of each nation may be dominated by its "grand figures" but they are not its sole authors; literary history is made up of the contributions of all those that have in one way or another left their mark on its trajectory, all those who, in life, may not have amounted to anything, all those whose talent was sacrificed or eclipsed by the emergence of a literary "giant." An exclusivist editorial policy serves to perpetuate the closed circle of "initiates," the altar on which the potential talent of the excluded is sacrificed:

> Custom houses for words, incinerations of words, cemeteries for words are organized. So we will resign ourselves to live a life that is not ours, they force us to recognize an alien memory as our own.... [P]erhaps writing is no more than an attempt to save, in times of infamy, the voices that will testify to the fact that we were here and this is how we were.[4]

Besides giving voice to national literary expression, past and present, the Cuban editorial movement, gave, without patronizing them, a privileged position to contemporary and classic literary movements and figures from those nations that had been cast aside by the transnational cultural industry. By including a wide range of voices, the objectives of each publishing house reflected a cultural dynamic that extended "from the national to the Latin American and Caribbean,

---

[4]Eduardo Galeano, trans., Bobbye Ortiz, *Days and Nights of Love and War* (New York: Monthly Review Press): 173.

and from there to the universal."[5] In the publishing houses studied, editorial policy has played an active role in the attempt to decolonize both the vision and criteria that shape literary and cultural expression.

To sum up the structure that was in place under the supervision of the Book Institute, founded in 1967, book publishing was organized into thirteen editorial "series",[6] each with a double function: to be responsible for receiving and processing, editorially, the broad range of genres and thematic lines within Cuban and universal literary production, and at the same time, to train qualified personnel who would be able to further define the collections and specialized departments that grew and evolved into the publishing houses in existence today.

In transforming the "series" into autonomous houses, it is interesting to note the increase in titles as well as the number of copies published in the period from 1967 to 1977, in the ten years that elapsed between the founding of the Book Institute and the creation of the Ministry of Culture. In 1967, 781 titles and 15.9 million copies were published; in 1977, it had risen to 1,143 titles and 31 million copies.

Cuban Publishing through the 1980s

The axis around which print culture revolved from 1967 to 1977 was the Book Institute, with its seven original publishing houses which have evolved into those existing today. The Institute served to link and unify all that goes into book publishing, integrating within its network the graphic arts workshops handling book production which were part of the Ministry of Industry; it organized all national booksellers, which had once been under the direction of the Ministry of Interior Commerce, into a coherent network that also handled import and export of books. The Institute sought to establish rational links and articulation among the different branches of book publishing and distribution so that the industry would be able to accommodate increases in production.

---

[5]Armando Hart Dávalos, *Cambiar las reglas del juego*, 21.

[6]These were: Edición Revolucionaria, Ciencia y Técnica, Pueblo y Educación, Ciencias Sociales, Arte y Literatura, Huracán, Gente Nueva, Cuadernos Populares, Ediciones Deportivas, Pluma en Ristre, Organismos, Ambito and Coordinación de Revistas.

From 1975 on, with the First Party Congress' resolutions on literary culture, the publishing industry began to branch out and evolve. The Ministry of Culture was created in response to the expansion of all forms of cultural activity across disciplines and the need to broaden the social infrastructure which supported arts and letters. Letras Cubanas was founded to fill the need for a publishing house capable of shaping, channelling and encouraging the small-scale "boom" that was beginning to occur in Cuban literature. The "editorial series" of the previous decade were transformed into autonomous houses, each one clearly defined, with the economic responsibilities of an enterprise in its own right.

It was around that time that the publishing house Oriente (1970) was founded, the only publishing house outside the capital. Oriente was an existing small print shop in Santiago de Cuba which evolved into a publishing house in the 1970s.

From their establishment as full-fledged publishing houses in 1977, all of them functioned as economically independent entities until roughly 1980. At that point, after weighing the experiences of their first three years as independent enterprises, the Ministry of Culture created two general divisions under which the publishing houses would from then on be grouped: Editoriales de Cultura y Ciencia, which incorporated Letras Cubanas, Arte y Literatura, Gente Nueva, Ciencias Sociales, Científico-Técnica and Oriente; and Pueblo y Educación, which coordinated publishing activity for all books destined for education, from elementary school to the university. Practical experience had shown that the publishing houses were too small to operate as autonomous economic entities, and that their integration into the Ministry of Culture's two supervisory divisions, Cultura y Ciencias and Pueblo y Educación would facilitate the coordination and economic planning needed by each house to meet its production goals. Outside this structure, there are three independent publishing houses that function as miniature enterprises: Ediciones Unión, of the Writers and Artists Union, which publishes the works of its members and those awarded prizes in the literary contests it sponsors; Ediciones Casa de las Américas, which publishes its own collections and the award-winning works from its annual literary contest, basically Latin American and Caribbean literature and literary criticism; and José Martí Publishers, which publishes Cuban literature in translation and foreign literature on Cuban themes for international distribution. In 1986, the Cuban Journalists Union founded the Pablo de la Torriente Brau publishing house, which also functions independently.

Editora Política was founded in 1970 and linked to the Party's Central Committee. Editora Abril, which publishes a collection of magazines for young people, is linked to the Young Communists' Union. From 1986 on, Editora Abril began to develop a publications list for book-length titles.

The other institutions not affiliated with the Ministry of Culture that publish books have their own presses or pay to have their books printed through one of the existing publishing houses or presses. In this category are the MINFAR, the Ministry of the Revolutionary Armed Forces which holds the largest of all the literary contests in terms of themes and genres represented and number of participants;[7] the National Library and the university presses. The Ministry of Public Health's Information Center currently publishes specialized journals and plans to set up a publishing house for books in the medical sciences and other branches of health care.

In this section we have attempted to provide a complete overview of the organization and structure of Cuban publishing, outlining all of the publishing houses and other institutions currently publishing books and periodicals nationwide.

It is important to stress the two-fold nature, both publication, and promotion and distribution, of the Cuban publishing industry: the active dissemination of all new titles that are published and the efforts at promoting literary culture among all sectors of society. Among the most notable aspects of the Cuban literary culture that evolved from 1959 on are its inclusive and participatory nature and the outreach projects to increase the level of participation of the masses in cultural life. Literary sociology, insofar as it is concerned to examine the relationship of literature and society over time, has alternated between taking as its object of study, the reader—following what a group or community reads and its responses at a given point in time—and the writer—examining how society is presented in literature and what values are transmitted by its creators through the narrative voice and vision. Both points of departure are valid, if somewhat partial, in terms of placing literary creation and its dynamic in social context. We have chosen to focus on the publishing industry as point of departure, the structure within which to carry out socioliterary investigation, because it is the essential point of contact where the activities and existence of writer, reader and editor converge; the center or axis which gathers up the fruits of the creative process and disseminates

---

[7]The "26 de Julio" Contest, organized by the MINFAR, was held bi-yearly for the following categories: novel, short story, *testimonio*, drama, poetry and *décima*, biography, history, music and the plastic and applied arts. The contest was open to all Cubans, and the prize-winning works were published by Letras Cubanas.

them through the printed volume. What the members of a given society read and what its creators produce has, historically, been influenced to an enormous degree by the state of publishing and what we have chosen to designate as the editorial system. In the history of Cuban literary culture, if the colonial period gave birth to the earliest expressions of national, vernacular literature, then the period from 1900 to 1958 may be characterized by the absence of social vehicles that would have allowed the promise of the literary phenomenon to be fully realized as an *act of communication*; from 1959 to 1976, creative energies in society are unleashed at the same time that a new social, cultural and material infrastructure designed to lend support and guarantee the continuity of literary production and the creative process is being forged. The literary heyday reached in the mid-1980s in no way represents the fulfillment of this promise as a *fait accompli*, but it does lay claim to a clearly defined literary movement and publishing industry to support it.

The 1980s witnessed the maturation of an industry, the fine-tuning of a literary infrastructure, which although still limited, had developed greater possibilities in terms of material and human resources and a superior level of organization. The basis for literary culture is consolidated on the editorial, technical and educational level attained by society, beyond the most essential indices of population, size of the national economy and basic literacy. Up to this point we have examined the structure and diverse manifestations of literary culture in Cuban society, while conscious of the fact that literary culture, in the social, global, essential sense, cannot be measured or interpreted in either strictly editorial or strictly literary terms. The Ministry of Culture, in its role as motive force in the creation of a general climate, an ambiance, which encourages the broadest participation in the cultural process, has in the process extended the parameters for literary activity. This is apparent in examining the entire gamut of vehicles and mechanisms, generated for the most part by the Ministry, designed to foster the creative impulse across the social strata. Programs that encourage the general population's engagement with and critical assimilation of the literatary heritage aim to make literature an integral part of the cultural life of the majority. Toward this end, a decisive role is played by the literary contests and workshops, the movement of *aficionados* of the arts, the campaigns to encourage reading, new mechanisms for promotion and distribution of literary works, expansion of the graphics industry, the training of professionals and technicians in the literary-editorial sphere, the foundation of graphic arts schools, and other measures taken to expand the realm of arts and letters.

Casa de las Américas

The oldest of the postrevolutionary literary contests is that of Casa de las Américas, held for the first time in October of 1959. It was the desire to break out of isolation and establish channels of cultural, intellectual and artistic communication throughout Latin America and the Caribbean, strengthening by extension Cuba's articulation with the rest of the world, that led to the decision to put out the call for original manuscripts and initiate what would become a tradition in the most intense moments of the blockade. All of the Latin American governments, with the exception of Mexico, had severed relations with the island, thus the extreme importance of keeping a range of channels and mechanisms for international exchange open. This effort has been the principal focus of the gamut of activities carried out by Casa in literature and the arts for over three decades.

Since it was first established, the Casa de las Américas literary contest has received over ten thousand manuscripts for consideration, with prizes awarded to over two hundred international writers and scholars.[8] The evolution of the criteria for selection and categories in which prizes have been awarded over the years parallels transitions in the focus of the *Casa de las Américas* review and demonstrates Casa's faithfulness to a guiding notion of solidarity based on the cultural values and elements of a common heritage that unite the nations of Latin America and the Caribbean. The categories for the first Casa contest covered the following five genres: novels, poetry, drama, short stories, and essays in Spanish. The original categories were later expanded to reflect changing trends in Latin American letters themselves. Throughout the late 1960s Casa received a growing volume of testimonial narrative and in 1970 added a new award for works in the genre. This would appear to correspond to a shift in the *raison d'être* of *Casa de las Américas* from an exclusively literary magazine from 1960 to 1965, to a vehicle concerned in equal measure with historiography and international politics in their relation to culture, from 1965 to 1971, "an agressive intellectual review rather than a literary magazine, " as Judith Weiss suggests in her study.[9] In 1973, awards in the categories of essay and *testimonio* were extended to include

---

[8]*25 Aniversario Casa de las Américas (1959-1984)* (Havana: Casa de las Américas, 1984): 1.

[9]Judith A. Weiss, *Casa de las Américas: An Intellectual Review in the Cuban Revolution* (Chapel Hill: Estudios de Hispánfila, 1977): 13.

works in Portuguese by Brazilian authors; since 1976 awards in all genres of fiction have included works by English-speaking West Indian authors; since 1978, by French-speaking Caribbean authors, and from 1978 on, Brazilian works in all categories and genres may be submitted in Portuguese. In 1975 a separate category for children's literature was added, open to writers in all of the admissible languages and geographic regions. The essay category is open to all international writers whose works deal with Latin American or Caribbean topics in literature, culture and the arts.[10]

Although initially conceived of as an international literary contest to be held annually, the growing diversity of genres and categories—seven new categories have been added to the original five—has led to the necessity to hold the contest every year but alternate the categories; six one year, the other six the next.

The establishment of a publishing arm of Casa de las Américas' own in 1960 was a benchmark with repercussions in the hemisphere, if not the world arena, and a tribute to its importance domestically, since scarce resources were allotted to book publishing essentially for foreign consumption. From that point on, in addition to the international recognition conferred upon the authors of the award-winning previously unpublished works, Casa de la Américas has at its disposal the means to transform those manuscripts into books and disseminate them worldwide. In the statistics gathered for its twenty-fifth anniversary, Casa's editorial production, excluding the literary prizes, consisted of 668 titles with a total of 6,469,858 copies printed throughout all six collections: Literatura Latinoamericana, for classics in Latin American literature; Cuadernos Casa for monographs, book-length studies in contemporary literary theory and criticism as well as socioliterary and sociocultural critique; Nuestros Países, no longer in existence, for brief monographs and interdisciplinary studies which are now being published in the *Casa de las Américas* literary journal; La Honda, for young writers and the shorter works of established writers; Valoración Múltiple, anthologies of literary criticism devoted to either an individual Latin American or Caribbean writer or a literary movement; and Pensamiento de Nuestra América, which as the title indicates, publishes the works of prominent figures in the tradition of Latin American thought such as Martí, Hostos, Guevara and Rodó, among others.[11]

---

[10] *25 Aniversario Casa de las Américas (1959-1984)*, 2.

[11] *25 Aniversario Casa de las Américas (1959-1984)*, 2.

Casa de las Américas' periodicals constitute another powerful vehicle for the dissemination of Latin American literature and criticism: the journal *Casa de las Américas*, published since 1961, is the institution's official organ, disseminating in its pages both contemporary literary production and interdisciplinary studies on all aspects of Latin American reality; *Boletín*, one of only three publications throughout the world specializing in Latin American music; *Conjunto*, another specialized journal devoted to publishing and encouraging the production of Latin American drama, a genre which has traditionally been one of the least recognized and disseminated on the continent; *Criterios*, a co-edition by Casa de las Américas and the Writers and Artists Union, devoted to theory and criticism; and *Anales del Caribe*, a scholarly journal for Caribbean specialists in all disciplines from linguistics and literature to history and the social sciences. *Casa* and *Criterios* are published bimonthly, with printings of fifteen thousand and a thousand, respectively. *Conjunto* and *Boletín* are both published every three months, with printings of seven and two thousand, respectively; *Anales del Caribe* comes out once a year.

There are two distinct mechanisms for the distribution of Casa de las Américas' books and periodicals. National distribution is handled by the Ministry of Communications; international distribution, by the Ministry of Culture. Internationally, Casa had, until the late 1980s,[12] proportionally few paying subscribers, with books and periodicals sent on a courtesy basis to intellectuals, artists, academics, researchers and others in the cultural milieu abroad who would, in turn, disseminate what they received within their home countries or set up a book and periodicals exchange through their institutional affiliations. It is important to underscore the importance of Casa de las Américas' extensive international distribution on a no cost, "courtesy" basis, as well as its repercussions: it represents an enormous economic sacrifice for the nation in order to keep channels of cultural communication and exchange open, despite the embargos on trade that could potentially impede the circulation of books and periodicals published by Cuban institutions.[13]

---

[12]In the late 1980s the U.S. Treasury Department loosened the regulations in force, permitting Cuban literary and graphic arts to be purchased with U.S. dollars. Subsequently, U.S. readers of the Casa journal could purchase their subscriptions.

[13]Much of the data on the evolution of Casa de las Américas' literary contest and collections was provided by Silvia Gil, Director of the Department of Subscriptions and Exchange at Casa, in an interview conducted on October 12, 1984.

The fact that Casa's publishing house began to function almost immediately after the first literary contest was held, in order to publish the award-winning works, highlights what sets the Casa de las Américas prize apart from its predecessors and emphasizes its raison d'être. Like all the Cuban institutions that lend their support to literary creation, both national and international, its function is not merely to confer a posteriori recognition on a work that has already been published and distributed, but to make it possible for a literary work to exist and make itself known by actually publishing and distributing the prizewinning texts. Casa de las Américas' literary contest brings to light year after year both new and existing, but little known, voices in Latin American culture, which consequently enjoy international exposure.

A history of Casa de las Américas, both the institution and its publications, however brief, would not be complete without addressing some of the internal tensions and controversies that characterized its evolution from one period to another, its growth from a literary magazine to an intellectual review which consistently took on more complex issues accross a range of scholarly disciplines, gaining in the process preeminence on the island and among the Latin American intelligentsia. The *Casa de las Américas* review's astonishing evolution in little more than a decade—a barometer of changes within the institution itself as a kind of artistic and intellectual "nerve center"—was not free of strife as was evidenced by shifting alliances and the dissolution and reconstitution of the entire editorial board and list of international contributors. The controversy with the greatest repercussions, both internal and external, was that generated by the well-known Padilla *affaire*. Cuban-American poet Lourdes Casal and scholar Judith Weiss both stress in their analyses the need to place the Padilla incident, set off by the publication of *Fuera del juego*, and all that ensued, squarely within the context of Cuban cultural policy and the role of Casa de las Américas as one of its principal exponents, if not shapers, in intellectual circles. Casal studies the Padilla affair against the backdrop of the tensions that led to the gathering at the National Library and Fidel Castro's "Words to the Intellectuals," and the ascendence of Fernández Retamar to the directorship of the *Casa* review:

As of 1990, Casa has reduced the volume of "courtesy" mailings, requesting that recipients become paying subscribers due to Cuba's growing need for convertible currency in light of the dissolution of the USSR.

It is only in relation to this entire backdrop that the Padilla affair and several of the episodes that constitute the affair begin to acquire meaning.[14]

Weiss, in her rigorous and sensitive study of Casa's evolution over the course of twelve years, shares Casal's criteria but offers a much more thorough analysis of the infinitely "larger picture" within which the Padilla incident, and the situation of the intellectual in general, must be understood, exploring theories of "alienation or of fragmentation," another name for "the dichotomy between 'pure' intellectuals and 'organic' intellectuals." She chronicles the growing international orientation of Casa's activities in literature, the arts, criticism and theory as well as counteroffensives such as the creation of a U.S.-based rival journal, *Mundo nuevo*:

> The pages of *Casa* became filled with more and more intense ideological discussion and reminders about the responsibility of the intellectual in the struggle for national self-determination. This period, then, between 1965 and 1969-70, may be called the "watchdog" or "conscience" stage of the *Review*. Occasionally defensive, generally polemical, the second period was one of growth on all levels. This is apparent in the literature as well.[15]

It was this period, with all its complexity, that culminated in the Padilla affair which, as Weiss rightly observes, must be understood in light of the self-definition of the intelligentsia and a squaring off of the "vanguard" and the "avantgarde." If *Casa* had been strictly literary in focus from 1960 to 1965, branching out to embrace intellectual, ethical and political concerns from 1965 to 1970, during this second period:

> The conscience of Latin American intellectuals grows gradually more impatient, and by 1971 there occurs a noticeable rupture between the militant vanguard and the artistic avantgarde that could not honestly become a part of the political movement. This might be postulated as

---

[14]Lourdes Casal, ed., "Introducción," *El caso Padilla: literatura y revolución en Cuba: documentos* (Miami: Ediciones Universal, 1971?): 6.

[15]Judith A. Weiss, *Casa de las Américas: An Intellectual Review*, 158.

the revolutionary-cultural gap, which occurred on two levels: the national and the international. On the national level this gap occurs in the continuing *cause-célebre* of Padilla....[16]

Weiss concludes, on all accounts, a thorough and balanced study of Casa in the national and international contexts by stressing that the period which ended with the unfortunate Padilla affair coincided with a necessary process of intellectual and artistic growth and maturation. In the final chapter she describes the "third" period, into which Casa moved after 1970-71, as being one of continued militancy, but a militancy which did not substitute rhetoric for critical thought but rather led to more rigorous scholarship on the part of Cubans and Latin Americans:

> It is worth noting, however, that solid scholarship is more of a distinctive presence in *Casa*: an indicator of the presence of a broader base of literary and cultural researchers trained in a rigorous historical method, and an indicator, quite possibly, of a stage of self-confident maturity and continuing support by excellent intellectual workers from Latin America. It reflects furthermore the consolidation of those rigorous methods of scholarship among an entire generation of writers and critics....[17]

It is because of *Casa*'s transformation from yet another Latin American literary magazine to a provocative, internationally oriented review, wedding literature to a gamut of disciplines and giving equal weight to theoretical currents, that it came to represent a "crystallization of many Latin American aspirations." Casa did more than just provide a forum for the expression of Latin American cultural and artistic aspirations, it established, after acquiring its own press, "a dynamic program of publications to divulge every worthwhile item of Latin American interest it possibly could..."[18] and thus became one of the most effective and far-reaching channels for the dissemination of Latin American literature.

---

[16]Weiss, *Casa de las Américas: An Intellectual Review*, 158.

[17]Weiss, *Casa de las Américas: An Intellectual Review*, 159.

[18]Weiss, *Casa de las Américas: An Intellectual Review*, 17.

Literary Workshops and Reader Reception

As we stated in Chapter I, the tradition of the literary *peña* or *tertulia*, pre-dominates in societies lacking a history of broad-based print culture, either because they do not possess the technology necessary to publish their literary expression—this was true for the majority of Spain's colonies in the Antilles until the end of the eighteenth century—or because the printing press is officially under the control of a ruling minority, to which the literary *tertulia* rose up in opposition, providing an alternate means of cultural, often popular, expression. In either case, the *tertulias* and *peñas* functioned, necessarily, as centers for the dissemination of the literary values and spirit of their time, without the aid of the official press—which would have multiplied a thousandfold literature's powers of communication—through public readings and the circulation of flyers, manuscript and mimeographed copies of literary works. The Cuban Revolution's literary workshops sprang from the historical tradition of the *tertulia*, although it should be pointed out that they no longer constituted an alternate, clandestine or underground channel for the dissemination of literary expression but existed at the very center of the dynamic in which readers participate as social actors for whom literary activity is no longer distant and "other."

The existence of workshops open to the public whose aim is to draw workers from all industries and sectors of the population into the nation's literary culture, came as a natural, logical outgrowth of the stated premises of the cultural policy of the Revolution; however, to establish points of reference, it is important to bear in mind that if we look at the history of print culture from a global perspective, past and present, the circulation of print literature among the general public is far from a common phenomenon. Until 1959, Cuba lacked a solid infrastructure for book publishing and the educated public was a small minority, in contrast to the industrialized nations of Europe. For the purposes of comparison, one might examine the relationship that existed between print literature and the labor force in Great Britain, a nation endowed early on with a powerful national paper industry and a growing publishing system from the mid-nineteenth century on.

In England, before the First World War, the daily life of the working masses was absolutely marginalized from the literary phenomenon. And fictional literature held no place within the classrooms of the universities. Workers had no access to literature and neither did the university students, despite their privileged status. Literature inhabited a social space relegated to the "sublime." All "well born" gentlemen and ladies read literary works in their leisure hours and, as such, it was presumed unnecessary to hold fictional literature up as an academic subject worthy of systematic study in the university. However, in the postwar period, the children of the English proletariat gained limited access to the university both as students and professors, as did literature. Since the study of literature did not yet exist as a formal discipline within the curricula of higher education, the professors who promoted its study had received their degrees in history, cultural anthropology and the social sciences which they drew on as analytical tools for constructing an interdisciplinary approach to the study of fictional literature.

The pioneers of this new mode of analysis, the founders of the literary magazine *Scrutiny* which also served as the mouthpiece for their theories, faced with a social order torn asunder by opposing forces in the decade from 1920 to 1930, rather than take on the challenge of opening literary expression up to the world, to *their* troubled world, chose instead to take refuge in literature, contenting themselves with the much narrower goal of transmitting an "enlightened" vision of belles letters from one generation to another of select university students, thus avoiding the elemental issue of addressing and examining the very factors that had given rise to an elite literary culture: the relations of production in an industrialized economy and the unfolding of a national literary culture, but by whom and for whom:[19]

> *Scrutiny* espoused this idealist "solution", however, because it was loathe to contemplate a political one. Spending your English lessons alerting schoolchildren to the manipulativeness of advertisements or the linguistic poverty of the popular press is an important task, and certainly more important than getting them to memorize *The Charge of the Light Brigade*. *Scrutiny* actually founded such "cultural studies" in England, as one of its most enduring achievements. But it is also possible to point out to students that advertisements and the popular press only exist in their present form because of the profit motive. "Mass" culture is not the inevitable product of industrial society, but the offspring of a particular form of industrialism which organizes production for profit rather than for use, which concerns itself with what will sell rather than with what is valuable. There is no reason to assume that such a social order

---

[19]See "The Rise of English," in *Literary Theory*, Terry Eagleton. (Minneapolis: University of Minnesota Press, 1983): 17-53.

is unchangeable; but the changes necessary go far beyond the sensitive reading of *King Lear*. [20]

It is precisely because a new social, human context—the vital landscape within which an inclusive literary culture may be generated—is not achieved solely through new sensitive and critical readings of the classics, particularly if carried out by the same minority readership, that one must examine the mechanisms that lend indirect support to literary creation by stimulating readers and encouraging novice writers such as the literary contests and workshops implemented by the Revolution's cultural institutions whose ultimate goal is to create an entire society of critical readers.

The central problems that inform theory and method for this study focus on *why* literary culture has been so highly valued and actively promoted in all of its facets and dimensions by Cuban society, and the hidden costs of such dedication to literary culture over the last four decades in an economy of limited resources. These are the fundamental questions which constitute the framework and initial point of departure; in formulating answers, we have tried to make sense of the complex socioliterary landscape of revolutionary Cuban society as well as the legacy of eighteenth- and nineteenth-century literary life.

Returning to our inquiry into the relations that are established, over time, between the forces of production, the labor movement and literary culture, there are strong parallels between the workers/writers movement in England in the 1920s and 1930s and the literary dynamic of the Cuban Revolution. Eagleton concludes his study of the evolution of literary theory with an examination of the situation of the working masses in relation to literary culture in the Great Britain of today:

> Silenced for generations, taught to regard literature as a coterie activity beyond their grasp, working people over the past decade in Britain have been actively organizing to find their own literary style and voices. The worker writers' movement is almost unknown to academia and has not been exactly encouraged by the cultural organs of the state; but it is one sign of a significant break from the dominant relations of literary production. Community and cooperative publishing enterprises are associated projects, concerned not simply with a literature wedded to alternative social values, but with one which challenges and changes the existing

---

[20]Eagleton, *Literary Theory*, 34.

social relations between writers, publishers, readers and other literary workers.[21]

I reiterate, at this point, my conviction that the literary workshops of the Cuban Revolution, like the worker-poets' movement of the Nicaraguan revolution and the British worker-writers' movement cited by Eagleton, constitute uncommon, isolated phenomena in the history of universal print culture. The social hierarchy, far from channelling the creative energies of the working masses, has tended to perceive those creative energies as a threat; this, in part, would explain their exclusion from the realm of "official" culture. The movement of worker-writers' or *aficionados* of literature in England today posits an interesting framework for comparison and contrast with the literary workshop as institution within the Cuban Revolution; the movement in England functions as a marginal, alternative channel, existing in the shadows of the established cultural industry which has turned its back on it. As Eagleton has so succinctly put it, what is indispensable is to make a change in the operative social relations among writers, editors, readers, the literary professions and the workers' movement in general. Until such change occurs, all genuinely popular movements will exist solely as marginal, alternative channels for literary expression and the artificial distinctions between "worker writers" and "real writers" will remain intact.

The complementary institutions of the reading/study circles and the literary workshops are powerful catalysts in the process of making such changes, organically, in the operative social relations among writers, editors, readers, cultural and other workers. The former, through close, analytical reading and discussion of literary works by members of each circle, seeks to create a society of active, critical readers; the latter offers orientation, stimulation and encouragement to those who, without necessarily being or aspiring to become professional writers, are interested in pursuing creative writing. Both the circles and the workshops constitute vital links between work and social life, in the broadest sense, and the world of literary culture, with an integral vision that highlights the work that goes into literary creation and the role of literary culture in the work place.

The early workshops seemed to arise and fall into place almost of their own accord until their proliferation signalled the need to organize the growing movement of literary aficionados at the national level. In 1974 there were more than 70 literary workshops, with over a thousand members in all and by 1983 there were 1,502 groups of aficionados throughout the nation. The literary workshops

---

[21]Eagleton, *Literary Theory*, 216.

function as study centers and literary laboratories for amateur and beginning writers where the concept of literary creation as practice, as a constant, sustained effort, predominates, in contrast to the "vague and chatty literary salon." The idea was to provide a setting in which aficionados could meet and work on ongoing projects rather than perpetuate the tradition of conversation among the "initiates" over work already completed. Anyone, after submitting a sample of their previous literary efforts, may participate except for members of the Writers and Artists Union, since professionals are not eligible for membership. Participants in the literary workshops generally meet once a week to read from and discuss works in progress, allowing for the opportunity to receive comments and criteria from the group. The national network is composed of base, neighborhood, municipal, and provincial literary workshops and readers' circles.

The "base" literary workshops are organized within secondary schools, pre-university programs, technical schools, factories, peasant organizations, military units, suburban or semi-urban neighborhoods and sugar mills. Workshops at the municipal level are composed of the most outstanding members of the "base" or neighborhood workshops and the members at the provincial level are selected from among the most outstanding members at the municipal level. Each year the National Encounter/Debate of the Literary Workshops is held, with a public reading of works selected at the municipal and provincial levels for critique and analysis by a jury of writers and academics. The Ministry of Culture and the publisher Letras Cubanas put out an annual volume entitled *Talleres literarios* which is an anthology of all the works that received an award or honorary mention at the National Encounter. One of the objectives of the literary workshops is to disseminate the production of its members, hence many publish their own journal or bulletin, either printed or in mimeograph form.

The readers' circle was the basic structure around which the National Campaign for Reading, launched in December of 1984, was organized. Twenty-six years after the literacy campaign—cornerstone of literary and editorial developments in the revolutionary period—the National Campaign for Reading was at once a movement for the dissemination of new literature, an invitation to the population at large to immerse itself in the world of literary culture, and a social measure designed to lend continuity to the adult reader's formation and development, so that the impetus generated by the literacy campaign and the subsequent massive editions of the classics put out by the National Printing House won't come to a halt. "Having completed the Literacy Campaign, this Campaign for

Reading should be understood as a second phase in the cultural growth of the nation."[22]

The decision to launch a campaign for reading at the national level brings to the public eye a host of problems for which solutions must be sought. Raúl Ferrer, director of the campaign, synthesizes the motivation behind the campaign as well as some of the problems facing contemporary readers:

> Although we can say with genuine satisfaction that we have the greatest annual, per capita consumption of books (five per inhabitant) in all of Latin America, this does not mean that everyone reads, it is an average; we are still deficient in certain dimensions and areas or zones of reading. And when I speak of reading I am not referring only to books but rather to the whole gamut of publications; journals, magazines, bulletins, etc. Many are content to read only the headlines or the section that interests them the most, and nothing more.... Much is said of the growing and dangerous competition inherent in the development of attractive mass media such as cinema, television and video cassettes.... But we take a dialectic approach and are convinced that the televised image can be an ally, that it is possible to promote the reading of books through a range of programs.[23]

The National Campaign for Reading rests on mechanisms for the promotion of literature and reading already in place, reflecting the dynamic relationship between literature and society: the readers' circles, literary workshops, cultural centers, book fairs and presentations, libraries and bookstores, except that once the campaign is underway the complex underpinnings of literary culture lend visible, public support to the campaign to provide a constant reminder to the Cuban reading public not to take the richness of the literary/editorial world for granted.

It is worth noting that coincidental with the campaign to promote reading, a campaign was launched to raise the reading level of the adults who benefitted from the literacy campaign of 1962 from the sixth- to the ninth-grade level. On

---

[22]"La universidad más económica: el libro." Interview with Raúl Ferrer by Basilia Papastamatiu in *Juventud rebelde* (September 30, 1984): 4.

[23]"La universidad más económica: el libro." Interview with Raúl Ferrer by Basilia Papastamatiu in *Juventud rebelde* (September 30, 1984): 4.

the one hand, a concerted effort to raise the average level of the adult reader who became literate in 1961; on the other, to awaken an active, sustained interest in reading on the part of the general public; two campaigns that converge and mutually support one another. Although the director of the national campaign for reading cites the proliferation of the image, of the audiovisual media, as factors that can have a negative effect on literary practice, these do not constitute, from our perspective, the principal motivation behind the campaign. Cuba is a nation with few or no illiterates; no one depends exclusively on audiovisual media, the only source of information and cultural enrichment available to the illiterate and semiliterate. Consequently, the point of departure for such campaigns in Cuban society is set at a different level: the goal is to further develop existing reading habits, not to instill them in a population in which many are of necessity dependent on mass-media. The twenty-three percent of the Cuban population that was totally illiterate in 1959, now reads, on average, at the sixth-grade level.

Most experts who study the problem of illiteracy agree that the most difficult task of the literacy worker is that of raising, grade by grade, the reading level of an adult. The most effective method for achieving a slow and steady increase in reading levels among adults whose lives, unlike those of children and young adults, do not unfold in the daily context of the classroom, is simply to stimulate an interest in reading as a daily practice. The campaign for reading has no set time frame; this "second phase" of a process is a lifelong task. To highlight the presence of books, of literature, in social life, as vehicles and instruments of knowledge and communication that enrich every discipline and human activity; that is the task of a campaign designed to increase readers' awareness, reminding the reading public that the five books per capita produced in Cuba each year are published in order to be read. The characteristics and composition of Cuban books, as physical objects, underscore this intention. They are made to last, to be read time and again; their pages, sewn into the binding with strong thread.

We will conclude these thoughts on readers and their role in literary creation by emphasizing the need to take into account their historical situation along with the social dimension of reading. Each reader's interpretation of a text is conditioned, to a great extent, socially and historically. A national campaign to promote reading does not hold the same meaning in Cuba in 1987 as it would in Haiti—with an illiteracy rate of 80%—in the United States—where it reaches almost 33%—in any other nation with an alarming index of illiteracy, or in Cuba itself in 1950. It would be misleading, or naive at best, to present the National Campaign for Reading, which coincides with the most prolific period for literary production in postrevolutionary Cuba, as an absolutely positive phenomenon, as if every citizen were the ideal reader that writers, educators, philosophers and editors dream of. There are undeniable problems that must be faced and combatted: the topic of television as a means of communication vis-à-vis reading still gives rise to unending polemics—the Cuban film, *Portrait of Teresa*, presents a scathing critique of television, among its many targets. It is undeniable that the readers who became literate as adults must be given incentives, that they do not approach literary works, demanding works, with the ease and self-confidence of a young college student. Neither should we forget that this was a campaign made for and directed at a society of readers, albeit with differing levels of education and cultural formation, where the specter of illiteracy no longer exists. Contemporary Cuban readers bring to their reading and assimilation of texts, a historical awareness of the initial educational campaign that involved the whole nation in the problem of illiteracy and its eradication. The reader's encounter with the text leads us to another essential facet of the socioliterary process: distribution of the literary product.

Channelling the Literary Product: Mechanisms for Distribution

Writers, editors, printers and booksellers alike coincide in emphasizing that the most dramatic change in the literary life of the nation, manifest immediately after the Revolution, was not a change in the order or spirit of literary creation and editions but rather in the *distribution*[24] of intellectual and literary products.

The role distribution plays in the cultural and socioeconomic dynamic of literary creation is one of undeniable importance. Escarpit, a pioneer in the sociology of literature, devoted more than thirty pages to principles and methods in socioliterary research; more than thirty pages to the study of literary production itself; and the rest—well over seventy pages—to circuits of distribution and consumption of literature. The epilogue to the Cuban edition of Escarpit's essay notes that as a methodological guide it has "the disadvantage of, for the most part, referring exclusively to capitalist societies, and particularly, French soci-

---

[24]Data on the present system of distribution and commercialization of Cuban books were provided by Mario Guillén Pandavenes, Director of Commercialization and Carlos M. Viciedo, Director of the Center for Research and Study on Demand, in interviews carried out on January 10, 1985.

ety."[25] Escarpit describes in detail how what he defines as the "elite" and the "popular" circuits for literary distribution operate; a preponderant and palpable division in literary culture in a market economy. A breakdown into the same categories is not applicable to Cuban literary history since, even in the Republic, the market economy, as such, was neocolonial and dependent, and the situation of readers, writers and literature itself quite distinct from that of France in the same period. The so-called "cultured" or elite circuit never really coalesced in Cuba and was by no means extensive; it was basically limited to the circulation of imported works. From 1959 on, cultural and editorial policy took pains to avoid, on principle, the emergence of a privileged circuit of distribution which would serve the needs of a "cultured" minority and a separate and distinct circuit for the masses, all of which would presuppose the existence of small, expensive editions of "good literature" for an élite public and inexpensive, popular editions, with an entirely different "tone" for the majority of readers. What distinguishes Cuban literary production throughout the revolutionary period is the fact that cultural and editorial policies converged, striving to meet a common overall goal: to extend literary and artistic works to the broadest sector while at the same time raising the cultural level of the masses so that they might take greater advantage of access to culture.

Since 1959 book publishing has been subsidized by the State; Cuban books are, without exception, sold to the public at a very modest price—the average price is eighty cents—and books intended for classroom use, at all levels, are distributed for free. As the cost analysis conducted by Letras Cubanas for all titles published in 1985 indicates, in the majority of cases, the price at which a literary work is sold to the population is far inferior to the total expense involved in producing it.[26] The Cuban classic *Cecilia Valdés*, for example, cost $10.91 to produce, in a print-run of just under 3,000 and sold for $4.05. This level of state subvention for literature was the norm.

The system of distribution for titles not destined for education, that is, the commercialization of Cuban books, was organized after 1959. Book production itself in the Republic was so negligible that it did not require the establishment

---

[25]Ana Victoria Fon, "Nota del Editor," in Robert Escarpit, *Sociología de la literatura*, 189.

[26]As the concluding chapter of this study indicates, since 1989, with the advent of Cuban books sold in dollars, such state subsidies, as a general rule, no longer exist.

of an efficient distribution network. Mechanisms that would ensure equitable distribution of the literary product had to be created from zero once the first Cuban publishing houses began to produce in volume. The very first titles put out by the nascent industry hit the street immediately in massive editions—the legendary 100,000-copy editions of *Don Quijote*, on sale to the public for twenty-five cents a volume, sold out immediately—and were sold in kiosks, improvised book stalls, and general stores in the rural areas, despite the fact that there was, at that time, still no concept of a consolidated system of distribution.

One can discern various stages in the development of the system for national distribution of Cuban books; but its study poses certain difficulties for scholars and researchers. Like book publishing in the early years of the Revolution, distribution was also carried out without the benefit of having first been organized in any systematic manner; therefore, we have little or no documentation in either case for the years preceding 1977.

In January of 1959, Cuba had the basic graphic elements necessary for book production, that is, the print shops for magazines, journals and newspapers examined in Chapter 5. Upon adapting existing equipment to meet the specific demands of book publishing, a limited yet functional system of production was quickly consolidated. This was not the case for distribution; although there were literary agencies and a retail sales network, they were, as was to be expected, devoted to the distribution of textbooks alone. What little volume there was of literary titles produced in Cuba before 1959 was distributed through the personal initiative of individuals and literary circles. From 1959 to 1967, more or less, commercialization of Cuban books was carried out in an ad hoc manner. The one fixed, stable, grounding principle was that of providing low cost books to the population at large, in order to guarantee access to an essential cultural product.

The Ministry of Culture's overall goal, in terms of the commercializaton of Cuban books, was to create a network of local bookstores that would extend to all municipalities, nationwide; provide each with trained staff where there had been none before and overcome the enormous difficulties in transportation and communication, with the center of literary and publishing activity concentrated almost exclusively in Havana. This initiative dates back to 1977, when the goal of establishing ten basic cultural institutions in each province was set, including museums, cultural centers, bookstores, and libraries, among others. It was never possible to calculate precisely how many bookstores there were in the Republic, nor to keep tabs on sales and distribution, since bookstores, as separate entities dealing exclusively in books, were rare. It is estimated that there was one bookstore for every sixty thousand inhabitants before 1959, the majority concentrated in the provincial capitals. As of 1985, there were three hundred and twenty bookstores nationwide; one for every thirty-two thousand inhabitants.[27]

Changes in the channels of distribution for literature since 1959 have been qualitative as well as quantitative, as a survey conducted in the early 1960s among members of an agricultural community bears out. Several of the respondents complained that, while the new bookstore had an abundance of titles in philosophy by Marx and Engels, there were none on agriculture and agricultural techniques.[28] The books they wanted existed, they were being published in Cuba, but the mechanisms of distribution were rather haphazard, and did not take into account readers' preferences by province or community. Later, the Ministry of Culture began to conduct research into demand, by geographic grouping. In addition to literary tastes and preferences, demand for technical books is analyzed according to occupational profiles and demographic traits of each province in an effort to channel texts on agricultural techniques to agricultural centers, and texts on the fishing industry to coastal fishing centers, for example.

The Network of Bookstore Specialists, REL (Red de Expertos en Librerías) provides current information on the titles in stock for all major bookstores and takes requests for those titles that have sold out in provincial bookstores. The REL also puts out a bulletin listing stocks of unsold titles—grouped by theme and publisher—in provincial bookstores. As part of this same effort at meeting readers' needs, the newspaper *Tribuna*, in the Friday literary section, publishes a list of ten or so of the titles appearing in the REL national bulletin.[29] Often, out of print or sold out titles requested by clients of one bookstore, turn up as remaining unsold stock in bookstores in another province.

One might ask, at this juncture, what the mechanisms for distribution and commercialization have to do with literary creation.... To paraphrase Escarpit, we reiterate that *distribution*—both sales and free distribution for classroom use—is essential "in order for the literary phenomenon to be complete," and

---

[27]"Algunos indicadores sobre la red del comercio del libro," document of the Esfera de Comercialización del Libro, 1984. In June of that year, the goal of establishing a bookstore in every municipality was met.

[28]See Fidel Castro Ruz, "Sobre la propiedad intelectual," April 29, 1967.

[29]Carlos M. Viciedo, "Importancia de la investigación de la demanda en la elaboración de los planes de promoción del libro," Department of Research on Demand, paper presented to the Reunión Nacional de Divulgadores del Libro, December 19 and 20, 1984, p. 13.

determines, to a great extent, the social function of literature. Contemporary theorist Wolfgang Iser echoes Escarpit in stressing that the "transaction" between text and reader is fundamental to the existence of the literary work:

> The work is much more than the text, for the text only takes on life when it is realized, and furthermore the realization is by no means independent of the individual disposition of the reader.... The convergence of text and reader brings the literary work into existence.[30]

The distribution circuit will shape the book's potential as a vehicle for the dissemination of culture, science and all other branches of knowledge; a potential which can only be realized through the reading public. As indicated earlier, Cuban book production is subsidized so that books, as merchandise, are within everyone's reach. The laws of the market economy discourage the stocking of titles not likely to sell quickly and massively. This, in part, explains the fact that specialized texts for scholars, technicians, volumes of poetry, social theory, and other categories that have historically enjoyed a lower level of circulation, are currently experiencing a worldwide crisis in production and distribution.

In Cuba the predominant factor, above all economic considerations, has been the intellectual, scientific or cultural value of the work; and the limited capacity for producing reeditions with speed and ease makes it essential that channels be developed to allow each title to reach the reader who needs it. Literature, in a noncommercial, editorial context, is not a "disposable" good whose value is established on the basis of how quickly it turns a profit.

It would be far from accurate to claim that Cuban literary production is totally exempt from considerations of an economic nature; the book publishing industry is, after all, an industry. Cuba is now in transition toward a mixed economy, but through the 1980s it was strictly centralized. The commission on economic planning set the price to the population for all products, including books, for a period of five years, during which time the price remained invariable. The pricing of Cuban books was extremely generous, falling far below what it could have been set at, without affecting the buying power of the population, allowing for fluctuations in the standard of living. Up until the late 1980s, it was cliché but true that every Cuban who stopped in each day at Coppelia, the ice cream parlor immortalized in the film *Strawberry and Chocolate*, could, for the

---

[30]Wolfgang Iser, cited in Susan R. Suleiman, "Introduction: Varieties of Audience-Oriented Criticism," *The Reader in the Text*, 22.

price of a milkshake, have bought one or two books a day. A volume of poems was often, in fact, much less expensive than a milkshake. The economic aspect, by design, did not loom large in the ensemble of factors that conditioned demand for literature. The other factors that can be cited as conditioning literary "consumption" or the buying of books, can be found within the readers themselves; literacy levels, leisure time for reading, interests and reading habits.[31] The society as a whole met the general conditions of competency and leisure. The remaining factor—interest—constitutes the major challenge facing editors, authors and book distributors. In a planned economy it is in both theoretical and practical terms much easier to design print-runs and distribution to allow for a close "fit" with the reading public, its needs and interests. In the communicational and creative chain that transforms ideas into manuscripts and manuscripts into printed volumes, booksellers have an extraordinary responsibility in the cultural process and development of society by virtue of being the only actors or agents in the complete circuit—manuscript to publishing house to print shop to bookseller to reader—for literary production in direct, daily contact with book buyers, with the potential for serving as principal "advisors" to readers... and editors as well. The knowledgeable bookseller, in his or her capacity as literary "advisor" to the clientele, has the potential to become a key figure in the work place, neighborhood or municipality.

Writers and editors also entered into direct contact—although less frequently than booksellers—with the reading public in activities designed for literary dissemination and promotion such as the book fairs and "Sábados del Libro." Initiated in 1977 in the Moderna Poesía, one of the largest and busiest bookstores in Havana—and which before the Revolution held a monopoly on the sale of textbooks—the weekly literary events christened the "Sábado del Libro" were quickly adopted by provincial bookstores as well. The "Sábado del Libro" is a miniature, Saturday book fair during which new titles are exhibited and sold in the open air, in a nearby park or green, public space. Authors and editors are present to dialogue with the public on the works exhibited, future projects and anything else of interest. Events like the "Sábado del Libro" changed the face of literary dissemination, once a passive affair involving little if any direct contact with readers, putting into practice the notion that the destiny of every work is "to make its way among men," and at which the creator is also present. Scholars and other dévotées of the history of print culture in Cuba will find it difficult to

---

[31]Wolfgang Iser, cited in Susan Suleiman, "Introduction: Varieties of Audience-Oriented Criticism, *The Reader in the Text*, 11.

resist the temptation of comparing the contemporary "Sábado del libro" with the melancholy and often absurd affairs that masqueraded as book fairs in the republican decades; exhibitions that were reduced to a passive spectacle with the population as onlookers or voyeurs. The prohibitive cost of the deluxe editions on display, coupled with massive illiteracy, limited such book fairs, at best, to a sad, spectator sport.

In mapping the trajectory of the Cuban book from the moment it leaves the creator's hands until it reaches the reader, one should not overlook the important role of the secondhand bookstore; an institution held very dear by all book lovers.[32] It reminds us constantly of the use value of the printed volume, which "is not used up through consumption but remains... for centuries in some cases,"[33] thanks to the quality of the paper or parchment and stable ink. The marks left by humidity or age, the patina acquired through repeated readings, the underlining and notes in the margin made by the reader or readers who came before, all enrich the enigmatic stock of the used bookstore. According to Escarpit, "for the moment the used book business has eluded all statistics,"[34] but is, nevertheless, of inestimable value as an alternative method of circulation, particularly in Cuba where books go out of print altogether too quickly and available technology does not yet allow for their immediate reedition. In view of this problem, the primary importance of used bookstores within the context of the Cuban publishing industry is not economic but cultural. Its inventory evades all the statistical instruments in place to determine stocks of titles throughout the national network of bookstores; the Cuban used and rare bookstore is a Pandora's box, for the assiduous and persistent habitué, which alleviates, in some measure, the inconvenience of the industry's limited capacity for reedition. I, one day, after failing to track them down through all conventional channels, found three out of print titles that were extremely important for this study, when I had all but given up, in a used bookstore in Old Havana.

---

[32]Sadly, current travelers often report finding personal libraries for sale, in dollars, on the sidewalks of Havana.

[33]Carlos Viciedo, "Importancia de la investigación de la demanda," 11.

[34]Robert Escarpit, *Sociología de la literatura*, 62.

CHAPTER 7. THE GOLDEN AGE OF REVOLUTIONARY PUBLISHING

The Boom Years: Cuban Books in the 1980s

> Comparing the figure of 1,065 titles published in 1984 with that of 1983, one can see that capacity for book production has doubled.[1]

As I wrote the final chapter of this study, Cuba was preparing for the Third Party Congress, in which the strategic plan for economic development played a significant role; a plan to be followed over the next fifteen years which included conservation of resources for energy, raw materials and other materials for industry in order to launch an import substitution campaign and generate exports that would bring in convertible currency. The essential elements of the plan were announced at the first National Forum on Energy:

> We have grown too accustomed to soliciting imports.... We sometimes create needs that generate imports, and almost never consider the opposite: to generate products for export, to generate export.[2]

Such a proposition implied moving from a society utterly dependent on imports to a fundamentally self-sufficient one, and from there, to develop a productive capacity that exceeded the basic needs of internal demand, permitting export. If an importing nation—an Antillean, Third World nation—were to transform itself into an exporting nation, not of raw material but manufactured products,

---

[1]*Granma*, October 2, 1984. The article referred to production plans for the Empresa Editoriales de Cultura y Ciencia.

[2]Fidel Castro, "Opening Speech, First National Forum on Energy," *Granma*, December 4, 1984.

in less than a half a century, it would mark the beginning of a new era in the global relations of production.[3]

The first chapter of this study opened with an appeal to the reader to employ what C. Wright Mills defined as the "sociological imagination"; imagination which enriches analysis, facilitating the linking of diverse elements within a global vision. It is not accidental that Mills, in characterizing "imaginative" analysis, uses the hypothetical example of the relations which may be established between literature and petroleum. The policy of conservation, effective in Cuba from 1985 on, referred to all fuel, principally gasoline, but the commitment to conservation extended to all essential national resources and raw materials. It is ironic that in 1989 when shipments of Soviet oil to Havana were suspended, all publishing activity was paralyzed in one fell swoop. Before this turn of events, Cuba had planned to double its export of books and periodicals. Instead, the nation experienced a double "blockade" with virtually no goods arriving either from the capitalist countries or the socialist block. At present, Cuban publishing is regrouping itself, at all levels, establishing new priorities and seeking new international collaborators. Many of the policies in force through the 1980s will no longer hold, as a consequence of Cuba's having to place itself within a globalized international market.

At this juncture, and from the perspective of literary culture in the 1980s, we will reexamine editorial policy and the effects of the blockade on the publishing industry.

Arte y Literatura

The publishing house Arte y Literatura, established in 1967 as one of the editorial series of the Book Institute, publishes world literature, from the classics to the most contemporary, in all genres. Titles in fictional literature are grouped according to geographical-political categories; each department handles the entire gamut of genres and literary themes from the geographical region or block of countries it is responsible for. There are four departments that cover geographical regions or blocks, divided as follows: Latin America and Spain; the socialist

---

[3]In 1991, Cuba was approaching the realization of this goal through its international exports of biotechnology. For more on Cuba's biotechnology industry, see Julie Feinsilver's study, *Healing the Masses: Cuban Health Care at Home and Abroad* (Berkeley: University of California Press, 1993).

countries; Asia and Africa; Western Europe and North America. The titles handled by the remaining two departments are not classified according to geographical origin but rather intellectual discipline or research area: Literary Theory and Criticism and Art History and Theory.

The order in which we have enumerated the different departments corresponds to the priorities established by the publishing house itself. We will attempt to explain the logic behind Arte y Literatura's editorial policy, its immediate and long-term goals, as set out in the publisher's own guidelines. Our two-fold task of documenting and analyzing, documenting and theorizing, leads us to use the data compiled as a springboard for socioliterary reflection across a wide range of issues.

Goethe, in his literary essays, explores the character of men and nations as revealed by their judgment and priorities:

> The insight and character of a man express themselves most clearly in his judgements. In what he rejects and what he accepts, he confesses to what is alien to him and what he has need of; and so each year designates unconsciously its spiritual state, the compass of its past life.
>
> Thus is it also with nations; their praise and censure must always be strictly consonant to their situation.[4]

The schema devised by Goethe is equally applicable to the literary culture of a given society, revealed in the works it rejects and those that it publishes, in its overall editorial philosophy. In the republican decades Cuba had no policy with regard to book publishing; it did not exercise this faculty since few literary titles were published, outside of schoolbooks, on any scale. Before 1959, contemporary foreign literature—and even Cuban literature which was preferably published abroad under contract with a publishing house—as a general rule, was shipped to Cuba at the request of individual readers. The books then circulated among the literati or "initiates," by nature a very limited circuit of distribution, both unofficial and random. The general readership had recourse only to what was available in the bookstores.

Cuba had received the literary influences first of Spain, later of France, England and the United States: it was the "classics" of these nations that were most prevalent in the bookstores, and most available books were imported edi-

---

[4]J.E. Spingarn, ed., *Goethe's Literary Essays* (New York: Frederick Ungar Publishing, 1964): 136.

tions. It was not until 1959, with access to a fledgling national publishing industry, that Cuban society began to exercise its own criteria in determining what might be made available, collectively, to readers. From its beginnings as a section of the Book Institute, Arte y Literatura attempted to fill the need for inexpensive editions of the classic works of European and North American literature, along with lesser known titles of Soviet and African literature, as well as contemporary and nineteenth-century Cuban literature.

In nations with a long publishing tradition, reprints of the classics offer the advantage of guaranteed, predictable sales. In the Cuban Republic, the "classics" of European and U.S. literature reached the bookstores in small quantities and did not circulate widely among the reading public. Following the massive editions of classic and contemporary universal literature put out by the National Printing House, the "Arte y Literatura" series of the Book Institute continued the tradition of popular editions for the general reading public with a wider selection of titles and a greater level of specialization, in keeping with increasing reading levels among the population and advances in the book publishing industry. After more than fifteen years of massive editions of major titles, of the "great books" of the European literary heritage, it was presumed that active readers had taken the opportunity to expose themselves to the classics, through the selections offered by Arte y Literatura. Without limiting publication and dissemination of the classics of Western literature, Arte y Literatura then began to expand its list of titles to include the contemporary literary production of countries not represented within the "grand pantheon."

The literature of Latin America and Spain currently holds first place among the collections of Arte y Literatura. Despite the cultural, historic and linguistic ties between Cuba and the rest of Latin America, the literature of the continent was not widely accessible and thus little known in Cuba before 1959. The task of publishing and disseminating Latin American literature is shared by Arte y Literatura and Casa de las Américas, but the ultimate destination of the editions varies. Casa de las Américas' editions, due to the very nature and raison d'être of the institution since its foundation, are produced, fundamentally, for the international community, whereas those of Arte y Literatura are distributed within Cuba. It is the huge demand for contemporary Latin American literature that has made it the highest priority among the collections offered by Arte y Literatura, suggesting the close correspondence between the literary interests and concerns of the Cuban reading public and selections, production and editorial policy of Cuban publishers. It is the expectations and demands of the Cuban reading public that conditions editorial policy and production, in a dialectical sense, and not the other way around—a situation that often exists in highly commercial publishing in which, through marketing and publicity campaigns, the aim is to have the literary product condition the taste and inclinations of the public, *a posteriori*, to boost sales. When García Márquez's *One Hundred Years of Solitude* came out, it was published by both Casa de las Américas and in the Huracán collection of Arte y Literatura. Both editions quickly sold out, and the same was true for the short stories of Julio Cortázar.

Each department within Arte y Literatura has its own set of problems and poses particular challenges to the publishing industry as a whole. In order to meet its goals, ambitious both in terms of volume and diversity, vast geographic and linguistic distances must be spanned, political differences resolved, and misunderstandings addressed, particularly those that arise, on occasion, over the negotiation of authors' fees. There have been numerous misunderstandings of this type in negotiations with authors from capitalist nations that do not enjoy diplomatic relations with Cuba.

Literature from Latin America and Spain

The essential problem in the publication and dissemination of works from Latin America and Spain is, quite simply, the volume of contemporary literary production. To attempt to disseminate Spanish and Latin American literature, from its origins to the present, including all the national literatures of the Iberian peninsula, Galician, Catalan, Basque, and that of the Canary Islands, for example, and the literatures of all the Caribbean nations, with the exception of Cuba, is an enormous task. The extensive networks of literary, cultural and artistic exchange throughout Latin America and the Caribbean developed by Casa de las Américas over thirty years have made possible the invaluable contacts and sources that allow Cuban editors to keep abreast of what is being written across the region in order to publish and distribute contemporary literature while it is still fresh. The greatest challenge is not the acquisition of works for publication but rather keeping on top of what is being produced in such a vast and dynamic geographic region. The greatest emphasis is placed on current production, in an effort to disseminate the most contemporary of Spanish and Latin American literature.

If we add to the list of first translations, the works of Latin Americans writing in Spanish who, either for political reasons or lack of an adequate publishing industry, choose to publish in Cuba rather than in their home countries, the task of publishing and disseminating Latin American literature, carried out jointly by Casa de las Américas and Arte y Literatura, constitutes the lion's share of literary publishing and an invaluable source for contemporary literature of the region.

Eastern European Literature

Twentieth-century Russian and Soviet literature, like that of Latin America, was virtually unknown in Cuba, a situation which Páginas publishers sought to remedy in the 1940s with its popular editions of world literature. For most readers in the Cuban Republic with limited access, Russian literature ended with Tolstoy.

This Department published literature from Eastern Europe and the People's Republic of Mongolia; everything from the *chansons de geste* and classic works from Russia and other Soviet republics to contemporary literary production including the detective genre, a genre relatively new to Russian letters.

African and Asian Literatures

This Department publishes literature from the African and Asian nations, excluding Mongolia, with particular emphasis on anthologies and selected works; the works are, in their majority, first translations into Spanish. Acquisition and dissemination of national and local literatures from Africa and Asia is a complicated task due to the level of diversity that exists. Historically ignored or overlooked by international publishers, there are few established, accessible sources of information at the disposition of editors on the lookout for new literature from African and Asian nations.

Cuban editors attempt to give voice and exposure to creators that have been traditionally marginalized through an editorial policy actively committed to publishing the literature of internationally underrepresented geographic regions. For the development of these collections, the task of increasing the corpus of publishable literary works and sources of information on contemporary literary production in the Asian and African nations is as important as the process of translation, editing, production and distribution.

Literature from Western Europe and the U.S.

The Cuban world of belles letters, from 1900 to 1959, no longer within Spain's orbit, had maintained the closest ties with French, English and U.S. literature. Hemingway's presence on the Cuban literary scene, like the imposing shadow cast by his "Cuban" house high atop a hill overlooking the town, was that of an overblown figure, one that came to loom disproportionately over the literary scene, both before and after the Revolution.

There was little of what could be considered clearly defined editorial policy in Cuba prior to 1959; it was a nation that, in the first half of the twentieth century, produced books in negligible quantities. Forced to import most of its books, with limited options due to the commercial trade agreements signed with the United States, Cuban readers read, for the most part, what they could get ahold of. Now, the literary works best known and most widely distributed throughout the world—those of Western Europe and the United States—are selected with the greater range and flexibility a national infrastructure for book publishing allows. Since its establishment, Arte y Literatura took pains to publish works from nations whose literary heritage has attained lesser prominence both in and outside Cuba, such as representative works from Canada, Portugal, New Zealand, Sweden, Switzerland, the Netherlands, Australia, and West German literature which, although widely read on an international scale, had been overshadowed by France, England, Spain and the U.S., and therefore not widely disseminated in Cuba.

Within this department, copyrights and royalties are a highly sensitive matter which, depending on the attitude and sensibility of the author to be published by Arte y Literatura, can throw a wrench into the plans for publication of the year's titles-pending list. The countries covered by this department do not, in their vast majority, have close commercial ties with Cuba. As a result, Cuban currency is not easily convertible to most authors' national currency. And this remains one of the thorniest issues and most stubborn of obstacles for publication and distribution in Cuba of contemporary Western European and North American literature.

The remaining two departments, those dealing with art history and theory and literary theory and criticism, because they handle works originating in the geographic zones already studied in terms of the mechanics of publication and distribution, present no new problems that have not been examined here, other than the greater graphic complexity of all art books that include reproductions.

Although it may not be apparent at first glance, there is an intimate relationship between the editorial policy of Arte y Literatura—responsible for the dissemination of works of universal literature—and contemporary Cuban literary production. The importance, for writers, of being able to read a representative sampling of the international production of their contemporaries cannot be underestimated. The broader and more rigorously universal the criteria employed in selection and publication of foreign literature in the home country, the greater the enrichment of the "soil" from which national expression springs, nurtured by the internationalist spirit which, as subsequent chapters will bring to light, has had its most immediate and direct exponent in contemporary Cuban poetry.

Before beginning an examination of Gente Nueva and Letras Cubanas, the two houses devoted to national literary production, we offer the following table of Arte y Literatura's editions between 1967 and 1986, based on a quantitative analysis of 1,380 titles grouped and published by nationality, epoch and genre.[5] It is on the basis of the historical comportment of titles or works published—their popularity and reception among the Cuban reading public—that the publishing house identifies genres or areas insufficiently represented and establishes future goals.

By nationality:

Latin America and Spain	509
Eastern Europe	241
Western Europe and U.S.	369
Asia and Africa	88
Miscellaneous (Art and Criticism)	173

By epoch:

Pre-nineteenth Century	75
Nineteenth Century	176
Twentieth Century	1083
Miscellaneous	46

By genre:

Novel	720
Short story	168
Poetry	126
Theater	74
Testimonio	52

---

[5]Empresa Editoriales de Cultura y Ciencia. Editorial Arte y Literatura. Statistical Report.

Essay	73
Criticism	80
Biography	24
Dictionary	1
Mixed	24
Other	38

Conscious of the disparity which exists between prose narrative and the other literary genres, corresponding to a tendency worldwide, Arte y Literatura has proposed compiling new anthologies of international poetry, theater and the essay, together with a greater effort aimed at promotion and dissemination of the classic works of Eastern Europe, Asia and Africa, and other literatures less familiar to the Cuban reader.

In the 1980s, Arte y Literatura attempted to infuse with greater rigor all Cuban editions of world literature, offering critical editions with notes and prologues directed at the Cuban readership, rather than following the format of the original; a project that has required a redoubling of efforts and even closer collaboration of specialists in a broad range of foreign literatures in the elaboration of critical editions.

Gente Nueva

The following will outline the objectives and operation of Gente Nueva, the publishing house that handles Cuban literary production for children and young readers. Considering that it is only one facet of national literary production in its entirety, it is unusual that Cuban children's literature has evolved to a point where it required a publishing house all its own rather than constituting a division or collection within a larger publishing house. This is due to two principal factors: the special emphasis placed on the literary formation of the population from earliest childhood on, since 1959, and the exigencies, from the production standpoint, of children's books. They are, in their majority, illustrated texts, requiring color reproductions and more demanding graphic design in addition to the permanent collaboration of advisors from primary and secondary schools, in their conception and elaboration, to make sure they are in keeping with young readers' development by grade and level. Children's literature experienced a renaissance as a result of the Revolution; the philosophical and social premises that prompted its emergence and subsequent development within the broader context of contemporary Cuban letters, from 1959 on, are outlined in Chapter 5.

Here, we will limit ourselves to analyzing the editorial philosophy of Gente
Nueva in its current phase, an overview of its offerings from 1967 to 1986.

Gente Nueva's editions include literary, artistic and scientific works for
young readers at all levels of development, from preschoolers and first graders
to high school students up to approximately fifteen years of age. Its publications
are grouped under four headings: Children's Literature, Historical and Patriotic
Works for Juvenile Readers, Literary and Social Works for Juvenile Readers, The
Juvenile Encyclopedia Series "Por los caminos de *La edad de oro*."

In the period from 1967 to 1986, Gente Nueva published a total of 968
titles in children's and juvenile literature.[6]

By nationality:

U.S.S.R.	77
Czechoslovakia	55
Germany	26
Bulgaria	3
Rumania	8
Poland	1
Mongolia	2
Vietnam	9
Spain	33
France	72
England	49
Finland	1
United States	33
New Zealand	1
Africa	1
Ireland	1
Italy	24
Norway	7
Greece	5
Holland	1
Japan	1
Denmark	4

[6]Statistics taken from the "Informe al Consejo de la Esfera." Empresa de
Editoriales de Cultura y Ciencia, Editorial Gente Nueva.

Switzerland	1
India	1
Chile	5
Colombia	12
Uruguay	4
Dominican Republic	1
Peru	1
Mexico	2
Guatemala	5
Argentina	11
Cuba	464
Other	47

By genre and topic:

Novel	209
Novella	3
Short Story	256
Poetry	60
Theater	22
Essay	40
Biography	47
Narrative	60
Testimonio	22
Legends	13
Fables	6
Graphics	2
Speeches	4
Hobbies	66
Comics	11
Fotonovela	5
Music, songbooks	11
Collected letters	4
Informational, current events	68
Journalistic	6
Monographs	7
Mixed	28
Catalogs	8
Other	10

Children's books are, with the exception of art books, the most technically complex in terms of graphics and production. Like many Cuban art books, the most complicated children's books rely on co-edition with foreign houses; a practice that allows works by Cuban authors to be produced in graphics shops with more sophisticated technology.

Statistics corroborate an upsurge in the literature for children and adolescents in Cuba dating from 1959, with 464 works by national authors published between 1968 and 1986:[7]

Year	Titles Published
1968*	14
1969	8
1970	5
1971	-
1972	11
1973	9
1974	17
1975	35
1976	24
1977	23
1978	-
1979	49
1980	48
1981	31
1982	11
1983	42
1984	44
1985	54
1986	39

*includes titles published in 1967

[7]Empresa Editoriales de Cultura y Ciencia. Editorial Gente Nueva. Statistical Report.

The sources for acquisition of new titles in children's literature are varied. Gente Nueva, like all Cuban publishing houses, evaluates manuscripts received "over the transom," even those by unknown, first-time authors. Many young writers work closely with editors from Gente Nueva, taking advantage of their close contacts with schools, cultural and scientific institutes, in order to keep up with young readers' concerns and interests. In addition to unsolicited manuscripts, Gente Nueva occasionally solicits works, within particular genres and on specific themes, from established writers. Since 1984, for example, Gente Nueva has made efforts to increase publication of works in art history and appreciation for young readers, working with Cuban authors and encouraging the collaboration of art critics, in the hope that juvenile literature might contribute to a greater knowledge and appreciation of art history among the young and even the very young. The same is true for literary criticism, monographs, biographies and the essay; the publishing house has attempted to both stimulate the cultivation of these genres among writers and increase their dissemination among school-age readers.

The predominant genres in children's literature are as follows, in descending order: short story, novel, essay and poetry. Many established authors, primarily known as writers of literature for adult readers, have worked with Gente Nueva's editors to create works for children, among them short story writer Onelio Jorge Cardoso and novelist Dora Alonso. Another project under way, which will include the poetry of Mirta Aguirre and Eliseo Diego, among others, is the collection of classics in children's and juvenile literature, to be published annually.

The privileged position children occupy in Cuban society and the active participation of a wide cross section of social sectors and spheres in their scholastic, artistic and cultural development, has given rise to an increasing number of creators of children's and juvenile literature.

In the early 1960s, when the publishing industry was just getting off the ground and there were relatively few national literary works for children, Cuba relied to a much greater degree on the editions of children's classics put out by foreign houses, particularly Soviet houses, like Progress Publishers, with foreign language editions. They were, and continue to be, imaginative editions produced, editorially, with great care, but they suffered from one irreparable defect: language. The translations into Spanish were, for the most part, done by republican Spaniards who had been granted asylum in the Soviet Union after the defeat of the Republican forces in the Spanish Civil War. In the highly sensitive matter of literary translation, it may be more accurate to lay the blame for the stilted translations on *Franquismo* and the historical circumstances that led scores of Spaniards to seek refuge in Russian cities than on the competence of individual translators. By the time the Soviet Spanish-language editions reached Cuba in the 1960s, more than twenty years had elapsed since their translation from the original.

By the 1980s, most of Gente Nueva's editors were writers and translators as well, who were careful to see that the Spanish translations of children's classics came across in "Cuban," adapting them whenever necessary so that they achieved a degree of simplicity, in contemporary terms, that approximated the feeling of the original.

In addition to the strictly editorial tasks, Gente Nueva participates in activities designed to promote extracurricular reading and an interest in literature on the part of young readers; among them, "The Author and His or Her Work," which takes writers to schools, summer camps and other educational and cultural centers so that children can meet and talk with them. Gente Nueva's editors collaborate with the Ministry of Education in research projects aimed at discovering techniques to improve students' reading habits and participate in colloquia sponsored by the Children's Literature Section of the Writers and Artists Union.

Letras Cubanas

Letras Cubanas, the last of the publishing houses we will examine here, was founded in 1977 to publish and disseminate classic and contemporary works of Cuban literature. Unlike the other two houses studied, Letras Cubanas is not an outgrowth of one of the editorial "series" of the Book Institute, it came into existence as a response to the "boom" in national literary output from the mid-1970s to the mid-1980s. Toward the end of the first phase of the Book Institute in the mid-1970s, prior to its break-up to form today's autonomous publishing houses, the increase in national literary production was beginning to make itself felt throughout all the institutions that supported, in one way or another, the wave of new Cuban literature. In addition, the structure and organization of the Writers and Artists Union, even with its own press, was not ideal for receiving and processing, editorially, all the new fiction that was being produced throughout the island. The UNEAC was intended to serve as a nucleus, a center that would bring established writers into contact with one another and provide assistance and support for novice writers through the workshops and literary contests it sponsored; it was never intended to develop into a full-fledged literary publishing house capable of handling the production of all national authors. As we indicated in the preceding chapter, the absence of publishing institutions capable of meeting the needs of the growing body of new writers was one of the most pressing problems in the realm of artistic and literary culture brought to light in the proceedings of the First Party Congress in 1975.

From 1959 to 1976, 1,544 titles by Cuban authors were published, in all. From 1977, the year it was founded, to 1986, Letras Cubanas published 958 titles; in less than ten years they had published more than half of the total number of titles published throughout the industry in the two preceding decades.[8] Together with Unión, the publishing wing of the Writers and Artists Union, whose members are, for the most part, established authors, Letras Cubanas' publications reflect the growth of the literary movement, its current rhythm and dynamics, while also including in its collections literary works from the nineteenth and first half of the twentieth centuries.

Of the 958 titles published by Letras Cubanas, twenty-four were the first published works of Cuban authors unknown to the reading public. To give a general idea of the tendencies at work in contemporary literary creation, we offer the following table which breaks the 958 titles published between 1977 and 1986 down by Department within the publishing house, genre or theme, reading public, edition, print-run, historical period in which the work was written and year of publication.[9]

Dept.	Titles Published	%	Print-run	%
Prose fiction	508	53.0	11,215,617	81.1
Poetry	195	20.4	1,141,415	8.3
Theater	61	6.4	304,130	2.2
Theory and Criticism	136	14.2	741,759	5.3
Art	58	6.0	429,348	3.1
TOTAL	958	100.0	13,832,269	100.0

---

[8]Empresa Editoriales de Cultura y Ciencia. Editorial Letras Cubanas. Statistical Report.

[9]Editorial Letras Cubanas. Statistical Report.

GENRE OR THEME

Genre				
Novel	190	19.9	6,110,485	44.2
Short Story	186	19.5	2,904,414	21.0
Testimonio	57	5.9	1,407,121	10.2
Biography	12	1.3	143,822	1.4
Epistolary	4	0.4	52,000	0.4
Journalism	25	2.6	300,364	2.2
Selected Works	10	1.0	62,425	0.5
Theater	61	6.5	304,130	2.2
Poetry	195	20.4	1,141,415	8.2
Music History and Criticism	19	1.9	94,485	0.6
Literary History and Criticism	88	9.2	392,441	2.7
Art History and Criticism	12	1.3	63,884	0.4
Drama History and Criticism	5	0.5	25,600	0.2
Film History and Criticism	2	0.2	10,300	0.1
Theory and Essays	9	0.9	120,122	0.9
Plastic Arts	8	0.8	45,681	0.3
Architecture	5	0.5	43,746	0.3
Photography	4	0.4	18,963	0.1
Dictionaries	5	0.5	135,306	0.8
Ethnology and Floklore	5	0.5	71,116	0.5
Dance	2	0.2	11,482	0.1
Other	52	5.4	366,974	2.6
Miscellaneous	2	0.2	5,993	0.1
TOTAL	958	100.0	13,832,269	100.0

READING PUBLIC

Public				
General	471	49.2	11,003,481	79.6
Specialized and Adult Education	487	50.8	2,828,788	20.4
TOTAL	958	100.0	13,832,269	100.0

EDITION

First	733	76.5	9,490,139	68.6
Second	202	21.1	4,042,174	29.2
Reprint	23	2.4	299,956	2.2
TOTAL	958	100.0	13,832,269	100.0

HISTORICAL PERIOD

Revolutionary	798	83.4	11,683,261	85.5
Period	78	8.1	823,038	5.9
XIX Century	78	8.1	1,309,789	9.5
XX Century	4	0.4	16,181	0.1
Other				
	958	100.0	13,832,269	100.0
TOTAL				

TITLES PUBLISHED ANNUALLY

YEAR	TITLES PUBLISHED	PRINT-RUN
1977	78	1,438,000
1978	56	985,000
1979	117	1,668,510
1980	88	1,860,400
1981	121	1,660,800
1982	86	1,771,000
1983	81	1,332,090
1984	136	1,475,190
1985	74	803,229
1986	91	838,050
TOTAL	928	13,832,269

The increase in new titles in traditional genres such as the novel, short story and poetry is immediately apparent, as is the appearance of genres that were rarely cultivated or could not find publishers and distributors in the decades prior to the Revolution, such as *testimonio*, journalistic works, drama and all branches of theory and criticism. Editions of art, architecture and photography are limited, not for lack of scholars and specialists working in these fields, but because of the complex graphics involved in reproductions which the industry is not technically prepared to handle on a large scale.[10]

Another tool of analysis at our disposal for examining the nature and characteristics of contemporary Cuban literary production, editorial philosophy and preferences among the reading public, is provided by the eight collections into which that production is grouped: Letras Cubanas, deluxe editions of nineteenth- and twentieth-century classics, as well as contemporary literature; Basic Library of Cuban Literature, more modest editions of literary works from the colonial and republican periods, Cuadernos de Arte, providing graphic material on the plastic arts and dance; Arte, the life and works of visual artists, in oversized editions; Girardilla, pocketbook editions of contemporary works in all genres; Radar, massive editions in the detective and science fiction genres; Saeta, massive editions of fiction in the "best-seller" category, and Espiral, for first-novels and other works of fiction by unknown authors. Another collection for new authors, Pluma en Ristre, which dates back to the Cuban Book Institute as part of the Arte y Literatura series, introduced the work of young writers, and was continued by Letras Cubanas, but has been discontinued, not because the output of young writers has diminished but because of a shift in the "classifying" function of all "collections" in the overall task of dissemination of literature. In the case of new authors, the labels of classification, as well as the purpose of special collections, becomes problematic; whereas other collections are grouped by the genre or epoch of the works themselves, Pluma en Ristre and Espiral covered *all* literary genres and grouped vastly diverse works under the common denominator of the writer's status as "novice." These collections served the purpose of stimulating the production of "virgin" writers, opening the doors to publishing houses and other means of access to the reading public. They were important vehicles which also enabled writers who had not had the means to publish their works before 1959 to emerge on the literary scene. While these important collections encouraged new literary production, they belong to a limited and specific stage in the literary trajectory of the nation which is in constant flux. The material foundations, literature's infrastructure, have evolved in accordance with the rhythms of the literary movement's development and the resources available; the mechanisms designed to stimulate the production of young writers and first-time authors do not remain static either. In a nation without book publishers, all writers are "novices" inasmuch as they remain unpublished and unknown to their

---

[10]Statistical information for this section covers the period up to and including 1986.

own reading public, even though they may have been writing for fifty years or have ten completed manuscripts stored away. As literary culture and its infrastructure grow, develop and broaden its scope, mechanisms, vehicles or institutions designed to foster literary creation that are no longer viable, rendered obsolete by a higher stage of development, must either evolve or disappear. This was the case with the concept of special collections for novice writers in the world of postrevolutionary Cuban letters. The publishers, who, day after day, and year after year, take the pulse of the corpus of creators and adapt to the rhythms of their production, are aware of this and made the decision themselves.

Such collections arose when the Cuban publishing industry was just getting off the ground and anxious to create vehicles for those authors whose works had never been disseminated nationally. The fledgling industry opened its doors to a small army of writers, both "novice" and "established" who welcomed the possibility of publishing their works, often for the first time, in Cuba. The existence of collections for unpublished authors, designed to encourage both those who were just starting out and more experienced writers whose works had remained in obscurity, was a powerful incentive, a vote of confidence, and led many "untried" talents to make a go of it.

By the mid-1980s, the function of such collections as a stimulus to unproven writers was better served by cultural institutions rather than editorial collections—through fellowships, prizes awarded to the winners of literary contests, and the publication of first-time authors in literary journals. The disappearance of all such editorial collections is inevitable; Pluma en Ristre has already been eliminated, only one remains:

> Nevertheless, Espiral should, in our opinion, be phased out slowly, so as not to produce a sudden gap in the programs and services available to young writers.[11]

The dichotomy existing between city and countryside has, for centuries, been a blight on the historical development of the Latin American continent as a whole, particularly with regard to cultural matters. If we examine the statistics for Cuban literary production from 1977 to 1986, reflecting the province in which each author resides, it becomes apparent that Havana and to a lesser extent Santiago—the traditional centers for the nation's cultural life—continue to domi-

---

[11] Empresa Editoriales de Cultura y Ciencia. Editorial Letras Cubanas. Statistical Report.

nate the literary panorama. The origins of the "Manigua" experiment recall the ingrained disdain toward "provincial" writers who could only gain national recognition by abandoning the provinces and immersing themselves in the literary life of the capital, at any cost. The statistical table of first-works has an impressive number by provincial authors who in the prerevolutionary decades would not have made their mark on the "cultural atlas" of the nation.

The first works of authors classified by province of residence have been recorded as follows:[12]

PROVINCE/YEAR	77	78	79	80	81	82	83	84	85	86	TOTAL
Pinar del Río											0
C. de la Habana	9	6	9	11	10	11	11	12	6	14	99
La Habana		1								1	2
I. Juventud				2							2
Matanzas					1						1
Villa Clara	1						1		1	1	4
Cienfuegos											0
Sancti Spíritus											0
Camagüey			1		1						2
Ciego de Avila	1										1
Las Tunas					1						1
Granma						2		1			3
Holguín									1	1	2
Santiago de Cuba	3	1	1							2	7
Guantánamo											0
TOTAL	14	7	12	11	15	13	12	13	8	19	124

It is clear that the capital, the "big city," still holds a strong attraction for young writers, despite the continued efforts of over a quarter of a century to extend cultural development more equitably throughout the nation so that the cultural level in Moa, for example, an extremely rural zone, will not be radically inferior to that of Havana. The historical background that inspired a mythology centering on the literary life of the capital is well grounded; Havana was the only place where one could nurture illusions of being a writer before 1959. The exodus of young writers from the countryside to the "big city" is not a problem peculiar to Cuba or to our times; it is an age-old, universal phenomenon. But in Cuba, by

---

[12]Empresa Editoriales de Cultura y Ciencia. Editorial Letras Cubanas. Statistical Report.

1987, relocation to the capital was no longer an obligatory "trial by fire" and "rite of passage" for all writers. A cultural and literary network was taking shape that allowed a writer from Camagüey or Pinar del Río to feel every bit as much a writer as his or her counterpart in Havana, without having to abandon the provinces in order to "make it."

In the strictest sense, one must take into account that the statistical table reflects authors' current place of residence but does not indicate where the ninety-nine authors who now make their home in Havana are from. It is most probable that not all are *habaneros* by birth.

Throughout the 1980s, most of the titles on Letras Cubanas publications lists are recent works; in past years, together with contemporary literature, they published and disseminated works by founding authors of the Cuban literary tradition of the nineteenth century. The classic authors of the nineteenth century have taken their place within special collections, notably the Basic Library of Cuban Literature. The debt to the founders of the national literary tradition had, in some small measure, been paid. The policy of limited reeditions, due, on the one hand, to the messy problem of warehousing case upon case of lead type, and on the other, to an editorial decision to give preference to the publication of new works over those that have already enjoyed wide dissemination, made for an editorial philosophy geared toward investing the greatest energy in current literature. The literary patrimony of the Antilles, in terms of print culture, has its origins in relatively recent history. This is fortunate for editors in that the literary "backlog" is a fairly manageable one, yet tragic when one considers the richness of the oral tradition that went unrecorded and all that was lost as a consequence of the late arrival of the printing press and its tight control by colonial authorities. If Cuban editors had been faced with more than two centuries of accumulated works to publish and distribute in accessible editions, they would never have been able to bring themselves up to date sufficiently to begin serving the living. It was a delicate balance that Cuban editors achieved and maintained when, with limited industrial capacity, they assumed the obligation of edition and distribution of a century and a half of accumulated works, often never before published on the island, while at the same time responding to the needs of a generation of contemporary writers, very much alive and productive.

The works of Cuba's prolific literary community were all printed on linotype equipment, and lack of warehouse space dictated that the boxes of lead type for each edition had to be melted down rather than stored. Such limitations severely affect the possibility of reedition for most works of literature. This, together with the commitment to publish the most current production, are the two greatest considerations in formulating editorial policy.

Critical studies and reviews of the most recent titles have been disseminated in articles appearing in weekly and monthly literary journals and this went a long way toward satisfying the need for literary criticism of what is being written today. It was being published regularly in the pages of periodicals like *Casa, El caimán barbudo, Gaceta, Bohemia, Conjunto, Revolución y cultura*. To this we may add the ongoing efforts of the National Library to fill in the gaps in the haphazard existence of Cuban bibliography in the first half of the century and the *Diccionario de la literatura cubana*, prepared by the Institute of Literature and Linguistics of the Cuban Academy of Sciences and published by Letras Cubanas.

In the interim, the Cuban editor has been called upon to assume, to some degree, the role of critic, without the aid and comfort of a wealth of critical treatises to support his or her assertions. In the absence of a "school" of works by veteran critics of contemporary literature, the greater part of the task of appreciation and critical analysis of recent works falls to the editor in the course of his or her work, before the printed volume reaches the reading public. To the multiple responsibilities of the Cuban editor we may add, in this sense, that of combatting the *idée reçue* of the editor as archenemy of the writer, in competition with the critic; an attitude which persists among even the most "illuminated" writers.... The following exchange between British writer Allan Sillitoe and two Soviet friends, a literary critic and a writer/editor, highlights the ironies of the situation:

> He [the critic] had written some excellent books. So we had a truce, and went over to the editors, whom I said, firing the opening shot, were just as much the natural enemy of the writer as the critic, even more so, perhaps. This was another gaffe, because Mark was an editor at the moment (or was it Frans?). You hardly meet a Soviet writer who isn't, hasn't been, or won't be, an editor.[13]

If we go back in history to the birth of the novel in England, coinciding with the disappearance of the Mecenas and the rise of the bookseller who fills in the vacuum, we find some of the root causes of the antagonism that characterizes the relationship between author and bookseller-editor in the market economy. Initially, booksellers fulfilled the function of editor and intermediary or

---

[13]Allan Sillitoe, *Road to Volgagrad* (New York: Alfred A. Knopf, 1964): 116-17.

agent to authors; further specialization occurred slowly, as the industry developed:

> Contemporary opinion was certainly much concerned with the new influence of the booksellers, and there were frequent assertions that it had had the effect of turning literature itself into a mere market commodity. This was expressed most succinctly by Defoe, in 1725: "Writing...is become a very considerable Branch of the English Commerce. The Booksellers are the Master Manufacturers or Employers. The several Writers, Authors, Copyers, Subwriters, and all other Operators with Pen and Ink are the workmen employed by the said Master Manufacturers.". . . Fielding went further, and explicitly connected this "fatal revolution" with a disastrous decline in literary standards: he asserted that the "paper merchants, commonly called booksellers," habitually employed "journeymen of the trade" without "the qualifications of any genius or learning," and suggested that their products had driven out good writing....[14]

Despite its lengthy historical tradition, the rigid compartmentalization of assigned duties in the literary arena is not an eternal "given," it is rather a function of production and distribution within the marketplace, whether it be literary works or automobiles. There is no good reason to divorce the act of writing from that of editing or critical analysis; there is an interrelation among the three activities, even though those who practice them individually are not fully conscious of this nexus. As long as writers remain aloof from the industrial mechanisms and procedures that are, in the end, essential to their vocation, they will suffer the consequences of their own ignorance.

The ideal might be, in the renaissance sense, to practice simultaneously all of the crafts involved; those of writer, critic and editor. This is precisely the tendency in noncommercial publishing, not only in Cuba but in many small independent presses in market economies as well.

At this juncture, let us consider the third point on the triangle: the critic. It is not within the purview of this study to offer a history of literary criticism in

---

[14]Ian Watt, *The Rise of the Novel* (Berkeley: University of California Press, 1967). Watt cites Daniel Defoe (William Lee, *Life and Writings of Daniel Defoe*, London, 1869, III) and Henry Fielding (*Social England*, eds. H.D. Traill and J.S. Mann, London, 1904), respectively, in *The Rise of the Novel*, 53-54.

Cuba. It is, however, instructive to examine some of the sociohistoric factors that have, since 1959, contributed favorably toward the development of the Cuban essay in general and literary studies in particular. The greatest contributing factor has been the postrevolutionary university and the astonishing increase in matriculated students in all departments. In 1984, one out of every three Cubans is enrolled in a course of study.[15] Studies at the university level allow—and demand—serious and constant application of critical and analytical faculties, the acquisition of an arsenal of theoretical and methodological tools, and the opportunity to use them in the context of the classroom; more Cubans have been formed in university classrooms since the Revolution than in all the republican decades, and the Humanities have benefitted enormously. Disciplines within the Humanities are traditionally the most vulnerable in times of economic crisis, when the student body tends, understandably, to concentrate on "utilitarian" majors; those that guarantee economic survival. There is a close relationship between access to institutions of higher education and the practice of criticism, analysis, research, and, of particular relevance to this study, their application to the literary phenomenon. The link between analytical work and the university ambiance is not a new one; the new and notable aspect is to be found in the educational development of Cuban society as a whole and the increase in those undertaking critical studies that begin to focus on contemporary literary production. In 1984, Letras Cubanas included nineteen previously unpublished volumes of essays and literary criticism. Together with the young essayists and critics, trained and in training, in the postrevolutionary university, other mechanisms were instituted in the 1980s, such as the Premio de la Crítica Literaria and the Premio Anual de la Crítica—awarded by a jury of established essayists and literary critics—which channeled energies toward a systematic analysis of new literary works. Mature, experienced researchers and critics, and graduate students in the universities, joined forces to channel literary analysis toward contemporary works.

The literary "avalanche," which was beginning to be felt in the decade of the 1980s, has been accompanied by corresponding works of critical reflection on the literary past, present and future. In terms of receptivity, reading public, and the industry, the 1980s offered optimum conditions for literary production of all forms.

---

[15]Miguel Cossío Woodward, "La planificación del sector cultural." *Revolución y Cultura* 4 (1984): 5.

Literature and the Blockade

The modus operandi of publishers, editors, designers and typographers for the last four decades has been to face the exigencies of edition and literary life as if the economic blockade did not exist. It was precisely this attitude that transformed what might have been been utter catastrophe for the nascent publishing industry into a grand challenge.

When one comes to know how books are produced in Cuba, how the industry was developed and the sacrifices involved—with appreciation for the *work* and the *book* which together constitute a vehicle for the transmission of knowledge and cultural values—there is little room or reason for objecting to the tone, more or less white, of the paper used or the degree of glossiness of the cover. Such considerations are part and parcel of a different approach to the literary product, considering each volume, in large part, in terms of its physical qualities, as merchandise, endowed with a greater or lesser degree of beauty or attractiveness.

On the international commercial market, Cuban books would be subject to the fierce competition which *all books* are subject to as rival merchandise in a market economy. Publishing houses that are not competitive are often "swallowed up" by transnational corporations able to avail themselves of the latest technology. A book's physical beauty as object and the cultural and intellectual merits of its contents are by no means at variance or in conflict, however, in a commercial market, the more superficial aspects can take on disproportionate weight; paper quality or cover design may be decisive in the life of a publishing house, independent of its significance as a disseminator of literature, culture and knowledge. Such considerations are hardly noble, and perhaps even a bit antiliterary, but they are real factors in the international book trade which Cuban houses will have to address in the future.

Anyone who has spent any length of time *inside* Cuban publishing may be initially astounded at the level of efficiency and meticulousness attained in all the phases and processes of editorial work, performed without the aid of modern equipment, which in the daily running of any publishing house in an industrialized nation would be inconceivable. Attributable to the ongoing blockade are the general absence of replacement parts for equipment in most printing presses, the absence of photocopiers, offset printers, and electric typewriters—even ribbons for the relatively few electric typewriters on the island are hard to come by. As a result, editorial work is twice as difficult and demanding as it would normally be. The overall lack of offset, wordprocessing and other time-saving equipment obliges most houses to print the majority of their books, except educational texts, on linotype machinery; an elaborate process which entails resetting lead type by hand for every revision, change or correction.

Long before a work arrives at the printing stage, the blockade has already complicated the editorial process. With the scarcity of photocopiers, manuscripts or typescripts are retyped in order to provide the multiple copies necessary for the editorial process.

A mechanical typewriter allows up to five copies to be made at a time with carbons. If ten copies of a manuscript are needed for editors, proofreaders and production, two typists will have to go to work; and manual typewriters are slow and noisy. Without photocopiers, limited reproductions of each manuscript circulate from hand to hand, making what should be simultaneous phases of editing and production consecutive.

And finally, one cannot fail to consider the number of presses and other equipment of U.S. origin and the impossibility of getting replacement parts for any of them. All Cuban magazines, more than one hundred, are printed in the same shop, on equipment from the U.S. in its entirety. They have been maintained and continue to function due to the contributions of the Asociación de Innovadores y Racionalizadores (ANIR) whose members, workers from all the nation's industries, invent and build "home made" parts to substitute for those that are unobtainable because of the blockade. What began spontaneously among workers and technicians at most factories in response to the blockade acquired, over time, the status of "method" and standard approach, making "invention" an indispensable part of daily life, the backbone of all branches of Cuban industry and a means for resolving, in some measure, the needs of Cuban industry exacerbated by the blockade; from creating a substitute for an imported screw to inventing a system for conservation of resources or upgrading technological processes. The ANIR's activities include: the substitution of national equivalents for imported raw and other materials; recovery and revitalization of dormant equipment; recovery and manufacture of replacement parts that were previously imported.[16] Replacement parts made by ANIR members, contributing to the longevity of essential equipment, can be found on display in many print shops, identifying the inventor of each part. The Cuban paper industry owes its renaissance, in large part, to the efforts of ANIR.

The sheer volume of production up to 1989 and the oil crisis, given inherent difficulties and those brought on by the blockade, are in and of themselves

---

[16]See Alberto Batista Reyes, "Las envidias tecnológicas de dios." *Química* 1.5 (January 1979): 12-13 for a more complete history of the ANIR.

a tribute to all branches of the book industry. The positioning of Cuban books in the global market will generate new exigencies in terms of the surface, physical aspect of literature and spur further development in graphics and design. Their export, when the U.S. trade embargo is lifted or new trading partners are found, may provide publishers with the greatest challenge they have faced to date.

From the Cane Fields to the Printing Press: The Bagasse Revolution That Almost Was

The raw material for paper now comes from two principal regions: North America and the Scandinavian peninsula, because of their forest lands. The introduction and cultivation of sugar cane on Cuban soil did away with the nation's precious woods, its forests, and the capacity to produce its own paper. It would be a singular example of "poetic justice" should cane sugar residue return to Cuba the capacity to produce paper after having been the cause of the elimination of its forests through the "slash and burn" policy of centuries ago. For roughly fifty years, various nations, including Cuba, have tried to produce paper, on an industrial scale, from sugar cane bagasse. The Cuban paper industry began production of a paper made from bagasse in 1837. In 1957, Jesús Azqueta, owner of the Papelera Moderna factory in Havana, decided to install another factory in Trinidad, on the outskirts of a sugar mill in order to take advantage of the bagasse that could be used as a raw material. The new factory was operational from 1959 to 1965 when it ceased production of white bond for book publishing.

Cuba has the greatest concentration of sugar cane residue, or bagasse, in the world, yet in the past only a small percentage of this cane byproduct was channelled for industrial use, the rest was used as fuel in the mills.[17]

Until the pilot plant was inaugurated in the 1970s, all of the paper produced in Cuba for printing and publishing continued to have a high percentage of imported wood pulp—up to sixty percent.

The Ministry of Culture bought white paper for book publishing abroad, but the sharp increase in the cost of paper in the early 1970s—in 1973, newsprint

---

[17]"Papel periódico procedente del bagazo de caña convertido en pulpa." *Química* 6 (June 1976): 35.

from the United States went from $187 to between $250 and $275 per ton[18]—unleashed a wave of experimentation with sugar cane derivatives that ultimately led to the production of a white bond paper at the Combinado de Papeles Blancos Jatibonico which is the only white paper in the world made from eighty percent sugar cane bagasse; the remaining twenty percent is wood pulp.

The Cuban Institute for Research on Cane Sugar Derivatives had been working intensely since the mid-1970s but it was not until the Jatibonico paper factory began to function that the extended phase of experimentation with cane residue yielded the long-awaited results, results which seemed to hold the potential for changing the course of industrial and editorial development not only for Cuba but for the "close to 45 underdeveloped nations whose economies rely almost exclusively on sugar exports."[19] In addition to solving the problem of providing a constant supply of high quality paper for the publishing industry, the Jatibonico factory also functioned, briefly, as a teaching facility for engineering students who would train workers, and there were plans to build a school near Jatibonico in order to train all those who will work in the nation's paper industry.[20]

The significance of the Jatibonico's experiment, even in the initial phase of production, has implications that extend far beyond the world of Cuban publishing; discovery of the industrial process by which sugar cane bagasse is transformed into bond and newsprint has enormous repercussions for the future of print culture:

> The Cuban experiment coincides with a call made by the FAO and the PNUD [Programa de Naciones Unidas para el Desarrollo] for coordinated world action to avert the potential paper and wood pulp crisis.

> In many developing nations there is a shortage of newsprint which has forced publishers to use a smaller newspaper format and reduce the number of school newspapers.[21]

---

[18]"Papel periódico procedente del bagazo de caña," 37.

[19]Gilberto Caballero. "Un papel dulce." *Prisma latinoamericano* 3 (1984): 46.

[20]"Pruebas de producción en el Combinado de Papeles Blancos de Jatibonico," *Granma* (March 20, 1984): 2.

[21]"Papel periódico procedente del bagazo de caña," 38.

This also had implications for the economic and industrial development of sugar-exporting nations in Latin America, Asia and Africa:

> By the time this paper is published, the "miracle" of transforming bagasse into book quality paper will have been consummated and the giant plant in Sancti Spiritus province will be producing its first "reams" and will have helped make the industrialization of the nation, one of the basic objectives of economic development in Cuba, something more than a dream. [22]

In terms of literary production and the editorial "machine," the ramifications are obvious; the potential for publishing books that were one hundred percent Cuban. When paper can be produced in sufficient quantities to cover the volume of national literary creation and production, there will be a much greater margin of flexibility with regard to the annual lists of titles pending, print runs and design, as well as the time frame for transforming manuscripts into books, having eliminated the "enigma" of international availability of quality, affordable paper for book publishing. This would allow literature to be published at a rhythm more in keeping with that of creation, rather than falling perpetually behind the creative "flow," with the publishing industry free of its dependence on a raw material that grows increasingly scarcer and more costly. After the first year of Jatibonico's "experimental" phase, Cuban houses began to publish the first books on "bagasse bond" in print runs of either ten or twenty thousand copies. Research was not continued beyond this phase, and the process of transforming bagasse into durable, quality paper has not yet proven viable on a large scale.

Paper consumption has always been an indicator of the cultural dynamism of a given society. The 1917 Revolution brought on a colossal increase in paper consumption in the Soviet Union:.

> In 1913 we consumed only 87 thousand tons of paper in the whole country. Two thirds of it was imported. And yet it was sufficient not only for us but for Poland and the Baltic Provinces as well.

---

[22] Abascal López, "Un gigante de papel," 22.

Now we use 675 thousand tons of paper, none of it imported. But it is not enough.[23]

Cuban publishers, who have come close but never achieved the self-sufficiency that domestic paper production would afford, echo the lament that "it is never enough," aware that creative potential surpasses the infrastructure's capacity to satisfy growing material needs in the cultural and literary spheres:

We continue to have limitations; when we develop polygraphic capacity, we discover that we're short on paper. We set the "Uruguay" paper plant in motion, with a significant production capacity, but it's not enough. Nothing is ever enough in an underdeveloped country because the historical accumulation of need is so great. And when it explodes—and it is exploding all around us every day—the poor editors want to jump out the window because they are constantly under pressure; writers want to see their work in print right away. They don't write in order to put their works in a drawer. Editors have the sensation that they are always in debt to someone.[24]

---

[23]Sergei Tretiakov, "Words Become Deeds: The Press and Books in the Soviet Union," *Communication and Class Struggle*, Vol. II, Armand Mattelart, Seth Sieglaub, eds. (New York: International General, 1983): 266.

[24] Interview with Rolando Rodríguez, January 30, 1985.

CHAPTER 8. FIN DE SIÈCLE: LITERARY CULTURE AT THE CROSS-ROADS

Expanding Horizons: Genre in Cuban Literature 1959-89

The film viewer who, after seeing an adaptation of a novel by Charles Dickens, wants to read the work itself, might find it unbearable reading because of all the subplots and digressions contained therein, so distinct from the abridged film version which followed the main plot and developed it in linear fashion straight through to the denouement. The reason for the abundant subplots and digressions was financial: Dickens wrote his novels in installments for the London newspapers of the day. The longer the novel, the better paid and fed was the novelist. Had these economic conditioning factors not existed, Dickens might have employed a different narrative style, exercised greater verbal restraint or even cultivated other literary genres.[1] What is certain is that literary genres are influenced, to one degree or another, by existing material conditions in the society in which they are cultivated.

In Cuba, in the republican period, the equation was inverted; everything seemed to favor brevity. The short story was the dominant genre because a vehicle for its dissemination was in place—the literary journal—there was a guaranteed reading public *and* remuneration. The pay was miserable, as we have seen, but the journals and magazines did pay the authors of short stories accepted for publication. The major journals and magazines of the day published four or five short stories in each issue; other genres did not enjoy the same good fortune, those that could not avail themselves of this channel for dissemination. The literary contests of this period, in which short stories, brief narratives and articles were the dominant genres, also contributed to the short story's growing dominance on the literary panorama.

It is a widely accepted generalization that the novel—due to its relatively long gestation period and the resources it requires—takes root more readily in societies with a stable book publishing tradition, whereas the shorter literary

---

[1]For more detail on Dickens and other novelists of his time, see Ian Watt, *The Rise of the Novel* (Berkeley: University of California Press, 1967).

genres tend to predominate in societies that lack mechanisms for the publication and dissemination of literary works or cultural institutions that support writers. This holds true, at least in the case of Cuba, if we compare the broad gamut of literary genres cultivated in the revolutionary period with their scant representation in earlier periods. The decades from 1959-89 fostered greater cultivation of the novel, testimonial literature and other lengthy narrative forms and expressions not widely published, for the reasons indicated above.

As noted, in the first years of the Revolution what was being published was overwhelmingly the finished manuscripts that had been put aside, stored in desk drawers and file cabinets with few or no outlets for publication. The first true literary explosion, in terms of genre, that the Revolution produced, occurred in the realm of poetry, as the statistics on titles published annually by Cuban authors indicate:

Year	Novel	Short Story	Poetry
1959	6	10	43
1960	11	14	52
1961	9	13	55
1962	14	16	69

This tendency began to experience a change of course in the early 1970s; in 1974, for example, sixteen novels by Cuban authors were published, with an equal number of poetry titles published the same year:[2] "It was always said that Cuba was a nation of poets and short story writers. No: Cuba is a nation of poets and narrators."[3]

If we take stock of Cuban literary production from 1959 through the 1980s, poetry stands out as the most cultivated genre, followed by the novel and prose narrative in general, which includes the essay and *testimonio* in addition to the short story, all of which caught up with poetry in the 1970s. Literary magazines publish journalistic articles, *testimonios*—the equivalent of the old "first hand

---

[2]Statistical Table: By genre and year of publication. Editorial Letras Cubanas, August, 1979.

[3]Interview with Luis Suardíaz, January 30, 1985.

accounts" that used to be published, in terms of their prevalence—excerpts from novels and, of course, short stories.

The majority of Cuban writers of this period cultivated several genres; short story writers, for example, experimented with the novel; poets cultivated testimonial narrative; novelists tried their hand at children's literature.

Cuban poetry reflected the revolutionary epic as it was occurring; it has been the most contemporary of genres in its themes, drawing its raw material from the everyday life of Cubans and their articulation with the world, to the rhythm of history unfolding. The Cuban short story, as well, due to its brevity and predominance among young writers, those born after the Revolution. With time, once the repository of unexploited historical themes has been exhausted, Cuban novels and testimonial narratives will increasingly exploit themes from contemporary reality, expressing their own historical epoch, setting, and problems, linking past and present in a vision that reflects the immediacy of the moment and projects into the future, as both cinema and the new song movment have done. The links that allow such fluidity exist. The novel, because of the elasticity and capacity for synthesis that characterize the genre, must eventually assume the challenge implicit in taking on immediate reality, recreating the world of the present in literature, beginning where the last word of Carpentier's contemporary epic, *Consagración de la primavera*, leaves off.

Postrevolutionary literature "unbound," in all genres, overstepped traditional boundaries and was everywhere at once, intermixing with the new song movement, film, the graphic arts and reportage; it escaped from within book jackets and the confines of academia to the street, to factories and sugar mills, to the posters and street signs on which the traveler's gaze rests.

The new relations forged between print literature and poster art, literature and cinema, *testimonio* and the new song movement reveal a dynamic, fluid concept of culture, of literary creation and its new function. Cinema and literature influenced each other mutually; themes treated in earlier films were echoed in a contemporary literature which was grappling with the past from a critical stance while newer literary works were brought to the screen, translated into the language of modern cinematography:

> [I]n silent film and the early days of talking pictures it was understood that dramaturgy for the theater was the principal source of dramaturgy for cinema.... This was an erroneous point of view; it is in prose literature that dramaturgy for cinema finds its most immediate source, just

as contemporary prose fiction has been profoundly influenced by cinema.[4]

To date, at least five works of national literature have been translated into film: *El siglo de las luces*, *Cecilia Valdés* and *El otro Francisco*, on or from the historical past, *Canción de Rachel* and *Memorias del subdesarrollo*, written in the early years of the Revolution. Cuban cinema has reflected with greater immediacy than the novel the challenges and contradictions of present reality.

All over the continent and on the Iberian peninsula, the union of Spanish-language poetry and song has been a constant; we need only remember the music composed by Serrat for the verses of Benedetti or Machado, or the phenomenon of the poet-troubador. In 1984, two books were published that underscored this relationship and highlighted the growing recognition which poet-troubadors have earned, as authors in their own right: *Hablar por hablar*, by Carlos Puebla, in which we find

> the voice of the bard, forever a poet, which recently made its presence felt in our reality in the feverish pages of what would be his first book.[5]

And *Silvio: que levante la mano la guitarra*, from which we include a fragment of the suggestive exchange between the editors—both poets and novelists—and the poet-troubador:

> —We know that you also write poetry; that is, poetry not sung. Why is it that certain themes become songs and others poems?
> —I don't think it has to do with thematic content. I believe that any topic is appropriate for a song (if it is poetry set to music), and the same is true of a poem intended to be read and spoken.[6]

---

[4]Miguel Torres. "Necesidad del guionista," in *Cine, literatura, sociedad*. Ambrosio Fornet, ed. (Havana: Editorial Letras Cubanas, 1983): 123.

[5]Carlos Puebla. *Hablar por hablar*, from the prologue by Joaquín G. Santana (Havana: Editorial Unión, 1984): 13.

[6]Silvio Rodríguez. *Silvio: que levante la mano la guitarra*, Victor Casáus, Luis Rogelio Nogueras, eds. (Havana: Editorial Letras Cubanas, 1984): 230.

Interesting distinction: poetry to be sung and poetry to be read. With its publication in book form, the "new song" poetry of Silvio Rodríguez will be read as well, like the poetry of Guillén, Neruda, Vallejo and so many other Latin American poets who gained wider readership after their verses were set to music and popularized by troubadors of the new song movement.

Literature and Revolution: Cuba in Context

There are those who believe that the use of quotations, as a modality, constitutes an abuse of the reader and a writer's vice. It is decidedly one of mine, since I consider the thoughts and formulations of others, past and present, to provide writers with raw material for new ideas and explorations.

I am not the first to have concerned myself with the origins and destiny of the printed volume. Scholarly curiosity in this realm was aroused at the time of the invention of the printing press and has been vital to the development of literary culture ever since. It is for all the reasons either expressed or suggested above that I would like to conclude my study with a beneficent dissection of the thoughts of two great thinkers—one from the nineteenth century, the other from our own, one from the "old" world, the other from the "new"—on the social destiny of print literature.

The lyric poet and prolific essayist Heinrich Heine, friend to Marx while exiled in Paris, great admirer of the Paris Commune—although he later fell victim to the ambiguity suffered by so many intellectuals when confronted with the very revolutionary processes they profess to admire—advocated the just cause of the masses against monarchical tyranny, while his youthful heart bleeds for the fate of poetry, fearing that conquest of the universal right to bread will bring about poetry's demise. His feverish mind visited a future in which the pages from his first book of verse would be ripped out one by one in order to wrap groceries. The mature Heine realized the error of such, often fatal, ambiguity:

> A terrible syllogism holds me in its grip, and if I am unable to refute the premise, "that every man has the right to eat," then I am forced to submit to all its consequences. From much thinking about it I am on the verge of losing my reason. I see all the demons of truth dancing trium-

phantly around me, and at length the generosity of despair takes possession of my heart and I cry: "For long this old society has been judged
and condemned. Let justice be done! Let this old world be smashed in
which innocence is long since dead, where egoism prospers, and man
battens on man! Let these old whited sepulchres be destroyed from top
to bottom, these caverns of falsehood and iniquity. And blessed be the
grocer who shall one day use the pages of my poems as paper bags for
the coffee and snuff of poor women, who in this present world of injus-
tice too often have gone without that solace. Fiat justitia, pereat mun-
dus![7]

With the pronounced diffidence of one who discovers that, in the end, he
has been faithful to a given truth, Heine's attitude is nonetheless elitist in the
order of its priorities—we suspect that, deep down, books always came first for
him and the masses, second. The times ahead, had he lived through them, would
have taught Heine a fundamental lesson. It would not be the humble masses in
their "ignorance" who would mutilate his books; this would be carried out, quite
intentionally, by the European aristocrats and officials who headed the forces of
repression in their campaign to preserve the status quo.

More than a century later, Ezequiel Martínez Estrada reexamines the problems posed by the German poet, his spiritual dilemma, placing them at the center
of his essay "Por una alta cultura popular y socialista," within the context of a
functional majority culture:

Heine's position was that of the poet who fears that the angry mob
might set fire to the libraries and loot the museums. But years later, in
Lutecia or *Confessions*, I don't recall which, he tells the tale, in his
inimitable style, of how he experienced terror at the thought that his
volumes of love poems might serve the needs of an old woman selling
groceries who, ripping out the pages, would use them to wrap coffee or
tobacco; after reflection he determined that if this were so that someone
who could never before do so enjoyed a cup of coffee or a peaceful
smoke, then it wasn't such a bad thing that his verses also had this
ultimate fate.

-----

[7]Frederich Ewen, ed. *The Poetry and Prose of Heinrich Heine* (New York:
Citadel Press, 1948), from the introduction, "Heinrich Heine: Humanity's Sol-
dier," 49-50.

I believe, in the same way, that only an egotistical hedonism would refuse to allow our poems to be used for such humble purposes, since we do not write them to preserve them from such foreseeable risks. In the end we can never know whether, by mysterious design of the gods, our books might serve, in decisive moments, some other purpose, in addition to reading them.[8]

Both thinkers, at different historical junctures and from very different perspectives, have expressed serious concern for literature's destiny in a functional, democratic culture; each has ultimately had to face the inexorable truth that once released from the poet's soul, the book no longer belongs to its creator, but to the men and women who, in reading and assimilating it, make it their own.

The Heinean image of coffee and tobacco wrapped in sheets of verse is, of course, hyperbolic. Once the "divine right to bread," to education, culture and human dignity has been won through profound social revolution, it is unlikely that the "humble masses" would ever tear the pages from a book of verse to wrap groceries; on the contrary, they would read and preserve such poetry as the most precious legacy. Or, accepting Heine's premise that such a situation might arise, they would, with heavy heart and full awareness of all that had been invested socially, spiritually and historically, in the existence of that printed volume of poetry, use its pages as wrapping paper, in a moment of great need, in order that someone might be able to take a bit of food home. In a recent independent film, *Smoke*, a novelist recounts to a young student the long shaggy-dog tale of how literary theorist Bakhtin was holed up, snowbound, with a tin of magnificent fresh tobacco and nothing to roll it in. In a punchline that echoes Heine's ultimate reconciliation with the world of the senses, Bakhtin "smokes his book" and, under the circumstances, does not regret it.

Such occurrences, imagined or real, do not, in the end, concern us greatly. Books are not written to be kept under lock and key. In addition to reading them, they may also serve to shore up a wobbly table leg, or preserve a flower between their pages for drying. Far from being a sacrilege, it seems logical and perhaps even beautiful that books may serve, after and in addition to reading them, many other purposes.

---

[8]Ezequiel Martínez Estrada, "Por una alta cultura popular y socialista," in *En Cuba y al servicio de la Revolución Cubana* (Havana: Ediciones Unión, 1963): 161.

Inquiry into the social destiny of print literature, an issue which has always generated controversy, is nonetheless a necessary task, more so all the time in our electronic age. And so, our attention is called to the fact that two such rigorous thinkers would choose as the point of departure for their analysis the printed volume as *fait accompli*; launching their ideas on culture and the literary product as if print culture, and all that supports its existence, were a fact, a social and material *given*; as if the entire, complex framework necessary for literary production were eternal. We have simply inverted the terms, not content merely to ask ourselves: What is to be the fate of literature in society after a work has been written and published? but also: How does literature come to exist fully, to realize its potential in the fullest sense? in examining the multitude of subtle social forces that condition its destiny, that inform and shape the relationship that is established between literature and society in the broadest sense, while at the same time presenting a historical and social inquiry into literature's existence as material fact.

A work of literature, once it has been published and disseminated, is immortalized in the readers who perpetuate its existence from generation to generation, and the literary process in its totality encompasses so much more than the solitary act of creation. This process, whose most immediate and tangible end-result is the printed volume, cannot be reduced to the sum of its material components, as human beings are so obviously much more than water and seven or eight basic chemical elements. Yet if one essential element is missing, the entire process comes to a halt: both the vital process that sustains life and that of literary creation. Readers of the anonymous Aztec poems that survived the Conquest, are invariably moved by the disturbing juxtaposition, in the verses, of the mortal, physical phenomenon of "the walls splattered with gore"[9] and the devastating spiritual reality of the systematic destruction of a civilization. The Aztecs were not afflicted by the false dichotomy of "body and soul" that has distorted so much of Western thought.

One encounters echoes of the same distortion in our understanding and perception of literary culture: purists have studied it as if it were all "spirit" with no ties to bind it to material existence, whereas many of the new critics, the structuralists and semioticians that followed, have reduced the literary phenomenon to the condition of *scarab*, to that of a linguistic schema devoid of historic dimension, of spiritual, social, human content.

---

[9]Miguel León Portilla, ed., *The Broken Spears: The Aztec Account of the Conquest of Mexico*, Lysander Kemp, trans. (Boston: Beacon Press, 1962): 137.

In chronicling the Cuban literary process in its totality, I wanted to pay tribute to both the "body" and "soul" of literature, acknowledging the essential role of the craftsmanship, intellectual, manual and industrial, too often relegated to anonymity, on which the existence of a poem or a novel rests, from its origins in the creator's imagination until it reaches our hands.

Diminishing Horizons: Print Culture in Transition

The myriad events marking 1992, primarily in Europe and the Americas, brought Cuban poet, essayist and director of Casa de las Américas, Roberto Fernández Retamar, and his wife, art historian Adelaida de Juan, to New York, as part of their lecture tour. Over dinner one evening, our conversation turned to the period of 1984-85 during which I conducted research in Havana and formed a network of friends and colleagues in the literary, academic and publishing spheres. Fernández Retamar made a casual observation, almost in passing, that my study of Cuban literary culture was now a "classic" in that it dealt with print culture and the social process up to and including its "golden age" within the revolution, when there was still access to paper, ink, technology and energy, without having to expend precious dollars in the effort.

Literary production continued pretty much apace with writers' output and readers' consumption through 1989, the collapse of the Soviet Union and the socialist block, and into 1990, while existing supplies lasted. But by 1991, my last trip to the island, print culture and the literary life were coming apart at the seams, struggling to survive in a radically altered landscape, and revealing the initial, dramatic signs of a crisis that would endure and deepen over the coming years.

Gifted editors I knew, who had always been overburdened and in constant demand, were sitting at home waiting out the storm; publishers were "on leave" writing books they hadn't found time for before, but that wouldn't be published in Cuba any time soon; writers were in crisis, regrouping energies or on fellow-ships in Mexico or Europe. Others were hard at work designing a new version of the old Book Institute—the umbrella organization that emerged in the turbulent 1960s to pool people and resources during *that* period of transition—in an attempt to navigate through the 1990s and keep alive at least a skeletal infrastructure for literary culture.

Crises, by definition, do not last forever, and the existential "slump," the necessary catharsis, must sooner or later give way to movement, to the vague first steps, however tentative and imprecise, that allow for transition toward new forms, mandated by changed circumstances. This holds equally true for individuals, cultures and societies. Crisis precedes a period of transition during which new links, and the cement with which to secure them more permanently, are formed.

The current crisis is certainly not the first in Cuba's history to unsettle literary life and change the trajectory of print culture. There is a cyclical pattern to literary life, and that spiral of rupture and continuity is precisely what this study has sought to reveal by taking the long view of print culture, focusing on the shifts in its development, from its origins with the arrival of the printing press in 1720, on.

Although the printing press operated under the severe restrictions imposed by the Spanish colonial administration, by 1860 and the onset of the Ten Years War (1868-78), there had already been one short-lived renaissance followed by a longer literary rut. When the major publishing "boom" of the 1840s went bust, the void was soon filled by the literary journals that provided an outlet for writers until the next "boom" of the 1890s.

The end of the nineteenth century, with the transition from Spanish colonial rule to the U.S. sphere of influence, did not have a marked effect on print culture, at least not until 1906 and the first U.S. intervention under the Platt Amendment. With intervention, the reality of the movement away from one sphere of influence and into another hit home, and brought on, among writers and intellectuals, a period of quietude, introspection and self-examination, not only in Cuba but throughout Latin America, in the wake of the Spanish-American War.

In Cuba, the decade from 1920 to 1930 witnessed yet another boom, followed by repression, censorship and a contraction in the public space for print culture, and the void was eventually filled once again by a proliferation of small literary journals.

What remains a constant throughout the nineteenth and the first half of the twentieth century are the factors limiting the steady growth of a market for literature: the lack of a stable, broad-based reading public able to afford books, or at least periodicals, on a regular basis. The educational and cultural campaigns of the revolution created that stable, mass readership, together with diverse state-subsidized publishing houses, removing both historical obstacles, but from 1989 on, Cuba could no longer afford to sustain the dynamic rhythms and steady growth of its own print culture. With the demise of the Berlin Wall and rapid global restructuring that ensued, Cuba lost with one blow all of its Eastern bloc trading partners and suppliers, now going through their own production crises and demanding convertible currency for goods. And individual Cubans had less "disposable income" with which to buy the dwindling literary output of Cuban houses.

The so-called dollarization of the Cuban economy has been an ongoing, though uneven process since 1989, sweeping in apparently random fashion across different sectors of the economy. With increasing numbers of Cubans buying food, clothing and other necessities in dollars on the black market, the process ultimately, or perhaps inevitably, grew to encompass literary production as well, with Letras Cubanas, Cuba's major literary house, opening a controversial "dollar" bookshop in its historic headquarters in an Old Havana frequented by tourists.

The social, cultural and psychological effects of a gradual dollarization of the Cuban economy have been apparent enough to anyone studying the process, as the haunting series of vignettes in the recent film "Mujer transparente" made clear. In the literary sphere, the repercussions, the stresses and strains, of this process have had an equal, though much less documented, impact. A statistical report of titles published by Letras Cubanas, the major literary house, through 1990, stops at 1988, when only five novels were published, down from 25 to 30 new novels per year in the early and mid-1980s; there is a corresponding drop in new titles in literary theory and criticism, with only four published in 1988, down from more than twenty new titles per year in the early to mid-1980s. After 1988, near silence.

Social theorists of literature from Robert Escarpit to Wolfgang Iser have long posited that it is the convergence of text and reader which brings the literary work into existence. One of the terrible ironies of the present crisis is its "timing." Cuba, as a society, invested so much in the literary life of the nation, in creating conditions that would bring forth the "ideal society" dear to reception theorists and sociologists of literature, a society with a mass readership in tune to and conversant with its literary tradition, only to have it virtually "shut down" in a period in which the better part of the so-called First World nations are undergoing a transition toward a more uniformly electronic age. At present in the U.S. and western Europe, what was once considered "serious reading" for its own sake and, in fact, almost all literary exchange, is fast becoming a marginal, elite activity.[10] Yet the ultimate destiny of print literature, and the cultural traditions and practices that have developed in its wake, is far too weighty a note to end

---

[10]This is the underlying thread running through the recently published reflection on reading and literary culture, Sven Birkerts, *The Gutenberg Elegies: The Fate of Reading in an Electronic Age* (New York: Fawcett Columbine, 1995).

on. The verdict is not yet in on literary culture's chances for survival into the twenty-first century.

The fin-de-siècle lull in Cuba's once vibrant literary life has more immediate, traceable origins in the twin forces of dollarization, on the one hand, and lack of resources to sustain a rather highly developed apparatus for the edition and dissemination of print culture.

One novelist's response to the dollarization of Cuban literary life has been to shop, on trips abroad, for desktop publishing software. With Cuban publishers buying supplies on the open market with convertible currency, and obliged, as a consequence, to sell Cuban literary titles in the dollar shops, no one, he argued, would read his novels. Tourists would buy lighter "beach" fare, and Cubans would conserve their scarce dollars for more essential goods. He determined, in the face of these pressures, to initiate a kind of neosamizdat, publishing his own literary works at home on his computer, in very limited editions, and distributing them through alternate channels, outside of the dollar circuit. That is one individual response to the current impasse but certainly not a strategy adequate to the task of bringing literary culture back to life.

From the perspective of those on the outside looking in, U.S. investors have looked on in frustration as European, Canadian and Latin American investors descended on Cuba while they are kept at arm's length by the embargo. *The New York Review of Books*, along with other publications, has noted the arrival in Havana of a virtual army of U.S. publishers in the last year or so. Aware of "idle" talent that could be put to use, of the scores of Cuban editors with decades of experience sitting around with nothing to do, U.S. publishers went on a scouting mission, testing the waters in anticipation of an eventual normalization of relations. It is no secret that all of the major trade publishers in the U.S. have begun publishing in Spanish for domestic consumption, breaking into the large but mostly untapped and unexplored Spanish-language market for literature. Once the site or "hub" of publication and distribution throughout continental Latin America of *Selecciones del Reader's Digest* and other periodicals in Spanish, Cuba, because of its geographical proximity and highly literate population—not to mention all of the experienced publishing professionals "in between projects"—would appear to be a "natural" partner in such a venture.

It is a rare historic privilege for a Caribbean island nation, any Caribbean island nation, given the colonial legacy of the region, one that tipped the scales *against* a common print culture for the majority of the citizens, to find itself experiencing the kind of "slump" in literary and publishing activity Cuba faces today. Most Caribbean societies have neither overall adult literacy nor a surplus of professionals in the graphics and publishing trades.

For the past five or so years, publishers, manuscript editors, printers and graphic designers have remained idle or abandoned the field altogether, while Cuban literature was often printed in Mexico, Colombia or elsewhere with a Cuban house's logo affixed, a posteriori. I am certain that the Cuban professionals and craftsmen who have dedicated themselves to print culture and the literary life will not remain idle much longer. What no one can be certain of is how these forces, now in hiatus, will regroup when Cuba's centuries-old literary dynamic regains its lost momentum. It is not just print culture, the foundations of a literary tradition, that is in transition, but Cuban society itself.

BIBLIOGRAPHY

Socioliterary

Abascal López, Jesús. "Un gigante de papel." *Cuba* 3 (1984): 21-27.

Acosta, Leonardo. "Cincuenta años de la *Revista de avance.*" *Revolución y cultura* (October 1977): 74-80.

Agüero, Luis. "La novela." *Casa de las Américas*, 22-23 (January-April 1964): 64-67.

Aguirre, Mirta. *Ayer de hoy.* Havana: Ediciones Unión, 1980.

Almendros, Herminio. "La imaginación infantil y las lecturas para niños." *Revolución, letras, arte.* Havana: Letras Cubanas, 1980. 467-80.

Alvarez, Imeldo. "Del Taller a los libros." *Revolución y cultura* (March 1985): 20-25.

—. *La novela cubana en al siglo XX.* Havana: Letras Cubanas, 1980.

Arias, Salvador, Adelaida de Juan, et al., *La cultura en Cuba socialista.* Havana: Letras Cubanas, 1982.

Augier, Angel. "Cuba: los escritores y la literatura en el proceso revolucionario." *De la sangre en la letra.* Havana: Ediciones Unión, 1977. 423-35.

—. *Nicolás Guillén: Notas para un estudio biográfico-crítico.* Las Villas: Editora del Consejo Nacional de Universidades, Universidad Central de las Villas, 1964.

Avilés Fabila, René. *El escritor y sus problemas.* México: Fondo de Cultura Económica, 1975.

Barthes, Roland, Henri Lefebvre, Lucien Goldmann, et al., *Literatura y sociedad: problemas de metodología en sociología de la literatura.* Barcelona: Ediciones Martínez Roca, 1977.

—. *Mythologies.* Annette Lavers, trans. New York: Hill and Wang, 1977.

—. *Writing Degree Zero.* Annette Lavers and Colin Smith, trans. New York: Hill and Wang, 1977.

Batista Reyes, Alberto. "Las envidias tecnológicas de dios." *Química* 1.5 (January 1979): 12-13.

—. "La narrativa: distintas vías para la imaginación." *Panorama de la literatura cubana (1959-1984).* Havana: Letras Cubanas, 1985. 36-41.

—. "Las voces de un testigo mudo." *Química* 3 (March 1978): 3-6.

Beiro Alvarez, Luis. "Veinte años del libro, otro triunfo de la Revolución." *Bohemia* (June 8, 1979): 10-13.

Beltrán, Luis Ramiro, and Elizabeth Fox Cardona. "Latin America and the United States: Flaws in the Free Flow of Information," in *National Sovereignty and International Communication*, Kaarle Nordenstreng and Herbert I. Schiller, eds. Norwood, N.J.: Ablex Publishing, 1979. 33-59.

Benedetti, Mario. *El escritor latinoamericano y la revolución posible.* México: Editorial Nueva Imagen, 1978.

—, and Alejo Carpentier. *Literatura y arte nuevo en Cuba.* Barcelona: Editorial Laia, 1977.

Biblioteca Nacional José Martí. *Bibliografía cubana 1959-1962.* Havana: Instituto del Libro, 1968.

Boletín ACNU (July-December, 1975). "Papel periódico procedente del bagazo de caña convertido en pulpa." *Química* 6 (June 1976): 35-37. Reprinted from *Boletín ACNU* (July-December 1975).

Boudet, Rosa Ileana. "Veinticinco aniversario del teatro de la Revolución." *Conjunto* 60 (April-June, 1984): 12-18.

Bueno, Salvador. *Medio siglo de literatura cubana (1902-1952).* Havana: Publicaciones de la Comisión Nacional Cubana de la UNESCO, 1953.

—. "La 'Revista Habanera'." *Revista de la Biblioteca Nacional* (July-September, 1957): 139-58.

Bullock, Warren B. *The Romance of Paper.* Boston: The Gorham Press, 1933.

Caballero, Gilberto. "Un papel dulce." *Prisma latinoamericano* 3 (1984): 46-47.

Cairo, Ana. "Apuntes para un estudio 'literario' de la Revolución del 30." *Santiago* 25 (March 1977): 91-141.

—. *El Grupo Minorista y su tiempo.* Havana: Editorial de las Ciencias Sociales, 1978.

Cámara Cubana del Libro. *El libro en Cuba.* Havana: Publicaciones de la Cámara Cubana del Libro, 1949.

Casa de las Américas. "Literatura y Revolución (encuestas)." *Casa de las Américas* 51-52 (November 1968-February 1969): 120-80.

—. "25 Aniversario de Casa de las Américas (1959-1984)." Havana: Ediciones Casa de las Américas, 1984.

Casal, Julián del. Cartas inéditas. Havana: Archivo Nacional, Fondos Donativos, caja 574, No. 33.

Casal, Lourdes, ed. *El caso Padilla: literatura y revolución en Cuba: documentos.* Miami: Ediciones Universal, 1971?

Casanovas, Martín, ed. *Revista de avance*. Colección Orbita, Havana: Instituto Cubano del Libro, 1972.

Casáus, Victor, and Luis Rogelio Nogueras, eds. *Silvio: que levante la mano la guitarra*. Havana: Letras Cubanas, 1984.

Castro Ruz, Fidel. "Discurso de clausura [Primer Congreso Nacional de Educación y Cultura]." *Referencias* 2.3 (1971): 56-62.

—. "Discurso de clausura [Primer Forum Nacional de Energía]." *Granma* (December 6, 1984): 2-5.

—. "Discurso, Primero de Mayo," 1966. *Documentos políticos*, Vol. II, *Política internacional de la Revolución Cubana*. Havana: Editora Política, 1966.

—. *La historia me absolverá*. New York: Center for Cuban Studies, 1981.

—. "Palabras a los intelectuales," in *Política cultural de la Revolución Cubana, documentos*. Havana: Editorial de Ciencias Sociales, 1977. 3-47.

—. "Sobre la propriedad intelectual." Discurso, April 29, 1967.

Centro Nacional de Derechos de Autor (CENDA). "Legislación del derecho deautor (1977-1983)." CENDA Archives.

Chaple, Sergio. *Estudios de literatura cubana*. Havana: Letras Cubanas, 1980.

Chío, Evangelina. "Aficionados: presente y perspectivas." *Revolución y Cultura* 128 (Abril 1983): 54-56.

—. "La lectura en ruedas." *Revolución y cultura* 4 (1985): 36-39.

"Comercio de libros cubanos." *Revista de la Biblioteca Nacional* 1.5-6 (May-June 1909): 123-30.

Consejo Nacional de Cultura. Dirección de Extensión Universitaria. *Talleres literarios y círculos de lectura*. Havana: Imprenta Universitaria André Voisin, 1974.

Cossío Woodward, Miguel. "La planificación del sector cultural en Cuba." *Revolución y cultura* (April 1984): 24-31.

—. "Toda la cultura. Entrevista con Armando Hart." *Revolución y cultura* 1 (January 1984): 2-9.

Costales, Manuel. "¿Es opuesta a la gloria del escsritor la retribución del trabajo literario?" *Revista de la Biblioteca Nacional* (January-March 1955): 9-25.

Cruz-Alvarez, Félix. "Los poetas del Grupo de Orígenes." Thesis, University of Miami, 1975.

Dalton, Roque, René Depestre, et al. *El intelectual y la sociedad*. Mexico: Siglo Veintiuno Editores, 1969.

Darnton, Robert. *The Literary Underground of the Old Regime*. Cambridge: Harvard University Press, 1982.

Day, Frederick T. *An Introduction to Paper*. London: Newnes Educational Publishing, 1962.

De Juan, Adelaida. *"La belleza de todos los días: notas sobre la gráfica cubana contemporánea."* *Unión* 14.3 (September 1975): 28-40.

—. "El objeto esencial que es el libro." *Revolución y cultura* (July-August, 1983): 17-20.

Dean, Warren. "The USIA Book Program: How Translations of 'Politically Correct' Books Are (Secretly?) Subsidized for Sale in Latin America." *Punto de Contacto/ Point of Contact* 1.1 (September-October 1976): 4-14.

Desnoes, Edmundo. "Los carteles de la Revolución Cubana." *Casa de las Américas* 51-52 (November 1968-Feburary 1969): 223-31.

Díaz Acosta, América. *Panorama histórico-literario de Nuestra América (1900-1943), (1944-1970)*. Havana: Casa de las Américas, 1982.

Diego, Eliseo. "Una ojeada cubana a la literatura infantil." *Revista de la Biblioteca Nacional* 1 (January-April 1970): 83-91.

Dulzaides Serrate, Elena Graupera Arango, and Elena Cabeiro Gil, eds. *Bibliografía cubana 1921-1936*. Havana: Editorial Orbe, 1978-79.

—, Marta and Norma Fernández Ugalde, eds. *Bibliografía cubana 1917-1920*. Havana: Consejo Nacional de Cultura, 1970.

Eagleton, Terry. *Criticism and Ideology*. London: Verso, 1978.

—. *Literary Theory*. Minneapolis: University of Minnesota Press, 1983.

—. *Marxism and Literary Criticism*. Berkeley: University of California Press, 1976.

Editorial Arte y Literatura. "Informe al Consejo de la Esfera." Havana: Empresa Editoriales de Cultura y Ciencia, 1984.

Editorial Gente Nueva. "Informe al Consejo de la Esfera." Havana: Empresa Editoriales de Cultura y Ciencia, 1984.

Editorial Letras Cubanas. "Autores publicados." Tabla. From the publisher's archives, 1984.

—. "Informe al Consejo de la Esfera." Havana: impresa Editoriales de Cultura y Ciencia, 1984.

—. "Informe al Primer Activo Nacional de Libreros y Editores." May 1980. From the publisher's archives.

—. "Literatura cubana: resumen de los títulos publicados." Tabla. From the pubisher's archives. October 1981.

—. "Modelo de evaluaciones." 1984. From the publisher's archives.

—. "Premios MINFAR, Premios MININT, Talleres Literarios, Premios CTC." Tabla. From the publisher's archives. 1984.

—. "Resumen de títulos publicados por años y por géneros." Statistical Table. From the publisher's archives. 1984.

—. "Títulos publicados 1977-1983." Statistical Table. From the publisher's archives. 1984.

Elizagaray, Alga Marina. *Niños, autores y libros.* Havana: Editorial Gente Nueva, 1981.

Empresa Editoriales de Cultura y Ciencia. "Historial del Centro." Havana, May 1983.

Escarpit, Robert. *The Book Revolution.* London: George G. Harrap; Paris: UNESCO, 1966.

—. *Sociología de la literatura.* Virgilio Piñera, trans. Havana: Instituto del Libro, 1970.

Esfera de la Comercialización del Libro. "Algunos indicadores sobre la red del comercio del libro." Havana, 1984.

Ewen, Frederick, ed. *The Poetry and Prose of Heinrich Heine.* New York: Citadel Press, 1948.

Febvre, Lucien, and Henri-Jean Martin. *The Coming of the Book: The Impact of Printing 1450-1800.* London: Verso, 1984.

Fernández Retamar, Roberto. *Calibán y otros ensayos.* Havana: Editorial Arte y Literatura, 1979.

—. *Para una teoría de la literatura hispanoamericana y otras aproximaciones.* Havana: Editorial Arte y Literatura, 1979.

Flores, Juan. *Insularismo e ideología burguesa en Antonio Pedreira.* Havana: Ediciones Casa de las Américas, 1979.

Fornet, Ambrosio. *En blanco y negro.* Havana: Editorial Arte y Literatura, Instituto del Libro, 1967.

—, ed. *Cine, literatura, sociedad.* Havana: Letras Cubanas, 1982.

—. "El cuento." *Casa de las Américas* 22-23 (January-April 1964): 3-10.

Galeano, Eduardo. *Días y noches de amor y de guerra.* Buenos Aires: Catálogos Editorial, 1984.

—. "In Defense of the Word," in *Days and Nights of Love and War.* Bobbye Ortiz, trans. New York: Monthly Review Press, 1985. 183-94.

García Espinosa, Julio. *Una imagen recorre el mundo.* Havana: Letras Cubanas, 1979.

Garrido, Jorge. "El reto de la cultura en las montañas." *Bohemia* (March 29, 1985): 26-27.

Gedin, Per. *Literature in the Marketplace.* George Bisset, trans. New York: Overlook Press, 1977.

Goethe, Johann Wolfgang von. *Goethe's Literary Essays*. J.E. Spingarn, ed. New York: Frederick Ungar Publishing, 1964.

González, Reynaldo. *Llorar es un placer*. Havana: Letras Cubanas, 1988.

González, Waldo. *Escribir para niños y jóvenes*. Havana: Editorial Gente Nueva, 1983.

Gorkey, Maxim. *On Literature*. Seattle: University of Washington Press, 1973.

Guerra, María, and Ezequiel Maldonado, eds. *El compromiso intelectual*. Mexico: Editorial Nuestro Tiempo, 1979.

Harris, Wilson. *Tradition, the Writer and Society*. London: New Beacon Publications, 1973.

Hart Dávalos, Armando. *Cambiar las reglas del juego*. Havana: Letras Cubanas, 1983.

—. *Del trabajo cultural*. Havana: Editorial de Ciencias Sociales, 1978.

Hauser, Arnold. *The Social History of Art*, Vol. IV. New York: Vintage Books, 1951.

Hernández, Erena. "La literatura soviética y las ediciones cubanas." *Revolución y cultura* (October 1977): 9-12.

Hernández, Josefa de la C. *Algunos aspectos de la cuentística de Onelio Jorge Cardoso*. Santiago de Cuba: Editorial Oriente, 1982.

Hernández, Olga. "Cómo incrementar el hábito de lectura en las bibliotecas." *Revista de la Biblioteca Nacional* 1 (January-April 1977): 43-58.

Herrera Ysla, Nelson. "Imagen de las letras cubanas." *Revolución y cultura* (April 1983): 7-12.

Ibarra, Jorge. *Un análisis psicosocial del cubano: 1898-1925*. Havana: Editorial de Ciencias Sociales, 1985.

—. *Nación y cultura nacional*. Havana: Letras Cubanas, 1981.

Instituto de Literatura y Lingüística de la Academia de Ciencias de Cuba. *Diccionario de la literatura cubana*. Havana: Letras Cubanas, 1980-84.

Izcaray, Jesús. *Reportaje a Cuba*. Havana: Ediciones Venceremos, 1962.

Jailer, Todd. "They Don't Care about You, Anyway." *The Guardian*, Literary Supplement, June 26, 1985, S3-S4.

Jitrik, Noé. *Producción literaria y producción social*. Buenos Aires: Editorial Sudamericana, 1975.

Kapf, Albert. "Sobre las tendencias actuales del diseño en el mundo: acerca del libro cubano." Conference paper, Instituto Superior de Gráfica y Arte del Libro, Leipzig, RDA, April, 1983.

Lapique, Zoila, and Miguel Barnet. "El libro en Cuba, 1723-1968." *Revista de la Biblioteca Nacional* 1 (January-April, 1968): 128-34.

Leal, Rine. "Sobre el libro y la escena," *Panorama de la literatura cubana (1959-1984)*. Havana: Letras Cubanas, 1985. 42-47.

Leenhardt, Jacques. *Lectura política de la novela*. Mexico: Siglo Veintiuno Editores, 1975.

León-Portilla, Miguel. *El reverso de la Conquista*. Mexico: Editorial Joaquín Moritz, 1974.

Le Riverend, Julio. "Palabras de clausura [Memorias del Primer Fórum sobre Literatura Infantil y Juvenil]." *Boletín para las bibliotecas escolares*, 3.2-3 (March-June, 1973): pag. unknown.

Lezama Lima, José. *Imagen y posibilidad*. Havana: Letras Cubanas, 1981.

Lissitsky, El. "The Future of the Book." in *Communication and Class Struggle*, Armand Mattelart and Seth Siegelaub, eds. New York: International General, Paris: International Mass Media Research Center, 1983. II.267-69.

López Dorticós, Pedro. "Una ojeada sobre la bibliografía de Cienfuegos." *Revista de la Biblioteca Nacional*, April-June, 1954. 161-90.

López, Oscar Luis. *La radio en Cuba*. Havana: Letras Cubanas, 1981.

López Lemus, Virgilio, ed. *Revolución, letras, arte*. Havana: Letras Cubanas, 1980.

Lowenthal, Leo. *Literature and the Image of Man: Sociological Studies of the European Drama and Novel 1600-1900*. Boston: Beacon Press, 1957.

—. *Literature, Popular Culture and Society*. Englewood Cliffs, N.J.: Prentice Hall, 1961.

Lukács, Georg. *The Theory of the Novel*. Anna Bostock, trans. Cambridge: MIT Press, 1977.

Marinello, Juan. *Ensayos*. Havana: Editorial Arte y Literatura, 1977.

—. "El libro, cuestión nacional." *Feria del libro* 1 (March 1943): PAGS.

—. "Sobre nuestra crítica literaria." *Vida universitaria* 219 (May-June 1970): 43-48.

—. "Sugerencias en la Feria del Libro." *Feria del libro* 1 (February 1943): 5-11.

Maritain, Jacques. *The Responsibility of the Artist*. New York: Charles Scribner's Sons, 1960.

Martí, José. *La edad de oro*. Mexico: Edición Porrúa, 1982.

Martínez Estrada, Ezequiel. *Leer y escribir*. Mexico: Editorial Joaquín Moritz, 1969.

—. "Por una alta cultura popular y socialista." *En Cuba y al servicio de la Revolución Cubana*. Havana: Ediciones Unión, 1963. 123-64.

Martínez, Raúl Víctor. "Presente, pasado y futuro del libro cubano." *Bohemia* 16.75 (April 1983): 16-19.

Marx, Carlos, and Federico Engels. *Sobre la literatura y el arte*. Havana: Editora Política, 1965.

Mattelart, Armand, and Seth Siegelaub, eds. *Communication and Class Struggle*: 2. *Liberation, Socialism*. New York: International General, Paris: International Mass Media Center, 1979-83.

Méndez Capote, Renée. *Memorias de una cubanita que nació con el siglo*. Havana: Ediciones Unión, 1964.

Mestre, José Manuel. "¿La propiedad intelectual es una verdadera propiedad?" *Revista de la Biblioteca Nacional* (July-September): 7-30.

Miranda, Julio E. *Nueva literatura en Cuba*. Madrid: Taurus Ediciones, 1971.

Molina, Roberto. "Mundo de papel." *Prisma latinoamericano* 3 (1984): 22-23.

Morawski, Stefan. *Inquiries into the Fundamentals of Aesthetics*. Cambridge: MIT Press, 1978.

Moreno Fraginals, Manuel, ed. *Africa en América Latina*. México: Siglo Veintiuno Editores; Paris: UNESCO, 1977.

Nogueras, Luis Rogelio. *Por la novela policial*. Havana: Ediciones Unión, 1982.

Norniella, José M. "Así vive el pueblo cubano hoy." *Granma* (June 25, 1984).

Nuñez Machín, Ana. *La epopeya*. Havana: Editorial de Ciencias Sociales, 1983.

Organo Central de Trabajadores. "Convocatoria al concurso literario XV Aniversario del Periódico *Trabajadores*." *Trabajadores* (April 18, 1985).

Ortiz, Fernando. *Orbita de Fernando Ortiz*. Havana: Ediciones Unión, 1973.

Otero. Lisandro. *Dissidences et coincidences à Cuba*. Havana: Editorial José Martí, 1985.

—. "El escritor en la Revolución Cubana." *Casa de las Américas* 36-37 (May-August 1966): 203-209.

—. "Notas sobre la funcionalidad de la cultura." *Casa de las Américas* 68 (September-October 1971): 91-107.

—, Roberto Fernández Retamar, Luis Suardíaz, and Juan Blanco. "Conversación sobre el arte y la literatura." *Casa de las Américas*, 22-23 (January-April 1964): 63-81.

Papastamatiú, Basilia. "La universidad más económica: el libro. Entrevista a Raúl Ferrer." *Juventud rebelde* (September, 30, 1984).

Pascual, José Antonio. *Peñas y tertulias. Revisión panorámica y casi crónicas*. Havana: Editorial Agora, 1965.

Pastor, Brígida. "Una feminista cubano-española: Gertrudis Gómez de Avellaneda ante la sociedad de su tiempo." *Association for Contemporary Iberian Studies* 8.1 (Spring 1995): 57-61.

Peraza Sarausa, Fermín. *La imprenta y el Estado en Cuba*. Matanzas: Amigos de la Cultura Cubana, 1936.

Perus, Françoise. *Literatura y sociedad en América Latina: el modernismo*. Mexico: Siglo Veintiuno Editores, 1978.

Piñera, Virgilio. Unpublished texts. Archives of Letras Cubanas Publishers, Havana.

Pita Rodríguez, Félix. *Poesía*. Havana: Letras Cubanas, 1978.

—. *Prosa*. Havana: Letras Cubanas, 1978.

Pogolotti, Marcelo. *La República de Cuba a través de sus escritores*. Havana: Editorial Lex, 1958.

Portuondo, José Antonio. *Astrolabio*. Havana: Editorial Arte y Literatura, 1973.

—. *Bosquejo histórico de las letras cubanas*. Havana: Editorial Nacional de Cuba, 1962.

—. *Capítulos de la literatura cubana*. Havana: Letras Cubanas, 1981.

—. *La emancipación literaria de Hispanoamérica*. Havana: Instituto del Libro, 1975.

—. *Itinerario estético de la Revolución Cubana*. Havana: Letras Cubanas, 1979.

Prieto, Abel E. "La crítica y el ensayo literario," in *Panorama de la literatura cubana (1959-1984)*. Havana: Letras Cubanas, 1985. 29-35.

Primer Congreso Nacional de Educación y Cultura. Documentos. *Referencias*. Havana: Universidad de la Habana, Instituto del Libro, 1971.

"Pruebas de la producción en el Combinado de Papeles Blancos de Jatibonico," *Granma* (March 20, 1984).

Puebla, Carlos. *Hablar por hablar*. Havana: Editorial Unión, 1984.

Randall, Margaret. *Risking a Somersault in the Air: Conversations with Nicaraguan Writers*. San Francisco: Solidarity Publications, 1984.

Resolución No. 93/94 de la Ley del Derecho de Autor. *Gaceta Oficial de la República de Cuba* 82.92 (December 1984): 1624-33.

Ricardo, José G. *La imprenta en Cuba*. Havana: Letras Cubanas, 1989.

Ríos, Alejandro. "El libro en Cuba." México: Centro Regional para el Fomento de la Literatura y el Libro Latinoamericanos, 1984.

Roa García, Raúl. *La revolución del 30 se fue a bolina*. Havana: Instituto del Libro, 1969.

Rodríguez Feo, José. "Breve recuento de la narrativa cubana." *Unión* 4 (1967): 131-36.

Rodríguez García, Rolando. "El libro cubano es obra de la Revolución." *Granma* (March 31, 1979).

Rodríguez Rivera, Guillermo. *Ensayos voluntarios.* Havana: Letras Cubanas, 1984.

Roig de Leuchsenring, Emilio. "Diez años de labor." *Social* (January 1926): 13, 91, 101.

—. "La función social del libro." *Feria del libro* 1 (February 1943): 9-10.

—. *Weyler en Cuba.* Havana: Editorial Páginas, 1947.

Rosales, Guillermo. "Algo sobre el papel." *Química* 6 (June 1977): 4-6.

—. "Una hoja de papel." *Química* 12 (December 1977): 9-11.

Said, Edward. *Culture and Imperialism.* New York: Vintage Books, 1994.

—. *The World, the Text and the Critic.* Cambridge: Harvard University Press, 1983.

Sammons, Jeffrey L. *Literary Sociology and Practical Criticism.* Bloomington: Indiana University Press, 1977.

Sánchez Vázquez, Adolfo. *Las ideas estéticas de Marx: ensayos de estética marxista.* Mexico: Biblioteca Era, 1972.

Segundo Concurso Nacional de Arte del Libro. Folleto. Havana, 1983.

Shatzkin, Leonard. *In Cold Type: Overcoming the Book Crisis.* Boston: Houghton Mifflin, 1983.

Sillitoe, Alan. *Road to Volgagrad.* New York: Alfred A. Knopf, 1964.

Sixto, Luis. "El lector de tabaquería no puede desaparecer." *Granma* (Oct. 18, 1984).

Smythe, Dallas W. "Realism in the Arts and Sciences," in *National Sovereignty and International Communications*, Kaarle Nordenstreng and Herbert I. Schiller, eds. Norwood, N.J.: Ablex, 1979. 99-110.

Suardíaz, Luis. "La poesía: un hecho editorial relevante," en *Panorama de la literatura cubana (1959-1984).* Havana: Letras Cubanas, 1985. 48-52.

Suleiman, Susan, and Inge Crosman, eds.*The Reader in the Text.* Princeton: Princeton University Press, 1980.

Taraporevala, Russi Jal. *Competition and Its Control in the British Book Trade.* London: Pitman Publishing, 1973.

Taubert, Sigfred, ed. *The Book Trade of the World.* Vol. II (The Americas, Australia, New Zealand). Hamburg: Verlag für Buchmarkt-Forschung; New York: R.R. Bowker, 1976.

Toledo Sande, Luis. *Tres narradores agonizantes.* Havana: Letras Cubanas, 1980.

Tolstoy, Leon. *What Is Art?* Maude Almyer, trans. Indianapolis: Bobbs-Merrill, 1981.

Torres, Miguel. "Necesidad del guionista." *Cine, literatura, sociedad.* Ambrosio Fornet, ed. Havana: Letras Cubanas, 1982. 121-28.

Trelles y Govín, Carlos M. *Bibliografía cubana del siglo XX*. Matanzas: Imprenta de la Viuda de Quirós y Estrada, 1916-17.

Tretiakov, Sergei. "Words Become Deeds: The Press and Books in the Soviet Union." *Communication and Class Struggle*, Vol. II, Armand Mattelart and Seth Siegelaub, eds. New York: International General; Paris: International Mass Media Center, 1983. II.265-67.

Viciedo, Carlos M. "Importancia de la investigación de la demanda en la elaboración de los planes de promoción del libro." Ponencia para la Reunión Nacional de Divulgadores del Libro, Havana, 19 - 20, December 1984.

Watt, Ian. "Publishers and Sinners: The Augustan View," *Studies in Bibliography*. Fredson Bowers, ed. Virginia: University Press of Virginia, 1959. XII.3-20.

—. *The Rise of the Novel*. Berkeley: University of California Press, 1967.

Weiss, Judith A. *Casa de las Américas: An Intellectual Review in the Cuban Revolution*. Chapel Hill: Estudios de Hispanófila, 1977.

Williams, Raymond. *Marxism and Literature*. Oxford University Press, 1977.

Sociological Theory and Methodology

Arato, Andrew, and Eike Gebhardt, eds. *The Essential Frankfurt School*. New York: Urizen Books, 1978.

Berger, Peter L. *Invitation to Sociology: A Humanistic Perspective*. New York: Doubleday, 1963.

Bottomore, T.B. *Elites and Society*. New York: Basic Books, 1964.

Clapperton, Robert Henderson. *Paper and Its Relationship to Books*. London: J.M. Dent, 1934.

Curtis, James E., and John W. Petras. *The Sociology of Knowledge*. New York: Praeger Publishers, 1972.

Dimaggio, Paul. "Market Structure, the Creative Process and Popular Culture." *Journal of Popular Culture* 11.2 (Fall 1977): 436-52.

—, and Michael Useem. "Social Class and Arts Consumption." *Theory and Society* 5 (1978): 141-61.

Dorfman, Ariel, and Armand Mattelart. *Para leer al Pato Donald*. Mexico: Siglo Veintiuno Editores, 1972.

Durkheim, Emile. *The Rules of Sociological Method*. New York: The Free Press, 1964.

Ewen, Stuart, and Elizabeth Ewen. *Channels of Desire: Mass Images and the Shaping of American Consciousness*. New York: McGraw-Hill, 1982.

Freire, Paulo. *La importancia de leer y el proceso de liberación*. Mexico: Siglo Veintiuno Editores, 1984.

García Canclini, Néstor. *Las culturas populares en el capitalismo*. Havana: Ediciones Casa de las Américas, 1981.

González Manet, Enrique. *Cultura y comunicación*. Havana: Letras Cubanas, 1984.

Gramsci, Antonio. *Selections from the Prison Notebooks*. Quintin Hoare and Geoffrey Nowell Smith, eds. New York: International Publishers, 1978.

Hamilton, Peter. *Knowledge and Social Structure*. London: Routledge & Kegan Paul, 1974.

Kozol, Jonathan. *Illiterate America*. New York: Anchor Press/Doubleday, 1985.

Landes, David. *Revolution in Time: Clocks and the Making of the Modern World*. Cambridge: Harvard University Press, 1983.

Marcuse, Herbert. *The Aesthetic Dimension*. Boston: Beacon Press, 1977.

Mills, C. Wright. *The Sociological Imagination*. New York: Oxford University Press, 1959.

Nordenstreng, Kaarle, and Herbert I. Schiller, eds. *National Sovereignty and International Communication*. Norwood, N.J.: Ablex Publishing, 1979.

Petras, James. *Critical Perspectives on Imperialism and Social Class in the Third World*. New York: Monthly Review Press, 1978.

Schiller, Herbert I. *Mass Communications and American Empire*. New York: Augustus M. Kelly Publishers, 1978.

Simmel, Georg. *On Individuality and Social Forms*. Chicago: University of Chicago Press, 1971.

History/Political Science

Alvarez Tabío, Pedro. *Antimperialismo y República*. Havana: Instituto Cubano del Libro, 1970.

Benjamin, Jules Robert. *The United States and Cuba: Hegemony and Dependent Development*. Pittsburgh: University of Pittsburgh Press, 1977.

Boorstein, Edward. *The Economic Transformation of Cuba*. New York: Monthly Review Press, 1968.

Bustamante, Luis J. *Enciclopedia popular cubana*. Havana: Imprenta Editorial Lex, 1948.

Cuba en la mano. Havana: Ucar García, 1940.

Figarola, Joel James. *Cuba 1900-1928: la República dividida contra sí misma.* Havana: Editorial Arte y Literatura, 1974.

—. *Un episodio de la lucha cubana contra la anexión en el año 1900.* Santiago de Cuba: Editorial Oriente, 1980.

Foner, Philip S. *The Spanish-Cuban-American War and the Birth of Amerian Imperialism, 1898-1902.* New York: Monthly Review Press, 1972.

Furtado, Celso. *Economic Development of Latin America.* Suzette Macedo, trans. New York: Cambridge University Press, 1976.

Galeano, Eduardo. *Las venas abiertas de América Latina.* Mexico: Siglo Veintiuno Editores, 1983.

Harnecker, Marta. *Cuba: los protagonistas de un nuevo poder.* Havana: Editorial de Ciencias Sociales, 1979.

Izcaray, Jesús. *Reportaje a Cuba.* Havana: Ediciones Venceremos, 1962.

Jenks, Leland Hamilton. *Our Cuban Colony.* New York: Arno Press, 1970.

Le Riverend, Julio. *Historia económica de Cuba.* Havana: Instituto del Libro, 1967.

—. *La República.* Havana: Editorial de Ciencias Sociales, 1971.

Mateo, Maricela. *Panorama cronológico 1902-1925.* Havana: Editorial de Ciencias Sociales, 1984.

Moreno Fraginals, Manuel. *The Sugar Mill.* Cedric Belfrage, trans. New York: Monthly Review Press, 1976.

Nuñez Machín, Ana. *La epopeya: historia de la campaña de alfabetización.* Havana: Editorial de Ciencias Sociales, 1983.

Partido Comunista de Cuba. *Documentos y discursos. Segundo Congreso.* Havana: Departamento de Orientación Revolucionaria del Comité Central, 1975.

Pérez, Louis A., Jr. *Intervention, Revolution and Politics in Cuba 1913-1921.* Pittsburgh: University of Pittsburgh Press, 1978.

Pierre-Charles, Gerard. *El Caribe a la hora de Cuba.* Havana: Ediciones Casa de las Américas, 1981.

Pino-Santos, Oscar. *El asalto a Cuba por la oligarquía financiera yanqui.* Havana: Ediciones Casa de las Américas, 1973.

Porter, Robert P. *Industrial Cuba.* New York: Arno Press, 1976.

Pratt, Julius. *Expansionists of 1898.* Chicago: Quadrangle Books, 1964.

Sarría, Juan, and Juan José Soto, eds. *Estudios sobre Martí.* Havana: Editorial de Ciencias Sociales, 1975.

Tesis y resoluciones. Primer Congreso del Partido Comunista de Cuba. Havana: Editorial de Ciencias Sociales, 1978.

Vázquez, Adelina, and Gladys Egües. *Apuntes de la prensa clandestina y guerrillera del período 1952-1958*. Havana: Unión de Periodistas de Cuba, 1974.

INDEX